IS
IRELAND
NEUTRAL?

Conor Gallagher is crime and security correspondent at the *Irish Times*. He lives in Cabra, Dublin. This is his first book.

IS
IRELAND
NEUTRAL?

THE MANY MYTHS
OF IRISH NEUTRALITY

CONOR GALLAGHER

GILL BOOKS

Gill Books
Hume Avenue
Park West
Dublin 12
www.gillbooks.ie

Gill Books is an imprint of M.H. Gill and Co.

978 07171 95992

Designed by Bartek Janczak
Edited by Michelle Griffin
Printed and bound by Scandbook, Sweden
This book is typeset in 11 on 16pt Minion Pro.

*The paper used in this book comes from the wood pulp of
sustainably managed forests.*

A CIP catalogue record for this book is available from the
British Library.

5 4 3 2 1

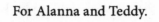

For Alanna and Teddy.

TABLE OF CONTENTS

CHAPTER ONE

GINGER GOES TO PARIS

Many Irish people whose views differ greatly in all other respects agree that neutrality is, in some sense, desirable ...
John Temple Lang (1985)[1]

On 26 January 1922, the Deuxième Bureau, the headquarters of French military intelligence in Paris, received an unusual visitor. The staff there probably assumed Major General J.J. 'Ginger' O'Connell, the deputy chief of staff of the Irish National Army, was in the French capital for the World Conference of the Irish Race, an international event aimed at promoting Irish culture. But O'Connell's real purpose was to ask the French army for assistance in training his young state's military officers. He arrived at the Deuxième Bureau with the offer that 12 Irish officers would train in military academies in France and, later, French officers would travel to Ireland where they could gather local intelligence and help the Irish build up its force of artillery, aircraft and tanks.

Colonel Fournier, the French officer who met with O'Connell, must have been taken aback by the proposal. Less than two months previously, Irish leaders had signed the Anglo-Irish Treaty in London, which essentially put the British military in charge of Irish external defence. Nevertheless, Fournier did not outright reject O'Connell's proposal, although he did inform the Irish general that the request should be made through diplomatic channels, and only after consultation with the British government. O'Connell responded that his government did not want to antagonise the British and asked that their conversation be kept secret, something Fournier seems to have complied with.

There the matter lay until February when O'Connell again appeared at the Bureau. This time his proposals were far more ambitious. O'Connell was now suggesting nothing less than a Franco–Irish alliance against England. In support of this, he presented Fournier with a remarkably detailed document detailing the Irish assessment of the geopolitical situation in Western Europe. After being victorious allies in World War I, Britain and France were destined to resume their centuries-long rivalry, the document stated. The development of aircraft and submarines meant that when this happened, Ireland could act as the 'left flank' of French forces. Cork was excellently positioned as an airfield for this purpose and the flying time between Ireland and France was not prohibitive. Ireland had more to offer than just geography, the memo continued, it had a race of people spread across the world, including in America, something which could be of great benefit to France.

It was a stunning offer and one which went far beyond merely bilateral military training. Such an arrangement would have been a flagrant breach of the Anglo-Irish Treaty, and if news got out it would have confirmed London's worst fears about Ireland being used as a backdoor to attack Britain, as had happened with Spain's forces in 1601 and the French army in 1798. The offer was all the more remarkable given that France and Britain were, in theory, still allies following the defeat of Germany four years earlier. O'Connell's proposal was a far cry from the suggestions of the Irish delegates during the treaty negotiations just a few months previously that Ireland would be a strictly neutral country which would agree to never allow itself to be used as a base to attack Britain. Had they known about O'Connell's trip, the British negotiators would have felt justified in their insistence that Ireland remain a dominion of the Empire and under the protection of the Royal Navy.

Surprising as they must have been, once again Fournier did not outright reject the proposals. In fact, there is evidence the document was given some serious consideration, at least initially. French intelligence passed the Irish memo to an informant with knowledge of Ireland who reported back that, while O'Connell was a 'most remarkable, honest and intelligent man', the Army was 'still only a bunch of badly armed and badly supervised bands but composed of extremely courageous people'. The informant's advice was to keep the lines of communication open.

The mystery continues to this day as to who sent O'Connell on this strange mission to Paris. UCC historian Jérôme aan de Wiel, whose work was responsible for bringing this episode to light almost a century later, said it is highly unlikely that the general was on a solo run. He suggested that Michael Collins, who had been the Irish Republican Army's (IRA) director of intelligence, was the brains behind it. Collins was known to have a keen interest in the use of aviation in warfare, and despite signing and campaigning for the Treaty, he was not opposed to continuing the war against Britain in more subtle ways, including sending arms to the IRA in Northern Ireland. Either way, de Wiel noted, the Irish side badly misjudged the climate. It was true tensions were high between France and Britain at the time, but French defence planners still firmly believed (accurately as it turned out) that their next war would be with Germany.[2]

Jump forward a century to 1 December 2022, when President of the European Commission Ursula von der Leyen visited the Dáil. There she discussed Russia's ongoing invasion of Ukraine and Ireland's role in shaping world affairs. Among those who addressed von der Leyen was independent TD Michael McNamara who, in pointed remarks, welcomed her to 'the building where we have sat for 100 years, each year of which has been as a neutral state'. According to McNamara, even when Irish citizens were under attack during the Troubles, Ireland 'eschewed a military solution for a diplomatic one'. He urged the EU to act similarly and pursue negotiations to bring the war in Ukraine to an end.[3]

Major General O'Connell's little-known visit to Paris in 1922 shows that McNamara's analysis of Ireland as maintaining a century-long history of neutrality is, at the very least, questionable. Despite his claims

– and that of every previous generation of Irish politician, both inside and outside government – in every year since independence, Irish neutrality has always, at the very least, had a large asterisk beside it. A reasonable argument can be made that Irish neutrality has been so flexible and paper-thin that the term should not apply at all.

So, is Ireland neutral? It is a seemingly simple question, yet even defining neutrality is a devilishly tricky task. For one thing, there's a seemingly endless variety of types of neutrality: classical neutrality, active neutrality, positive neutrality, permanent neutrality, qualified neutrality, limited neutrality, military neutrality, political neutrality and, one which seems to only be used in Ireland, traditional neutrality.

It gets even trickier when trying to apply those definitions to Ireland, particularly when each side of the debate has its own interpretation of the term. Typically, when people debate neutrality, they are at cross-purposes. Those on the Irish left tend to view it as a very broad concept encompassing a commitment not just to staying out of military alliances but to avoiding any international agreements or agencies which are military in nature, aside from perhaps United Nations peacekeeping missions. At the most extreme end, this includes withdrawing from the EU due to its increasing focus on security and defence matters. On the other side of the debate, recent governments have come to define neutrality in increasingly narrow terms. To them, neutrality means that Ireland stays out of military alliances and not much else. It's fair to say the majority of public opinion falls somewhere in the large space between these two views.

Problems of definition are further compounded by the fact that throughout Ireland's 100 years of independence, the government has repeatedly adapted its interpretation of what is and isn't neutrality. For the first decade, neutrality was something the government claimed to pursue, despite Britain protecting Irish waters and controlling some Irish ports. In the 1930s, de Valera embraced the concept of collective security through the League of Nations and was open to the idea of sending Irish troops to enforce the decisions of the organisation. He reverted to claims of neutrality ahead of World War II, only to stretch the definition well past breaking point through his assistance to the Allies. Following the war, Ireland was happy to abandon neutrality and join NATO on the condition it brought partition to an end. When this failed, it sought a defensive alliance with the US.

This conditional approach to neutrality continued through the Cold War when, although not in NATO, Ireland placed itself unambiguously in the Western camp. When applying for membership of the European Economic Community (EEC), the government made it clear it was willing to one day abandon its claim of neutrality in interests of greater integration. Later, when the US requested the use of Irish facilities to prosecute its wars in the Middle East, it did not have to ask twice. This takes us up to the present day and a version of neutrality which, following the launch on 24 February 2022 of Russia's illegal and unjustified attack on Ukraine, involves Ireland providing Ukraine with military supplies, albeit non-lethal ones, and assigning troops to the EU's overseas crisis management force. For every decade of its existence, the neutrality of the Irish State has been caveated in one way or another.

On the other hand, Ireland has remained out of foreign wars – or at least direct combat in those wars – for its entire history since independence, something which is surely the most important characteristic of a neutral state. It has also, particularly in the 1960s, adopted an independent position between the two powers in the United Nations, one which could reasonably be likened to neutrality. This stance was key to progressing the cause of nuclear disarmament, something Ireland could not have credibly pursued if it was under the protection of NATO's nuclear umbrella. And in every European Treaty since 1987, Ireland has insisted on recognition of its special status as a neutral nation in the face of a push towards a common defence agreement. The diplomatic efforts of Irish officials over the decades mean that, under the current rules, the EU will never become a true common defence union without the Irish public first approving it by referendum.

Poll after poll shows a significant majority of Irish people believe we are neutral and that we should stay that way. The Irish public may not agree exactly on what neutrality is, but they like its broad contours.

Neutrality may be one of the few things most of us can agree on. As John Temple Lang, a lawyer for the European Commission, wrote in 1985:

> Many Irish people whose views differ greatly in all other respects agree that neutrality is, in some sense, desirable ... that without it Ireland would be less distinctive and more provincial, and they feel that this would be a loss.[4]

With all these contradictions and definitional problems in mind, to answer the question of whether Ireland can call itself neutral, one must go back through the events, foreign and domestic, which have shaped Irish attitudes towards war, peace, security and defence – from the Conscription Crisis in 1918, through the League of Nations, the Emergency, the Cold War and, eventually, to the return of war to Europe in 2022 – and evaluate some of the myths surrounding neutrality which have taken hold in the Irish psyche. The most pervasive of these seems to be that claiming neutrality requires us to be defenceless, when in fact it is the commonly accepted duty of a neutral country to be able to independently defend that neutrality. Both sides of the debate have been guilty of spreading such myths. For example, neutrality purists often put forward the naive, and occasionally smug, thesis that neutrality is responsible for Ireland being regarded as a particularly altruistic player on the world stage. The same group has also been arguing for years that the government is constantly on the verge of joining NATO. The fact that no movement has been made in this regard for nearly 25 years has done little to disabuse this view.

On the other hand, recent governments have sometimes been guilty of misrepresenting Irish involvement in foreign military initiatives and operations as purely humanitarian in nature. The truth is often more complex. Ireland takes part in EU crisis management missions in Africa for the same reason as its neighbours: to prevent the problems of failed states, including terrorism and mass uncontrolled migration waves, from arriving on its doorstep. This is also, at least in part, the reasoning behind its 2022 commitment to help train Ukraine's military.

The use, and misuse, by government of our amorphous concept of neutrality for political purposes is nothing new of course: just look at former Taoiseach Charles Haughey's attempt to rally his base in 1982, when he insisted that neutrality prevented Ireland from continuing with sanctions against Argentina after the invasion of the Falklands; and this just a few months after he raised the prospect of an Anglo-Irish defence alliance with Margaret Thatcher.

In the last few years, several discrete events have converged to make a debate about Irish neutrality not just timely but vital. Russia's invasion of Ukraine has signalled a return to the Europe of the bad old days, a continent dominated by great power bullying and the shadow of nuclear war. It has shown that the era of war in Europe did not end with the peace agreements in the Balkans in the 1990s. It has also raised the question of what legal and moral obligations EU countries owe each other if they come under attack. The presence of Russian warships in Irish waters in August 2022, combined with the devastating cyberattack on the Health Service Executive (HSE) in May 2021, has shown that Ireland can no longer rely on its geography as a security policy. Neither can it rely on its military apparatus; something made clear by a major government report released in early 2022 which stated that the Defence Forces are unable to offer a credible response to a major external attack.[5]

Meanwhile, NATO is in a state of flux, with Finland and Sweden set to join, leaving the already small club of EU neutrals down two members. Domestically, there are increasing calls, including from Sinn Féin, for a referendum to enshrine neutrality in the constitution, while senior government ministers are advocating for a citizens' assembly to discuss the concept.

There's little point, however, in the Irish people discussing whether they *want* to be neutral before defining what that neutrality means and whether the country has ever fulfilled its criteria. For that, one must trace the origins of this slippery concept in Ireland, going back a lot further than Ginger O'Connell's 1922 visit to Paris.

CHAPTER TWO

THE HOTTEST PLACE IN HELL

Before you commit ourselves, decidedly, to war or peace,
it behoves you well to consider the consequences of both
to Ireland.
Wolfe Tone (1791)[1]

I n 1791, Britain was preparing for one of its favourite traditions – war with Spain. It would be the seventh time the two countries went to war that century and this time the *casus belli* was transatlantic trade. As members of parliament in London debated the pros and cons of war with Spain, over the Irish Sea, an ambitious young barrister by the name of Theobald Wolfe Tone sat down to write a pamphlet on the matter.

In comparison with his later revolutionary career, the pamphlet, *Spanish war! An enquiry how far Ireland is bound, of right, to embark in the impending contest on the side of Great-Britain?*, was a minor event. Through the prism of a study of the history of Irish neutrality, it takes on a greater importance. For the first time in print, someone was raising the idea that Ireland could become a neutral country in its own right, despite being controlled by Britain. The document was addressed to the members of both Irish houses of parliament. The Parliament of Ireland had existed in various forms for five centuries, but it was only in 1782–3 that it had been granted the power to pass legislation, a concession from a British Crown worried about the contagion of rebellion spreading from the American colonies into Ireland. Tone hoped to persuade the Irish MPs to use their newfound powers to declare Ireland's neutrality in Britain's expected war with Spain.

'What, in the first place, are the grounds of the quarrel as to Ireland? And what are the profits she has to look to from the contest between Spain and England?' he asked. Like later proponents of Irish neutrality, his arguments against war with Spain were based not on morality, but on the fact that war would do little to serve Ireland's interests. Ireland should no more be compelled to take part in a war between Britain and Spain than it would in a war between the 'Emperor of Japan and the King of Korea'. Tone argued that 'The quarrel is merely and purely English … Shall we eat, drink or sleep one jot the worse whether the Mandarins of Pekin line their doublets with furs purchased from a Spanish or an English merchant? No.'

Tone believed that, if an Irishman were to kill a Spaniard in such an unjust war, it would be murder; if he seized Spanish property, it would be robbery. The young barrister anticipated the argument that Spain would simply ignore Irish neutrality in any conflict. But what if the Spanish king was informed of Ireland's 'absolute neutrality' before conflict broke out? Surely, Tone reasoned, Spain would be more than happy to treat Ireland as a customer for its goods rather than an enemy?[2]

The pamphlet made the case for an independent Ireland (albeit with some connections to Britain) and Tone also used it to call for an Irish flag and independent Irish military. In practical terms, it had little immediate impact. Although the Crown had granted the Parliament of Ireland power to enact legislation, the Irish still had no control over foreign relations. Perhaps more importantly, the armed forces present in Ireland, and the Royal Navy in her waters, remained firmly under the control of London.

As it turned out, Britain had to wait another six years, until 1796, for war with Spain. This one would form part of the Coalition Wars against Napoleonic France which, by that time, had Spanish support. When war did come there was no objection from the Parliament of Ireland, and

Irish men fought and died in the ensuing conflict just as they had always done, and just as they would do for another 120 years.

Two years later, Tone and the United Irishmen would set in motion the ill-fated 1798 Rebellion. This led directly to Britain abolishing the Parliament of Ireland through the passage of the Act of Union of 1801, rendering the question of Irish neutrality moot for over a century.

The origins of the concept of neutrality in an international context are much harder to pin down. Of course, nations have claimed neutrality in war since the idea of a nation first came into being. Even before this, Greek city states often invoked a form of neutrality when their neighbours went to war.

Debates on the morality of neutrality have a similarly long history: in the fifth century, St Augustine of Hippo, the Christian philosopher and North African bishop, laid out his theory of what did and didn't constitute a just war. Augustine believed that remaining peaceful in the face of an evil that can only be stopped by violence would be a sin – an argument which would be used to justify wars for the next 15 centuries and counting.

The debate was taken up by St Thomas Aquinas in the thirteenth century when he set out the criteria for a just war. These were: a) that the war be waged under the command of a rightful leader, b) that the nation being attacked must have done something to deserve it, and c) that the warriors must have righteous intentions. These arguments clearly had an influence on Dante Alighieri who, in 1321, described in the *Divine Comedy* a special place in Hell for the 'neutrals' – those angels who could not choose between God and Satan.

However, it is only in recent centuries that the idea of neutrality started to be codified in law, and then only in fits and starts. Some historians have traced the origin of the modern concept of neutrality to the Peace of Westphalia of 1648, which brought an end to the Thirty Years' War. In extremely simple terms, the war was a struggle between Catholic and Protestant territories within and around the Holy Roman Empire. It was one of the most destructive conflicts in European history and, by some estimates, claimed up to eight million lives. The Peace of Westphalia, which was negotiated by 16 European states and 66 territories of the Holy Roman Empire, did far more than simply end the conflict. It solidified the notion of a sovereign nation state. According to the concept of what would become known as Westphalian sovereignty, every state, no matter how small or large, had a right to exist without interference from another.

Much of the history of neutrality in early modern Europe is tied up with the history of maritime trade. It's no coincidence that the early European neutrals, such as the Netherlands, Denmark and Sweden, tended to be seafaring states. In the eighteenth century, these countries were becoming increasingly frustrated with their ships being seized or sunk by countries who happened to be warring with each other. The Royal Navy in particular were notorious for ignoring the neutrality of ships at sea for fear they may secretly be aiding the enemy. By one estimate, during the American War of Independence, the Royal Navy's actions meant that one-in-five merchant vessels failed to make it to port.[3] This prompted Empress Catherine the Great of Russia to establish the League of Armed Neutrality in 1780, which counted as members Sweden, Denmark–Norway, Finland, Prussia, Austria, Portugal, the Ottoman Empire and the Two Sicilies. League members committed to defend the neutrality of each other's merchant shipping and to retaliate, with force if necessary, if that neutrality was compromised.[4]

This was followed in 1793 by the Proclamation of Neutrality by the United States. President George Washington declared his country would take no part in the wars between Revolutionary France and its neighbours and would prosecute any American citizen who assisted the belligerents. It was a bold decision for the young nation and caused some frustration within Washington's cabinet. Secretary of State Thomas Jefferson suggested the government play for time 'and make countries bid for [American] neutrality'.[5] But he was outvoted. America, which was just a decade removed from its War of Independence, could not afford to become involved with either side of the conflict.

The nineteenth century has been called the 'Golden Age of Neutrality' and for good reason.[6] The period between the end of the Napoleonic Wars in 1815 and the start of World War I in 1914 was a heyday for the growth of international law, particularly as it applied to war. The Congress of Vienna ran between 1814 and 1815 with the aim of undoing, as much as possible, the changes Napoleon had wrought across Europe. The main aim of the delegation from Switzerland was to secure a guarantee of its permanent neutrality from the major powers. Switzerland had previously declared its neutrality during the War of the First Coalition, which saw the European monarchies line up against Revolutionary France following the overthrow of King Louis XVI, but this did not save it from being invaded by the French in 1798, leading to the downfall of the Old Swiss Confederacy and the establishment of the Helvetic Republic. It then became a sister republic, essentially a puppet state, of Napoleonic France.

At the Congress of Vienna, which began after the capture of Paris and the exile of Napoleon to the island of Elba, the Swiss pleas for a recognition of its neutrality fell on deaf ears. The major participants were more interested in trading territories than pondering the question of neutrality. While the conference was ongoing, Napoleon escaped Elba and regained control of France, and again Switzerland was dragged into war. It was only then that the major powers agreed to consider Swiss neutrality. On 9 June 1815, nine days before Napoleon's final defeat at Waterloo, all parties to the Congress agreed to recognise the permanent neutrality of all 22 cantons of Switzerland. Since then, it has managed to maintain this neutrality through the two world wars which engulfed its neighbours right up to the present day.

Although permanent neutrality was guaranteed for Switzerland in 1815, and later for Belgium in 1839, it was only because the great powers permitted it. The idea that a small European country could declare neutrality without the permission of its larger neighbours only became credible following the Hague Conventions of 1899 and 1907. The genesis for the conventions date from 24 August 1898 when Count Mikhail Muravyov, the foreign minister to Tsar Nicolas II of Russia, circulated a document which became known among St Petersburg's diplomatic corps as the 'Tsar's Rescript'. The Rescript laid out the Tsar's wish for a conference to restrict the proliferation of weapons of war and introduce a new era of international cooperation. It is the 'supreme duty' of modern states 'to put an end to these incessant armaments', Nicolas wrote.[7]

Reading it today, there is little unusual about the document's idealistic allusions to fraternity and cooperation, but at the time it appeared to the world as a remarkable gesture of goodwill, especially as it came from an absolute monarch who commanded a military of three million troops. Although it was warmly received by the public, the announcement was met with a mixture of shock, incredulity and mockery from the diplomatic corps and world leaders. The Tsar's cousin Kaiser Wilhelm II of Germany called it 'humanitarian nonsense' while future king of Britain, Edward VII, said it was 'the greatest nonsense and rubbish I have ever heard. The thing is simply impossible.' The US, France and the Ottoman Empire expressed similar sentiments.[8]

Immediately, the question turned to what Russia was looking to get out of this endeavour. Some historians believe the Rescript was likely the work of Count Muravyov and other senior ministers in the Tsar's cabinet, and that the idea behind it was probably less noble than it first appeared. Russia could not keep pace with its rivals' advances in military technology and it was instead suspected of trying to restrict these advances under the guise of peace. Others, however, believe the Rescript was motivated, at least in part, by the young and naive Tsar's genuine commitment to peace, which was underpinned by his intense religious faith.

Whatever the motivation, and despite the international community's doubts, the First Hague Conference took place one year later in May 1899 in the Dutch city of Den Haag, or the Hague. It ran for just over two months and by its end, the delegates had agreed something quite remarkable in its ambition: a broad-ranging multilateral treaty governing the laws of war. Among the many points were a ban on chemical weapons, rules against looting and harming prisoners of war and the establishment of a permanent court of arbitration to settle international disputes. At this first conference the topic of neutrality was barely addressed, despite efforts by Denmark and Norway to have the conference recognise them as permanent neutrals. The issue would have to wait until the Second Hague Conference in 1907, which was suggested by US President Theodore Roosevelt as a way of updating and expanding the 1899 agreement. One of the jobs of the 1907 gathering was to address issues that had arisen during the Russo-Japanese War of 1904–5, which had ended in a disastrous defeat for the Tsar's forces, and severely disrupted the maritime activities of non-belligerent nations.

Most of the points agreed at the second conference dealt with the more granular issues of war, including rules on how a war is declared and how sea mines could be used. But delegates also, for the first time in international law, set down in writing the 'rights and duties of neutral powers' in war at land and at sea.[9] Across 58 articles, the delegates agreed detailed rules on the protection of neutral countries and what they must do to retain their neutral status in times of war. It begins by stating simply 'the territory of neutral powers is inviolable' before detailing how neutral nations may not host troops from belligerent countries or allow their ships to dock at port for more than 24 hours.[10]

The rules set in place at the Second Hague Conference were limited in scope and realistic in nature. For example, neutrals may not allow recruitment for belligerent militaries on their territory, but their citizens may travel abroad to enlist in those militaries. Any belligerent military personnel found on neutral territory must be interned, but neutrals may allow the passage of sick and wounded troops through their lands. Neutrals also reserve the right to respond with force to any invasion of its territory, while still retaining their neutral status. Curiously, much of the section on neutrality concerns the obligations which do not fall on neutral countries. Neutral nations are not obliged to stop private companies within their country from trading with belligerents or even from sending them military equipment. Nor are they obliged to prevent warring parties from using their communications infrastructure. And, crucially, neutrals must impose the same restrictions on both sides of the conflict.

The Hague Conventions were broadly praised at the time as ushering in a new era of international rule of law and cooperation. It was a reputation that was short-lived. Many of the provisions, including the rules on neutrality, were roundly ignored by both sides in World War I.

Before the outbreak of hostilities, Belgium had reaffirmed its neutrality in the looming conflict. Just two weeks later, on 4 August 1914, the German army crossed Belgium's borders as part of the Schlieffen Plan to invade France via a surprise attack through the Low Countries. It was this violation of Belgium's neutrality that formed the technical basis for Britain's entry into the conflict that same day.

Neutrality would also be widely ignored during World War II, when the Low Countries again found it to be a thin defence against a German invasion (as did Iceland, which was invaded by Britain). But, after the war, the reputation of the Hague Conventions improved somewhat and they were used as the basis for the prosecution of the many war crimes committed by the Axis powers. The judges at the Nuremberg trials of Nazi war criminals declared the 1907 convention was 'recognised by all civilised nations, and were regarded as being declaratory of the laws and customs of war'.[11] The implication was that even countries that did not sign the convention were bound by its terms, including countries, such as Ireland, that had not existed when those terms were written.

The Golden Age of Neutrality had little impact on the Ireland of the nineteenth century. The 1801 Act of Union, which abolished the Parliament of Ireland and made the country unambiguously a part of the United Kingdom, put an end to any credible arguments by people like Wolfe Tone that Ireland could remain neutral in Britain's wars. Furthermore, the relative peace of the era offered few opportunities for Irish leaders to protest at being dragged into Britain's wars: between the Battle of Waterloo and World War I, there was no war in Europe that involved all the major powers; and, until World War I, there hadn't been a European war involving Britain since the Crimean War of 1853–6.

Britain's entry into the Great War played a formative role in shaping Irish attitudes towards neutrality. The threat of conscription was a driving force in solidifying resistance to British rule and in giving Sinn Féin a mandate to launch the War of Independence following their victory in the 1918 election. This put an end to the political power of the Irish Parliamentary Party of John Redmond (and previously Charles Stewart Parnell), which had advocated for a type of independence that would oblige Ireland to take part in Britain's wars. But even after more radical figures took the lead in the struggle for Irish independence, many doubted Ireland could maintain a credible neutrality in Britain's future wars. Overall, neutrality played a relatively minor role in the debates and struggles for Irish independence between 1916 and 1922. When it did arise, it was almost invariably in a purely pragmatic context. Revolutionary leaders for the most part were not in favour of neutrality for moral reasons. Rather, declarations of neutrality were a way of resisting conscription and demonstrating independence from Britain.

This is not to say there was unanimity on the issue of neutrality among the Irish leaders. The events of the 1910s showed there was a distinct lack of coherent policy among Irish nationalists on the issue. As historian Patrick Keatinge said, 'Irish nationalism pursued almost as many foreign policies … as it contained different groups'.[12] When asked about Sinn Féin's foreign policy, its founder, Arthur Griffith, put it in extremely simple terms: 'In any issue I find out where England stands. Ireland will be found on the other side.'[13]

Roger Casement probably thought more about neutrality than all of the other revolutionary leaders combined. Through his diligent work with the British Colonial Service, he developed a deep hatred of imperialism and war. His enquiries into imperialist abuses in the Congo, Peru and South Africa shaped his worldview. It was this acute sense of social justice which caused the Antrim man to resign from the Foreign Service in 1913 and embrace the cause of Irish independence. His correspondence around this time described his vision of Ireland as independent, peaceful and neutral, and when he helped found the Irish Volunteers in 1913, he gave it an overtly neutral manifesto: 'The object proposed for the Irish Volunteers is to secure and maintain the rights and liberties common to all the people of Ireland. Their duties will be defensive and protective, and they will not contemplate either aggression or domination.'[14]

But Casement's later actions demonstrate, to put it charitably, an elastic definition of a neutral Ireland. In the run-up to the Easter Rising of 1916, he travelled to Germany to seek assistance for an Irish uprising in the form of men and arms. This was done not just because Germany was at war with England, but because of Casement's genuine preference for the German imperial model over the British one. He was a great admirer of German culture and frequently spoke out against Germanophobia in the British press. It was a position that caused significant damage to his reputation, both inside and outside the independence movement.[15]

Casement's efforts in Germany focused on recruiting Irish members of the British Army who were being held as POWs to an 'Irish Brigade' which would fight for independence. In this, he was less than successful. Some soldiers reacted with indifference, others with open hostility, and in the end none would be sent to Ireland. In December 1914, while still in Germany, Casement drew up a document outlining the founding articles of his theoretical Irish Brigade. Clause Two stated the brigade would fight 'solely in the cause of Ireland'. But, in contrast, Clause Eight suggested it could be used to expel the British from Egypt to assist Germany.[16] This was a stark contrast to Casement's impassioned letter to the *Irish Independent* just four months earlier in which he stated, 'Ireland has not blood to give any cause but that of Ireland. Our duty as a Christian people is to abstain from bloodshed.'[17]

Further evidence for Casement's preference towards Germany can be seen in the document he authored, *Ireland, Germany and the Next War*, which he had published a year previously under the pseudonym Shan Van Vocht. In it, he suggested that if Germany emerged victorious in the coming conflict, as he expected it to, it would act as a guarantor of Irish neutrality while also occupying the country. He wrote:

> [Ireland], severed by a sea held by German warships, and tempo-rarily occupied by a German army, might well be permanently and irrevocably severed from Great Britain, and by common assent erected into a neutralised, independent European State under international guarantees.

The country, Casement continued, would become an 'Atlantic Holland, a maritime Belgium'. In such circumstances, he reasoned, Britain would never be able to muster international support to stage a reconquest of the country.[18]

Germany's disregard for Belgium's neutrality at the beginning of the war did little to alter Casement's position. When confronted by evidence of German atrocities against Belgium, he appeared to have tried to justify it on the basis of atrocities committed by Belgian officials in the Congo, which Casement had documented extensively in his previous career. While being given a tour of the Ardennes by his German hosts, he was shown a wall where the Germans had shot hundreds of Belgium men in revenge for an ambush on an escort. Casement was almost moved to tears by the sight and its 'pitiable evidences of a sorrow'. But he also said he felt 'there may be in this awful lesson to the Belgian people a repayment. All that they now suffer and far more, they or their king, his government and his officers wreaked on the well-nigh defenceless people of the Congo basin.'[19] Despite these comments, the scene at the Ardennes seems to have deeply affected Casement and made him question his support for the Germans. Before leaving on a submarine back to Ireland ahead of the Rising, he wrote, 'Why did I ever trust a Govt such as this – They have no sense of honour, chivalry, generosity … They are Cads … that is why they are hated by the world and England will surely beat them.'[20]

Casement was not the only 1916 revolutionary with a preference for Germany. Joseph Plunkett, during his own visit to Germany to seek arms for the Rising, joined with Casement in suggesting to his hosts that a German invasion at the mouth of the Shannon in Limerick would be enough to rid Ireland of its occupiers. The plan was for 12,000 German troops to sail the long way around the north of Scotland before landing on Ireland's west coast. They would carry an extra 40,000 rifles to arm the Irish Volunteers and turn Limerick into an 'impregnable' base.[21] Plunkett's ideas had little basis in the realities of the war. The most the Germans would agree to was another shipment of guns (which ended up being scuttled off the coast of Cork) and a statement saying if it ever invaded Ireland it would do all it could to advance the cause of Irish liberty.[22]

There is some evidence to suggest that Plunkett, ostensibly an ardent republican, would have been satisfied not just with a German invasion but with some sort of German rule. In 1966, on the fiftieth anniversary of the Rising, the *Irish Times* published a posthumous eyewitness account by rebel Desmond FitzGerald. In it, FitzGerald – the father of Taoiseach Garret FitzGerald – said that during the Rising he'd had a conversation with Patrick Pearse and Joseph Plunkett about a German prince ruling Ireland following Germany's victory in the war. This prince, Joachim of Prussia, the sixth and youngest son of Kaiser Wilhelm II, would act as a figurehead of a 'republican monarchy' with Pearse as prime minister. The revelation caused quite the stir in the Ireland of 1966. It soon received credence from veteran republican Ernest Blythe, who said he had discussed the same issue at length with Pearse and Thomas MacDonagh in 1915.

It's difficult to see how an independent Ireland could claim any pretence of neutrality if it swapped a British monarch for a German one. In any case, the plan did not progress much beyond fantastical discussions between naive revolutionaries. Germany would get a mention in the 1916 Proclamation, with its reference to 'our gallant allies in Europe', but poor Prince Joachim never did become king of Ireland. He shot himself in his castle in Potsdam in 1920, following Germany's defeat in the war and the exile of his father to the Netherlands. The idea of German intervention in the independence struggle was definitively abandoned following the entry of America into the war in 1917 on the side of the Allies. The large Irish diaspora in the United States, which was a major source of funding and support for the independence movement, would have regarded such activity as treasonous to their adopted homeland. From then on, Germany would no longer be a factor in the fight for independence.[23]

The next phase of the Irish neutrality debate took place in the context of opposition to conscription of Irish men into the British armed forces to fight in World War I. The promotion of neutrality to oppose conscription was nothing new. During the Boer War of 1899–1902, where British forces attempted to suppress breakaway republics in South Africa, Irish nationalists advocated a neutrality which was framed in opposition to British recruitment campaigns in Ireland (although some nationalists did travel to fight on the Boer side). But it was the World War I conscription campaign, which was to be on an infinitely greater scale, that truly focused the minds of nationalists. Britain's attempts to introduce conscription in Ireland in 1918 were met with what historian F.S.L. Lyons called, 'the most massive demonstration of nationalist solidarity that had been seen since the beginning of the war'.[24]

The opposition can be traced back to the foundation of the Irish Neutrality League in 1914. The idea of a league had originated at a conference organised by Éamonn Ceannt, a member of the Irish Republican Brotherhood, in the library of the Gaelic League offices on Parnell Street on 9 September of that year. In attendance were eight future leaders of the 1916 Rising, including Pearse and James Connolly, as well as Sinn Féin leader Arthur Griffith. Two weeks later, John Redmond, the leader of the pro-Home Rule Irish Parliamentary Party, which at that time was still the dominant nationalist force in the country, made his famous Woodenbridge Speech, where he urged the Irish Volunteers to make themselves available to fight for the British in the war: 'Go on drilling and make yourself efficient for the work, and then account for yourselves as men, not only in Ireland itself, but wherever the firing line extends in defence of right, of freedom and religion in this war.'[25]

His call to action resulted in 170,000 Volunteers signing up for the British forces, where they were scattered through the army structures and defanged as a political or military entity. Only 11,000 Volunteers ignored Redmond's call and stayed behind. They went on to form the core of the IRA, which would fight the War of Independence. Redmond's reasoning for supporting British war aims was threefold. He believed Irish support for the war was necessary to ensure London kept its promise to grant Irish Home Rule at the end of the hostilities. And he believed, as did almost everyone else at the time, that the war would be short and the human costs involved would be relatively minor. Lastly, he had a genuine affection for Britain and a belief that the war was a just one to defend the rights of small nations such as Belgium.[26]

On 5 October 1914, two weeks after Redmond's speech, Sinn Féin's Seán T. O'Kelly and Seán Milroy circulated a document publicly announcing that the purpose of their new Irish Neutrality League was to define Ireland's attitude towards the war 'as one of neutrality, preventing employers from coercing men to enlist, and taking steps to preserve the food supplies of Ireland for the people of Ireland'. The inaugural meeting was held a week later on 12 October and was attended by a who's who of the Irish republican movement, including Connolly, who was elected its president.[27] But despite this auspicious start, the work of the League stalled. Aside from organising a few public lectures, it was finished before it got started. It never had more than a handful of subscribers, causing Irish Republican Brotherhood (IRB) member and Irish Parliamentary Party MP William O'Brien to describe it as 'an organisation of leaders without members'.[28]

It is perhaps not surprising that the Irish Neutrality League failed to get off the ground. At that stage, the staggering bloodshed of the Somme and Ypres was still in the future and there was still broad support for the war, even among some nationalists.

That attitude had changed dramatically by 1918 when Westminster introduced conscription into Ireland for the first time. By that point, the war was not going well for Britain. There were drastic troop shortages on the Western Front, despite the introduction of conscription on the island of Great Britain two years earlier. Germany's spring offensive, which began in March 1918, broke through British and French lines in several areas. In one sector, Allied troops were outnumbered four to one.[29] The British needed more men and fast. The purpose of the Military Service Bill of 1918 was to extend conscription to the island of Ireland and to broader age and worker groups in Britain. When British Prime Minister David Lloyd George introduced the bill in Westminster in April 1918, it provoked immediate and fierce resistance in Ireland. This resistance was not confined to republican or even nationalist organisations. The labour movement and, crucially, the Catholic hierarchy, also came out forcefully against conscription.

As soon as the bill was introduced in Parliament, John Dillon, who had taken over leadership of the Irish Parliamentary Party from John Redmond the previous month, led his colleagues in a walk-out. The nationalist MPs returned home to Ireland, where they joined in the broad movement that had emerged to oppose conscription. An anti-conscription committee was convened, which brought the Irish Parliamentary Party together with Sinn Féin and Labour. It was far more successful than the Irish Neutrality League had been. Mass rallies were organised and a general strike took place on 23 April 1918, which brought the country to a standstill. The Catholic bishops decided an anti-conscription pledge should be taken at the doors of every church, stating, 'Denying the right of the British government to enforce compulsory service in this country, we pledge ourselves solemnly to one another to resist conscription by the most effective means at our disposal.'[30]

Much of the anger related to Lloyd George's overt attempts to link conscription with the passing of Home Rule, the latest version of which had been adopted at the Irish Convention in Dublin at almost the exact moment conscription was introduced. In the end, this strategy meant that neither would happen. As resistance in Ireland grew, and as the troop shortage became more acute, the British government decided that desperate times called for desperate measures. Stuart Hay, a British Army captain was tasked with overcoming Irish anti-conscription sentiment. The result was the Hay Plan, which involved asking the bishops to persuade Irish men not to join the British Army but to join their Catholic brothers in the French army. The plan received some support from the Primate of Ireland, Cardinal Michael Logue, but ultimately went nowhere due to political rivalries within the upper echelons of Lloyd George's government.

An even more desperate attempt came in what became known as the German Plot, a claim by the British authorities that Sinn Féin was consorting with Germany to stage an invasion of Ireland. It perhaps wasn't all that fanciful a notion, given Irish republicans' affection for the German cause just two years previously. Britain used the invented German Plot to justify the arrest and imprisonment of 150 Sinn Féin leaders, thereby neutralising them as opponents to conscription. But in the end, like many decisions by the British government during this period, it merely served to increase support for the party. Very few people believed the British allegations of a German plot and the main impact of the arrests was to leave Sinn Féin in control of people like Michael Collins who was more in favour of using military means to achieve independence.

In the end, the Conscription Crisis was overtaken by events. A successful Allied counteroffensive, aided by the arrival of American troops in Europe, pushed the Germans back and suddenly the manpower shortage was no longer such a crisis. Plans for conscription were dropped by the London government. But the indirect consequences were seismic. Sinn Féin's leading role in opposing conscription helped it to steal the crown of the Irish Parliamentary Party as the representatives of nationalism. The Conscription Crisis also became part of the foundational myth of Irish neutrality. In the decades since, the episode has been pointed to as evidence that neutrality was always part of the Irish republican ideal.

But the majority of public opposition to conscription was based on a simple objection to sending more Irishmen into the European killing fields. Many, including the Catholic hierarchy, supported voluntary enlistment but opposed forced levies of troops. Few, if any, opposed conscription due to a commitment to pure neutrality. This was also the case for the republican movement. When Ireland's revolutionary leaders, from Tone to Connolly, thought of neutrality, they thought of it as a means of demonstrating independence from Britain, not an ideal in itself, and this had not changed much by 1918. For Sinn Féin, opposition to conscription was just another way to alienate British authorities in Ireland rather than a demonstration of neutrality. The party's ultimate aim was an Ireland free to choose which wars it wanted to fight rather than an Ireland locked into a permanent neutrality. Few Irish revolutionaries of the era – with the exception of Casement with his entirely unique and often contradictory concept of neutrality – wanted an Irish Switzerland, a nation that would be prevented by international law from deciding which wars it could involve itself in. After all, Tone's objection to war with Spain wasn't that war was inherently immoral, it was that Ireland had nothing to gain from such a conflict. 'First of all,' he had implored Irish MPs, 'take care of ourselves.'[31]

CHAPTER THREE

MORE PRESSING MATTERS

*Ireland is quite ready by treaty to ensure England's safety
and legitimate security against the danger of foreign
powers seeking to use Ireland as a basis of attack
against her.*
Éamon de Valera (October 1920)[1]

How can a country be independent if it has no navy? Or if it doesn't control its own ports? Or if its neighbour can take over any other facilities as it sees fit? These were the questions an embattled Erskine Childers asked as he sat across the table from Winston Churchill during the Anglo-Irish Treaty negotiations in October 1921. He would not get any satisfactory answers. The final treaty would make any notion of Irish neutrality an impossibility for many years. But by the end of the negotiations, most of the Irish delegates didn't seem to much care. They were far more concerned about the implications of the treaty's other, more immediate provisions, such as the partition of the country. These were the matters, and not the abandonment of any possibility of neutrality, that would trigger the Irish Civil War and guarantee a split in the nationalist movement which lasts to this day.

Like their predecessors, the men who led the struggle for independence during the War of Independence held a wide variety of views on neutrality, but it was never a priority in the movement. On 21 January

1919, the first shots of the war rang out in Soloheadbeg, County Tipperary, as ten IRA volunteers ambushed an explosives shipment being escorted by the Royal Irish Constabulary (RIC). That same day, some 200km away, the first meeting of Dáil Éireann was taking place in the Mansion House in Dublin. On the agenda that day was a reading of the Message to the Free Nations of the World: the document formed part of Sinn Féin's plan to achieve independence by obtaining a place at the peace conference in Versailles planned for later that year, and by gaining recognition from the international community. The hope was that American President Woodrow Wilson's public support for the notion of self-determination for small nations would lead the US and others to support Irish independence. In high-minded rhetoric, the *Message to the Free Nations of the World* spoke of 'frank co-operation between the peoples for equal rights against the vested privileges of ancient tyrannies.'[2]

However, in announcing the Republic of Ireland to the world, the Dáil made only the vaguest reference to the notion of neutrality, with a passage detailing how its harbours must be 'open to all nations, instead of being the monopoly of England.'[3]

Two other foundational documents were also produced that day: the Declaration of Independence and the Democratic Programme for the First Dáil. Both spoke of the need to establish international recognition and foreign trade and the Declaration of Independence demanded the removal of the 'English Garrison' from Ireland. But neither mentioned neutrality even in passing.[4] These omissions reflect a surprising truth; the Sinn Féin leadership recognised even then that the goal of neutrality would likely have to be sacrificed on the altar of independence. Of the republicans who gave the issue any thought, most recognised that, to gain independence, some concession would eventually have to be made to British security concerns, particularly as that country had just emerged from a war which had killed almost a million of its citizens.

The clearest demonstration of this came the following year, in February 1920, when the War of Independence was in full swing. President of Dáil Éireann, Éamon de Valera, was on a tour of America to raise funds and support for the Irish cause. During an interview with the *Westminster Gazette*, an influential London newspaper, de Valera posed this question: why couldn't Britain do with Ireland what the US had done with Cuba, and reach an agreement in which an independent Ireland would guarantee that it would 'never enter into a treaty with any foreign power which might pose a threat to British security'?[5]

Here de Valera was referring to the Platt Amendment, an agreement between America and Cuba in which Cuba agreed never to enter into an alliance against the United States. It was part of the Monroe Doctrine, a long-standing policy of the US government which prevented European countries from meddling in the affairs of South America and potentially posing a threat on the US southern flank. An arrangement similar to the Platt Amendment would be of great benefit to Britain, de Valera reasoned, because:

> An independent Ireland would see its own independence in jeopardy the moment it saw the independence of Britain seriously threatened. Mutual self-interest would make the people of these islands, if both independent, the closest possible allies in a moment of real danger to either.[6]

On the face of it, it was a reasonable suggestion. But de Valera's comments caused anger among Irish Americans and even within his own cabinet. It was seen in some sectors as a step back from the goal of achieving full independence from Britain. The *New York Globe* went so far as to call de Valera's suggestion 'a withdrawal by the official head of the Irish Republic of the demand that Ireland be set free'.[7] This was certainly not de Valera's intention. It seems more likely that at the time he did not fully understand the details of the relationship between the US and Cuba. Although on the surface the Platt Amendment of 1903 appeared to reflect an agreement between two sovereign nations of equal standing, in reality Cuba was firmly under the heel of Washington. Not only was Cuba forbidden from entering into alliances against America, but the agreement also permitted America to intervene in Cuban affairs and forced Cuba to lease lands to America for coal and naval purposes (the location of a US military base and notorious prison at Guantanamo Bay today is a direct consequence of the treaty).

De Valera had consulted nobody about the proposal and appears to have been taken by surprise by the backlash.[8] By that time, six months into his US tour, relations were becoming strained between him and prominent Irish American republicans such as Judge Daniel Cohalan of the New York Supreme Court and John Devoy, a leading Fenian. Much of the tension related to the conflict between the Irish Americans' isolationist views and de Valera's wish for the US to become more involved in international affairs. The Cuba comments threw fuel on that fire. Devoy's newspaper, the *Gaelic American*, said the proposal 'will be hailed as an offer of surrender'.[9] In the eyes of his critics, de Valera's comments were a signal that he was willing to do something much worse than abandon Irish neutrality; he was willing to sacrifice independence.

Cut off from news from home, de Valera was worried about how his comments were being interpreted in Dublin, particularly as some of the Sinn Féin leadership had been against his trip to America in the first place. He wrote to Arthur Griffith stating the controversy was simply due to a clash of personalities with the American Fenians and asserting that 'no American has a right to dictate policy to the Irish people.'[10] De Valera also dispatched Dr Patrick McCartan, the Dáil's envoy to Washington, back to Ireland to defend his position. McCartan's personal view was that de Valera's comments showed he was 'prepared to accept much less than complete sovereignty for Ireland' and that de Valera had specifically chosen a London paper to publish the comments so that they would reach the ears of Britain's prime minister, Lloyd George.[11] Nevertheless, back in Ireland, when Michael Collins called a meeting of the cabinet to hear de Valera's explanation, McCartan defended his boss. He told the cabinet the president had merely wanted to open the conversation with the British on defence arrangements and that his reference to the Platt Amendment was a way of showing that Ireland was willing to consider London's security concerns. The Irish Americans, McCartan continued, had sought to put their own slant on the comments due to their own animosity towards de Valera.[12]

De Valera's cabinet was initially split on the issue. At first, Collins was critical of the comments, while Cathal Brugha, Countess Markievicz and Count George Noble Plunkett displayed 'marked hostility' to the proposal. Arthur Griffith defended de Valera, saying, 'We know the president better than we know the men who are opposed to him in America. It is our business to be perfectly loyal to him.'[13] In the end, Collins and Griffith moved the conversation on and nothing further was said on the matter at cabinet.[14]

It was arguably the nascent Irish Nation's first political dispute over neutrality. It would be far from the last. The entire episode demonstrated two things. First, that de Valera was a committed republican who, nevertheless, had a realist approach to neutrality. He recognised, in the words of biographer Ronan Fanning, that 'small states within the spheres of influence of great powers must accept the constraints on their liberty of action in the conduct of foreign policy.'[15] Secondly, the matter highlighted a severe lack of knowledge and direction in Sinn Féin's foreign policy and security aims, a failing that would become apparent during the Anglo-Irish Treaty negotiations two years later.

De Valera was wise enough not to make any more comparisons between Ireland and Cuba. But he did not resile from his pragmatic view of independence and neutrality. In October 1920, during the closing stages of his American tour, he made one last appeal to President Wilson to recognise Irish independence. In an open letter, he told the president, 'Ireland is quite ready by treaty to ensure England's safety and legitimate security against the danger of foreign powers seeking to use Ireland as a basis of attack against her.'[16] He received no reply.

By the spring of 1921, the war in Ireland had reached a stalemate. Lloyd George was under increasing domestic pressure to bring the conflict to an end and the Republican leadership believed the IRA, suffering from a lack of weapons and ammunition, could not hold out for much longer. It was in this context that war ended on 11 July 1921 with a truce, with plans for negotiations to 'determine how the association of Ireland with the community of nations known as the British Empire may best be reconciled with Irish national aspirations.'[17]

From the start, it was clear the question of whether Ireland would be a neutral nation would form a key part of the discussions. One-third of the draft treaty prepared by the Irish delegation as a basis for the talks dealt with the issue in some way or another. However, it soon also became clear the question mattered a great deal more to the British government than it did to the Irish side. The matter was first raised by the British in July 1921, three months before the start of the negotiations, when the government made a preliminary proposal offering Ireland dominion status within the empire. On the face of it, this would grant Ireland the same status as Canada, Australia, New Zealand and South Africa. However, a closer examination showed Ireland was actually being offered a type of dominion-lite arrangement.

Ireland would have autonomy in areas such as finance, taxation and justice and would be allowed to retain its own army 'for home defence'. But in nearly all other areas of defence, it was firmly in the control of the British. It is essential, Lloyd George told de Valera, 'that the Royal Navy alone should control the seas around Ireland and Great Britain' and should have the right to use Irish ports. Ostensibly, this was to protect British food supplies and communications with her other territories. What went unmentioned was Britain's fear of a submarine war with America or France in the Atlantic, which might be assisted by the Irish government.[18]

The proposal also suggested Ireland's on-island army should be no larger, on a per capita basis, than Britain's. Lloyd George loftily, and unconvincingly, proclaimed this was to protect the global movement towards arms limitation in the wake of World War I. Britain's RAF would also have the use of 'all necessary facilities' in Ireland for both military aviation purposes and communication. Ireland would not be obliged to supply men to fight in Britain's wars. But hopefully, of its own free will and 'in proportion to her wealth', it would agree to meet a portion of the financial cost, Lloyd George wrote, and would continue to allow recruitment in its territory for British forces.[19]

The subtext was clear. The Royal Navy would control Irish waters, meaning, unlike the other dominions, Ireland could not maintain its own navy. Furthermore, Britain would control Irish ports and airfields, making it virtually assured that Ireland would be dragged into any future European conflict involving its colonial master. Neutrality was not a possibility. Childers, more than the other Irish leaders, was incensed by the proposals. That was because he had seen them before: he had acted as secretary to Lloyd George at the Irish Convention, the abortive effort in 1917 to pass a form of home rule that unionists and nationalists would agree to. The defence provisions proposed to the Convention by the British War Office were almost identical to those being submitted five years later, by which time Childers had abandoned any commitment to home rule and had become an uncompromising republican.

As an experienced yachtsman and adviser to the British Admiralty, Childers knew an island country with no navy and no control of its harbours could never call itself neutral. To allow Britain to defend Irish waters was to deny Ireland's existence as a free nation 'and to submerge it in the political and strategical system of that other power,' he said. Furthermore, the provision allowing the RAF to use Irish facilities for military and communications purposes was, he contended, 'the most extreme extension of militarism ever pronounced'.[20]

These proposals formed the basis for the British position at the treaty negotiations, which began in London on 11 October 1921. Although he was not a member of the Irish cabinet, Childers joined the negotiating team as an adviser on defence and other issues. He was less than impressed with the preparation carried out by his fellow delegates in the area. He wrote later in his diary that Griffith, who was responsible for foreign affairs, admitted during one meeting that he had read no defence documents and that Collins, who would soon become the Irish Army's first chief of staff, showed 'complete ignorance of the matter'.[21]

The Irish delegates arrived in London with a document known as *Draft Treaty A* which, while never presented to the British side, formed the foundation of their opening position. The document outlined how Ireland would be a neutral state, with that neutrality guaranteed by the British Commonwealth in perpetuity. A guarantee of Ireland's neutrality would also be sought, with Britain's support, from the United States and the League of Nations. However, reflecting de Valera's previously expressed views, Ireland would also 'in friendly regard for the strategic interests of the British Commonwealth' promise to not enter any alliance that would endanger British security or allow its territory to be used as a base for an attack on Britain.[22] Aside from this, they proposed under the draft treaty, Ireland would have total control of its foreign relations while maintaining an 'external association' with Britain.

These proposals were the closest the Irish delegates believed they could get to a true neutrality, but these were never going to fly with the British. On the first day of talks, the British side, whose delegates were led by Lloyd George, insisted it must have a more robust defence guarantee from Ireland. It was agreed the matter would be handled by a subcommittee, consisting of Churchill for the British and Collins for the Irish, with Childers as an expert adviser. This subcommittee met for the first time on 13 October, during which Britain made it clear that one of their primary concerns was the use of the Irish coastline by hostile submarines. In support of this, they showed the Irish team a map of the locations British ships had been sunk by German submarines during the war.

It was at this meeting that what would become known as the Treaty Ports were first raised. Britain wanted control, during periods of both peace and war, of three ports on Ireland's Atlantic coast: Cobh (then called Queenstown) and Berehaven in Cork and Lough Swilly in Donegal. It also wanted control of Belfast Lough on the northeast of the island. Further demands included an agreement that Ireland would not maintain a submarine force, an issue assumedly far from the minds of Irish delegates and one later conceded without argument.[23]

From the start, the Irish strategy was to not argue defence and neutrality issues on the basis of international law but to come at them from a strategic viewpoint. Collins and Childers disputed the importance Britain placed on the western Irish coastline to its security. They argued that Britain's map showed that far more British vessels had been sunk by submarines in the English Channel, off the coast of the Netherlands and in other areas far away from the Irish coast. Collins also made the reasonable point that, until these negotiations, the Royal Navy had not believed a major naval base was required in Ireland. Churchill replied that Cobh was one such important base, despite the fact that its dockyard at Haulbowline had just been shuttered.[24]

The first day of negotiations raised a question in the minds of the Irish delegates: just who was Britain so afraid of? There was little chance of Germany, its most recent enemy, posing any fresh threat, naval or otherwise. Aside from the fact that it was bankrupt, the Treaty of Versailles had placed strict limitations on the size of the German navy, including forbidding it from maintaining submarines. That realistically left only the US and France, Britain's two principal allies, as potential naval threats. In 1919, just after the end of World War I, Britain's Admiralty believed the United States Navy might pose a threat, while in 1921 Arthur Balfour, the head of the Committee of Imperial Defence, raised war with France as a possibility.[25]

Britain's fixation on the western and southern coast of Ireland led Childers to believe it most feared an attack from America. He pressed his British counterpart, Admiral David Beatty, on what opposing power they had in mind. Beatty replied that he was not in a position to specify.[26] Churchill realised the diplomatic consequences of implying Britain feared an attack from the US. At one point in the discussions, he told the Irish delegates:

> We do not want you to think that we want these ports as facilities for war with the United States. You are forcing me into a position, and I do not want you to say that you are prepared to agree to everything but that you broke because we want facilities for war with the States.[27]

Despite the hard-line position taken by the British, Childers was upbeat after the first day of the defence discussions. 'Very interesting, they are not as stiff as we thought,' he wrote in his diary.[28] He would soon realise he was mistaken. On the issue of the ports and neutrality, Britain was not for turning. Following the first meeting of the defence subcommittee, the Admiralty produced a memo stating that, as well as requiring the perpetual use of the four ports mentioned previously, Britain would reserve the right to possess any other locations 'deemed necessary for the adequate development of the bases required for the use of the fleet'. It should have this right both in times of war and in times of 'strained relations' with other powers.[29] This new position was a big jump from requiring access to a small number of specific ports.

The Irish delegates again argued against the proposals from a strategic point of view. There was no need for the Royal Navy to occupy any ports, they reasoned. A small, defensive Irish navy, consisting of coastal patrol boats, submarine chasers and minelaying craft, would be perfectly capable of deterring any belligerents from using its coastline for an attack on Britain. On 18 October, in a memo to their own government, the Irish delegates said they doubted Britain was as afraid of a naval attack as it claimed to be. There was 'no reasonable possibility in the future of any European power being able to undertake a naval war with Great Britain', the memo stated. The possibility of attack from Bolshevik Russia had also been mentioned at the first meeting, but Russian submarines would have to navigate great distances to even reach Ireland. The same was the case for submarines coming from a base thousands of miles across the Atlantic. No submarine was currently capable of such a journey. Britain wanted dominion status for Ireland, but no dominion would stand for the conditions it proposed, the memo added.[30]

Although Childers was the main defender of the idea of Irish neutrality, Collins and Griffith did make efforts to push the issue with the British. Collins argued an independent Ireland, with its neutrality guaranteed by the great powers, would be more beneficial to British security than the occupation of ports and naval bases. Churchill strongly rejected this, stating that if Ireland had been neutral during the recent world war, it would have caused Britain 'great difficulty'. Britain's Austen Chamberlain said granting Ireland neutrality would mean allowing Ireland to be outside the British Empire, something which was never on the table. Griffith accurately pointed out that Britain was offering a watered-down version of dominion status because, unlike Canada or Australia, Ireland would not have the right to build a navy.[31]

This was the high point of Irish resistance to British defence demands. The talks broke apart soon after with Britain insisting the Irish delegates return with answers to its proposals. The Irish returned on 24 October with a memo abandoning its claim to neutrality and replacing it with a proposal for 'guaranteed integrity'. Ireland would enter into no alliance against Britain nor allow its territory to be used against it. Instead of guaranteeing neutrality, Britain, the US and the League of Nations would guarantee Irish 'freedom and integrity'. If the League of Nations or the US declined to become involved, the matter should be decided by an 'imperial conference' and the Irish government.[32] The substitution of the word 'neutrality' with 'freedom' was a subtle but important change. Under the proposals, if Britain went to war, Ireland would too, at least on paper.

It was a major concession from the Irish side, but they were prepared to go even further. On the same day the memo was presented to Lloyd George and his ministers, Griffith also agreed that Britain would be able to maintain facilities in Ireland. The British delegates had emphatically won the day on the issues of defence and neutrality. Childers continued to protest, but his influence had waned since the conclusion of the work of the defence subcommittee. As the talks went on, the British delegation attempted to extract further concessions from Ireland on defence matters. Over the next week it demanded that, as well as having no navy, Ireland would have no air force. It also won the right to determine the exact extent of the naval facilities Britain would occupy, rather than leaving them as a matter for future negotiation.[33]

Throughout the process, the British side made some attempts to sugar-coat its demands with assurances or vague promises to revisit the issues down the line. It insisted that it wanted the ports purely to defend against a naval attack and not to claim any political or military control over Ireland. On 30 October, Lloyd George suggested to Griffith that Britain was prepared to back away from the air force demand. He also said the ban on an Irish navy would not include small craft such as revenue vessels or gun boats and that Ireland may be allowed an army of up to 40,000 men.[34]

By 5 December, the Irish delegation was prepared to sign the treaty, albeit reluctantly. The loss of neutrality was well down the list of their worries. Delegates were far more concerned about the provisions regarding dominion status for Ireland, partition and the swearing of an oath to the king. With Lloyd George promising a renewal of 'immediate terrible war' if they did not sign, the delegates agreed to the Anglo-Irish Treaty just after 2 a.m. in the cabinet room of 10 Downing Street.

Issues of defence were dealt with in Articles 6, 7 and 8 of the Treaty. Article 6 stated 'the defence by sea of Great Britain and Ireland shall be undertaken by His Majesty's Imperial Forces'. This meant there would be no Irish navy. However, there were two important concessions. Firstly, Ireland could maintain ships to protect revenue and fishing rights and to intercept smuggling, something which would prove to be an important loophole during the then-looming Civil War. Secondly, the matter was to be reviewed at a conference of the two governments in five years' time 'with a view to the undertaking by Ireland of a share in her own coastal defence'.[35] The format and terms of that conference were left purposely vague. Article 6 caused little controversy when the Treaty was debated over the following months. In any event, despite the concerns of Childers, the Sinn Féin government had no pressing desire to establish a navy and was certainly not in a financial position to do so.

The matter of the Treaty Ports was dealt with in Article 7. Part A stipulated that the Irish Free State, as the 26 counties were to become known under the Treaty, would allow Britain control of the ports in Cobh, Berehaven and Lough Swilly (the issue of Belfast Lough being rendered moot by partition). There was no expiry date for this provision and the ports would remain in British control during times of both war and peace. This would include harbour defences and air defences in the vicinity of the ports.[36]

Part B went much further. It required the Free State to make available any 'harbour and other facilities as the British government may require' for its defence. This was to be the case in war and in times of 'strained relations with a foreign power', an incredibly vague term which would be defined solely by the British side.[37] It was as true then as it is now that there is rarely a period when Britain does not have 'strained relations' with someone somewhere. Like the naval ban, the Treaty Ports provision did not cause much controversy during the subsequent debates. Curiously, the much boarder provision contained in Part B which granted the British rights to occupy any facility it saw fit received hardly any attention at all. This is perhaps partly explained by the generally held view at the time that, in the wake of World War I, Britain had few viable rivals who would dare to challenge it on the high seas. But it also reflects the fact that neutrality was simply not a matter of major concern for most of the delegates.

Article 8 dealt with the issue of the Army which must 'not exceed in size such proportion of the military establishments maintained in Great Britain as that which the population of Ireland bears to the population of Great Britain.'[38] This text was virtually identical to Lloyd George's proposal to de Valera in July 1921. Again, the issue caused little controversy during the negotiations. Britain could have pushed for Ireland to have an even smaller army to ensure it posed as little threat on land as it did at sea, but the negotiators were aware that British security interests were best served by the Free State being able to keep its own house in check.

In terms of foreign relations, the Free State would theoretically have the same rights as Canada, Australia, New Zealand, and South Africa. But what these rights entailed was not exactly clear. Dominion status in the British Commonwealth of the twentieth century was an evolving concept with different countries having different statuses on the world stage. For example, Canada took a leading, independent role in the League of Nations from its foundation in 1919, while the other dominions mainly followed Britain's lead. However, it was to be inferred from the comments of the British side during negotiations that it was prepared to allow Ireland some autonomy in foreign relations, providing it did not impact British security. On the other hand, if Britain went to war, Ireland was also at war. It would not have to provide troops, money or supplies to the British war effort, but it would nevertheless surely be a legitimate target for Britain's enemies if war did break out.

Two days after the Treaty was signed, the Irish Cabinet voted four to three to recommend it to the Dáil. It would later be accepted by a majority in the Dáil after an acrimonious debate, with de Valera leading the anti-Treaty side. In the aftermath of the vote, in an attempt to rally support for the anti-Treaty side, he published his alternative to the Treaty, a text which became known as *Document No 2*. The document again advanced his notion of 'external association', meaning Ireland would be an associate of the British Commonwealth but not a dominion.[39] However, when it came to matters of defence, it differed little from the Treaty. Britain would still retain the ports and would, in times of war, have access to other facilities. Irish military numbers would still be restricted, and Britain would still defend Irish waters. In one area, he went even further than the Treaty and proposed that Ireland would be an active participant in repelling any threat to British security. In any event, the document was rejected by the pro-treaty side and received little support from anti-treaty hardliners.

The split over the Treaty and the subsequent Civil War was due, in the main, to the clauses concerning dominion status and partition. Issues of neutrality and defence, if they were discussed at all, were far down the list. Historian Ronan Fanning goes so far as to say there was a 'bi-partisanship' between the pro and anti-treaty sides on the issue of neutrality, which would be echoed again during World War II.[40] The Irish had always recognised 'in their hearts' that defence, and with it, neutrality, 'touched Ireland's honour least and British security in British eyes the most,' as Lord Longford wrote in his 1935 account of the Treaty negotiations.[41] Even Childers came around to the view that neutrality in the short term was a pipe dream. In the months after the Treaty was signed he spoke out in support of de Valera's *Document No 2*, which contained no mention of neutrality at all.

In the areas of defence and neutrality, the British negotiators achieved all their aims and more. Virtually every security provision they demanded was conceded. The Free State would not offer Britain's enemies a backdoor to attack it. 'Not one jot or tittle of the naval security of Britain has been inroaded upon, or whittled upon,' Churchill told the House of Commons afterwards. Churchill conceded that the issue of naval defence would be discussed again in five years' time, but he suggested Britain might use this as an opportunity to ask for even more ports.[42]

However, it is also a fact that the Treaty granted far more freedom than was offered under the various forms of Home Rule that had been drafted over the years. Under the agreement, British forces were to evacuate the vast majority of the island and, to a limited extent, the Free State would be free to chart its own course in foreign relations, including by joining the League of Nations, which it did in 1923. The Treaty Ports rendered neutrality an impossibility in times of war but had little impact on the security situation on the island as it then existed. The ports were to be lightly garrisoned and would be of limited use to the Irish military in any event, which was then purely focused on putting down the on-island threat to the State posed by the anti-Treaty IRA. Furthermore, it soon became evident that Britain would, to serve its own interests, turn out to be quite flexible in relation to the provisions limiting army numbers and naval vessels. Bitterly disappointing as it was to so many, the Treaty gave Ireland, in the words of Collins, 'the freedom to achieve [freedom]'.[43] It also gave the country the freedom to one day achieve neutrality, or at least a pretence to it.

CHAPTER FOUR

A COCKPIT FOR BELLIGERENTS

*There is no question here of neutrality; it may be that, by
their giving facilities, neutrality goes ...*
Viscount Cave (December 1922)[1]

I t was dubbed the 'Queenstown Outrage' by the *Irish Times*. On
Friday, 21 March 1924 a contingent of British soldiers and civilians
boarded a vessel on Spike Island, the fort in the middle of Cobh
Harbour, to take them into the town for an evening's socialising.
There was nothing unusual about this – the Treaty had been signed
three years previously, and the presence of British soldiers had been
accepted in the town, despite their evacuation from most of the rest
of the Free State. Local businesses and hostelries were glad of their
custom and British troops even socialised from time to time with their
counterparts in the Free State army.[2]

That evening, as the party came alongside the quay in the town,
a civilian Rolls-Royce car containing five men pulled up. One of the
occupants shouted, 'Now, ready!' before another raised a Lewis machine
gun from between his legs, rested it on the edge of the car and opened
fire. After spraying the quayside with bullets, the attackers fled, leaving 19-year-old Private Herbert Aspinall dead and another 23 people
wounded, including two women. Reports from the time suggested the
ambush party were wearing uniforms of Free State Army officers, but

that they appeared unshaven and dishevelled.[3]

The reaction in both Britain and Ireland was fierce. In the House of Commons, Secretary of State for the Colonies J.H. Thomas called the attack 'a blot on Irish honour' while other MPs demanded to know why the Free State government was unable to protect unarmed British troops on its territory. The Irish government was equally appalled. On the night of the shooting, President of the Executive Council W.T. Cosgrave telegrammed British Prime Minister Ramsay MacDonald to assure him that 'this cowardly crime will arouse the same horror and detestation throughout Ireland as it has caused to myself and my colleagues' and that 'no efforts will be spared' in bringing the perpetrators to justice.[4]

The Irish government offered a £10,000 reward for information, a staggering sum for the time, and agreed to pay a large amount in compensation to the victims. However, despite a massive Garda manhunt and the arrest of seven men, no one was convicted of the murder. It was accepted by the Irish and British sides that the likely culprits were a group of about 130 republicans who were living in the mountains of Cork and were determined to resume the war against the British. Cosgrave told the Dáil the motive was 'clearly to provoke a diplomatic conflict' between Ireland and Britain.[5] The British government agreed. If this was indeed the motive, it was unsuccessful. Although one MP asked if it was time the Irish 'had another Cromwell', the Labour Government showed a surprising amount of understanding and promised 'all the help and sympathy' it could give the Free State.[6] Nevertheless, from then on British soldiers in Spike Island were confined to quarters and the ferry service was put under armed guard.[7]

The Queenstown false flag attempt raised concerns among the British authorities that they had perhaps made a mistake in campaigning so forcefully for the retention of the Treaty Ports during the negotiations of 1921. It was becoming clear that the ports of Queenstown, Berehaven and Lough Swilly, as well as the seven forts and 800 men that guarded them, may have had more to fear from land-based enemies than those coming from across the sea. The IRA had mostly laid down its arms the previous year following its defeat in the Civil War, but it remained a potent force in parts of the country. The Queenstown Outrage was not the first incident since the Treaty signing. Westminster MPs were told that a destroyer docked in Queenstown, the HMS *Scythe*, which had also been hit in the attack, had previously come under machine-gun fire and kept its guns trained on the land side as a result.[8] The military also feared an attack from the IRA on its officers' quarters on Bere Island, off Berehaven, and the relationship between soldiers and locals around Lough Swilly in Donegal continued to be frosty.[9]

It is not hard to see why the British treaty negotiators believed possession of the ports was vital to their interests. The military significance of all three ports went back to at least the time of Henry VIII. His successor, Queen Elizabeth I, had used Bere Island as a staging post for the final suppression of the Gaelic lords of Ireland, and 90 years later it was the location of the Battle of Bantry Bay, one of the largest naval battles ever to occur in Irish waters. A century later, the bay was the intended landing site of the French navy dispatched to aid Wolfe Tone's United Irishmen rebellion. Queenstown became an important naval hub during the Napoleonic Wars of the early nineteenth century when the British used it to protect the entrance to the English Channel and maintain a blockade of France.

All three ports were used as gathering points for transatlantic merchant convoys during World War I. In 1914, the Royal Navy's Grand Fleet was temporarily relocated to Lough Swilly, which was judged to offer greater protection from submarines than its home base of Scapa Flow in Scotland. In Queenstown, the Royal Navy built Q-boats, which were intended to act as decoys for convoys crossing the ocean and, from 1917 on, the US Navy made extensive use of Berehaven.[10]

But times had changed by the mid-1920s. Despite Churchill's view that Britain's food supply during war relied on the Irish ports, the Admiralty believed naval bases on the island of Britain could fulfil the same tasks almost as well. Massive upgrade work was also needed to modernise the facilities at the Treaty Ports: Bere Island alone would require £1 million to upgrade its guns to make it suitable for coastal defence, a figure which was not forthcoming. Britain also came to realise that, if it was to go to war with another power, the ports would be of limited use if it also had to defend them against hostile Irish forces, be they the IRA or the Free State army. Troops stationed at Bere Island and Lough Swilly also complained about the poor facilities, the isolated nature of the postings and the hostility of the locals.[11] And the British government did not want to improve the landward defences of the ports for fear of implying the Free State government was not in control of the security situation in its country.[12]

This left the British in a position of not wanting to maintain the facilities but not wanting to hand them over either. By contrast, Ireland wanted them back but, having no navy or coastal defence capabilities, did not have the means to staff them. For the Irish government, the ongoing occupation of the ports was a constant reminder that Ireland was not a neutral state, despite occasional claims to the contrary. The presence of foreign troops in military installations meant that if Britain was to go to war in Europe, Ireland would also be at war in both practical and legal terms. To this end, in 1927 the Free State made a move to gain control of the facilities. The Treaty had promised a conference after five years to determine if Ireland should take over its coastal defence. To the relief of the penniless Free State government, this never took place. Instead, there were a series of informal technical discussions of the matter between officials. During these, Ireland requested it be granted control of the ports during peacetime.

The British government was split on the issue. The Dominions Office favoured granting the Irish request as a way of improving relations; so did the War Office, which no longer wanted to provide the troops required to guard the facilities. But the Admiralty insisted retention of the ports was vital to British security interests. In the end, its opinion won out. According to internal documents, the Irish government realised the British were aware Ireland did not have the means to staff the facilities and that the Irish bid for control 'was based on questions of general prestige, and not defence considerations'.[13] The matter would have to wait another decade before being resolved in Ireland's favour.

Despite the practical and legal barriers to neutrality, some in government continued to speak and act as if it was the de facto position of the Irish Free State. For the most part, Britain was content for Irish leaders to maintain this position as there were no military threats on the horizon which would put it to the test. Britain permitted Ireland to include a vague allusion to neutrality in the 1922 Irish Free State Constitution, which was drafted to give effect to the Treaty. This came in the form of Article 49: 'Save in the case of actual invasion, the Irish Free State (Saorstát Éireann) shall not be committed to active participation in any war without the assent of the Oireachtas.' On paper, this suggested the Dáil, and not Westminster, would have the final say over whether the country was at war. The article, therefore, caused some concern among British government members, but they were assured by the Lord Chancellor, who said there was 'no question here of neutrality; it may be said that, by their giving facilities, neutrality goes.'[14] Furthermore, the preamble to the Constitution, as it appeared in legislation, stated any provision of the document which was 'in any way repugnant' to the Treaty would be 'absolutely void and inoperative'. In other words, it hardly mattered what the Constitution had to say on the matter of neutrality. The Treaty reigned supreme and true neutrality was still a fantasy.

Nevertheless, the term neutrality continued to be used by politicians and in government documents as if it carried much greater meaning. The Cumann na nGaedheal government was able to get away with this during the first decade of independence due to the fact that Irish neutrality, notional or otherwise, faced no major tests. The list of conflicts involving Britain during the period is made up mostly of the suppression of revolts in the Middle East, none of which impacted Ireland in any way. The matter was the subject of a spirited Dáil debate in 1927 when Irish Labour Party leader Thomas Johnson asked the government to remove the factors which might bring Ireland into a British war, i.e. the Treaty Ports. In his response, Minister for External Affairs Desmond FitzGerald spoke of the need to maintain 'our neutrality and freedom' but also stated Irish neutrality would mean little if Britain were attacked.[15]

Defence and security documents from the period also talk of neutrality while conceding it was entirely contingent on the wishes of Britain. A memo drafted by the Department of the President in September 1925, which effectively became the Irish Free State's first defence policy, stated that the National Army – which had been renamed the Defence Forces the previous year – must be capable of defending against a violation of neutrality in 'full and complete coordination with the forces of the British government'.[16] It was a long way from J.J. O'Connell's attempts to forge an alliance with France in February 1922. The main difficulty here was that the Defence Forces believed Britain was the party most likely to violate Irish neutrality. One of the tasks of its intelligence bureau was to plan for this threat, including by planning a military survey of each county and beginning work on code breaking and signal interception. In 1925, plans were drawn up by Commandant William Brennan-Whitmore for a censorship bureau to ensure the 'maintenance of neutrality' during a war. If Ireland had any hope of staying out of a war involving Britain, the media and communications systems would have to be strictly monitored for any expressions of sympathy for any of the belligerents. The proposals languished until 1938 when they became a key part of Irish preparations for the coming global conflict.[17]

When de Valera re-entered constitutional politics in 1926 he took full advantage of the vagaries of the Cumann na nGaedheal government's approach to neutrality. As leader of the newly founded Fianna Fáil, he argued 'the right of maintaining our neutrality is the proper policy for this country.'[18] Gone for now was the de Valera of 1920 who conceded full neutrality was a pipe dream. Fianna Fáil frequently raised the issue in the Dáil throughout the rest of the decade, much to the frustration of the government. Some of its members reverted to the earlier republican goal of seeking the great powers to 'guarantee' Irish neutrality, as they had done for Switzerland. One Fianna Fáil deputy, Patrick Little, suggested this course would have the added benefit of reducing the beleaguered State's defence budget. Desmond FitzGerald, now minister for defence, mocked the proposal and pointed out that Switzerland spent considerably more on its military than Ireland and that, as things stood, the Irish Defence Forces would be 'quite useless' in defending the State against a major power.[19]

FitzGerald's 1928 declaration of the uselessness of the Defence Forces did not cause much controversy. By then it was well known that Cumann na nGaedheal had resigned itself to the fact that the Free State would always have an ineffectual military. In fact, a toothless army was the party's strong preference, lest it pose a threat to the government. During the Civil War, the National Army had been rapidly and massively expanded. When that conflict concluded, the Army numbered some 55,000 men. Just over a decade later, Irish military planners declared that 'in the usual European sense the [Irish State] can hardly be said to have a Defence Force at all.'[20]

Following the Civil War, the government reduced the Army numbers just as quickly as it had built them up. Within the year there were just 16,382 members. This rapid demobilisation caused significant anger among officers and enlisted men, many of whom were also angry that IRA men who had fought and won the War of Independence were being excluded from the senior ranks in favour of former British Army officers. Members of Michael Collins' War of Independence assassination unit, known as the Squad, were particularly angry. They felt they should have been rewarded with senior army commissions.

Tensions were further heightened in the autumn of 1923 when the government ordered the demobilisation of 900 officers. This caused 60 officers to protest, leading to their dismissal without pay and further inflaming the situation. These frustrations led to the Army Mutiny the following March, when the Irish Republican Army Organisation (known as the Old IRA), who represented the disgruntled army officers, gave Cosgrave's government an ultimatum, demanding a halt to demobilisation at once. Otherwise, they would take unspecified action to halt 'the treachery that threatens to destroy the aspirations of the nation.'[21] In a bid to gain public support for the drastic move, the Old IRA maintained its chief grievance was a lack of government action in ending partition, rather than frustrations over demobilisations. In sympathy with the demands, 49 officers resigned their commissions and another 50 deserted their posts with their weapons. Publicly, the government took a hard line, with Cosgrave calling the action 'a challenge to the democratic foundations of the State' and Minister for Defence General Richard Mulcahy ordering the arrest of the mutineers.[22]

In private, however, the government sought to end the crisis quickly and quietly and engaged in negotiations with the Old IRA. It agreed to cease searching for the AWOL officers and to set up an inquiry into alleged incompetence in the Department of Defence. In return, the Old IRA agreed to withdraw the ultimatum. However, this did not end the crisis. Mulcahy received intelligence that the Old IRA leadership was meeting at Devlin's Hotel in Dublin in contravention of the agreement worked out with the government. In response, on 19 March, 40 of Mulcahy's men surrounded the building and, following an armed stand-off, arrested the mutineers, bringing the crisis to a close. Over the following weeks, the government ordered the resignation of the entire army leadership, cementing civilian control over the armed forces.[23]

The mutiny had affirmed the government's view that the Army was not to be trusted. It placed the Defence Forces at the mercy of the Department of Finance, which was particularly keen to reduce its status as an institution. This process was already well in motion by the time of the mutiny. From the foundation of the Free State, all government bodies were obliged to seek permission from Finance before spending any money or making any appointments, meaning even the purchase of ammunition or rations by the Army required departmental sign-off. In 1923, Finance officials declared 'semi-spectacular' services such as a cavalry corps or an air force were not required and would do 'grave injury' to the country's finances if pursued. The readiness of civil servants in Finance to decide what was and was not needed to defend the country was a source of great frustration to military officers. This was further compounded by a ruling from the department in September 1924 that the members of the Army were not sufficiently professional to warrant a full wage.[24]

The civil servants found a listening ear for these policies in Cosgrave's government, particularly after the Army Mutiny. In June 1924, the Ministers and Secretaries Act was signed. This stripped power from the Army chief of staff and allowed the minister of the day to give orders directly to the chief's subordinate generals. Around the same time, procedures were put in place where almost all proposals from the Army leadership would have to be conveyed to the minister through officials in the Department of Defence. This further reduced the status of the Army leadership and removed them from the decision-making process.[25]

The emasculation of the military can be seen most clearly in the government's response to a document produced by the Council of Defence in July 1925. In stark terms, the council, which was made up of the minister and the three most senior army generals, had warned that the Defence Forces were not capable 'as at present constituted, of taking any really effective part in the defence of the country against a modern army, navy or air force'; that there was no chance of Ireland being able to defend its neutrality militarily and, just like Belgium in World War I, it was likely to become 'a cockpit for the belligerents in a war between England and any other power'. Irish neutrality, the council predicted, would be imperilled by war, even if Britain was not involved, and that a war between the US and France, Germany or Russia would pose a great danger to Ireland.[26]

The council proposed three ways forward. The government could a) develop Irish defence capability into a 'complete Defensive machine'; b) organise the Defence Forces to form a part of the British armed forces and to come under British command in the event of war; or c) abandon all matters of external defence to Britain and retain a domestic force for the sole purpose of dealing with internal threats, such as those from the IRA, communists or disgruntled ex-army personnel.

It is clear from the tenor of the document that its authors favoured the first option, that of a viable, independent Defence Forces. In a series of remarkably ambitious proposals, the council called for the establishment of a force which could resist invasion by Britain and others. Among its proposals were an Irish air force, a 'chemical warfare service' and a coastal defence system. 'The construction of submarines is not feasible in the immediate future but there is no reason why we should not keep the matter in mind,' it added. Needless to say, Cosgrave did not agree. In a handwritten note on the margins of the document, he wrote, 'do not visualise anything but alliances with [Great Britain].'[27]

The official government response to the document came in October 1925 in the form of a memo from Cosgrave's office, outlining what would become Ireland's official defence policy. Ireland would maintain a standing army of up to 12,000 troops which would form the 'nucleus' of the Defence Forces and which could be expanded in the event of an attack. The army should be able to defend Ireland against invasion and also be capable of 'full and complete coordination with the forces of the British government' in the event of a breach of neutrality by a common enemy.[28]

In reality, the Army would be capable of neither: as well as being completely incapable of resisting invasion, very little was done to build ties with the British military. Aside from some limited cooperation in the area of procurement, there was little contact between the two countries' militaries over the next decade. Instead, the Irish Army turned to the US for training and inspiration.[29]

This enfeeblement of the Defence Forces became permanent government policy, a policy which persisted after Cumann na nGaedheal left power for good. For the next century, a weak military became a defining characteristic of the State's ambivalent attitude towards neutrality. Most interpretations of international law on neutrality suggest a nation must have a military force capable of defending its neutral status against incursions by all sides. The Free State had no such thing and was mostly content with that situation. Despite allusions to a desire to defend neutrality through military means, in the style of Switzerland, the State in the 1920s and beyond instead planned to rely on immediate British assistance if an attack did come. And if Britain was to attack, the policy seems to have been to hope for the best. Either way, government policy in the 1920s meant that if war did break out the Free State *would* likely be 'a cockpit for the belligerents'.

Further evidence of the State's early flexible attitude to neutrality can be seen in its eagerness to join the League of Nations, a body founded on the concept of collective security – the idea that an attack on one member would draw a response from the others. In its most benign form, this meant members could be obliged to comply with economic sanctions against nations that violated League principles. At the other end of the spectrum, League members could theoretically be duty-bound to go to war against violators. It was a far cry from the old view of neutrality where a state would do all it could to avoid taking sides in a conflict. In this new world order, League members could find themselves having to take sides in inter-state conflicts that had nothing to do with them; even ones on the other side of the globe.

Support for joining the League was far from universal in Ireland. It is an indication of the perilous finances of the Free State during the period that the yearly cost of membership of the League, £10,000, was cited as a valid reason it should not seek membership. Such a price may indeed be too high, a pamphlet from the Irish League of Nations Society conceded in 1923 on the eve of Irish membership, but, it said, 'for £10,000 a year Ireland could not maintain fifty soldiers. The protection given by membership of the League is worth more than a platoon of infantry.'[30]

Other objections against joining were the claims that the League was ineffectual as an organisation and that joining it would alienate Irish allies in America, which was not a member despite being instrumental in its founding.

The Irish public, distracted by more pressing events at home, showed little interest in foreign affairs. This view was often reflected in the Dáil where the Department of External Affairs was mostly ignored by TDs; in 1927 it had only seven parliamentary questions to answer – and on one occasion, it was suggested there was no need for a department at all. Republicans remained either ambivalent or outright suspicious of the League of Nations. Part of this attitude was no doubt related to the first Dáil's failed attempt to gain a seat at the peace conference which founded the League in 1919. Subsequently, de Valera had described the League as a form of 'tyranny' which existed to 'perpetuate power for those who had got it.'[31]

But for Cosgrave's government, the League was a way of demonstrating Irish independence on the world stage, and of forging international relations without having to go through Britain. Minister for External Affairs George Gavan Duffy also believed Ireland could bring a great deal to the League because it would not be afraid to say things 'that the other powers are too cowardly to be the first to say.'[32]

So eager was the government that it appointed almost its entire cabinet as annual delegates to the League after Ireland joined in September 1923.[33] When Irish delegates took their seats at the League headquarters in Geneva to a standing ovation, their priority was to register the Anglo-Irish Treaty with the League as an international agreement. This would be a coup for the Free State as it would frame the Treaty as an agreement between two equal nations, rather than a piece of internal Commonwealth business. Britain objected in private, preferring to keep Commonwealth matters out of the League, but it did not formally object when the Treaty was registered.

The Free State government gave little consideration to the impact League membership would have on its occasional aspirations to neutrality. Far more important was that it would give Ireland an independent voice on the world stage. In its defence, it could point to the fact that Switzerland, that paradigm of neutrality, had also joined the League. But in the case of Switzerland, the League had specifically recognised its neutral status. It did not do so for Ireland, nor was it asked to.

On the other hand, it is clear Cosgrave's government viewed League membership not as a military alliance but as a way to peacefully settle disputes. Through membership, Ireland pursued an early version of a policy that would come to be termed 'positive neutrality'. It frequently took a moral stance on issues before the League, including condemning the weapons trade and calling for disarmament. In 1928 it was one of the first to sign the Kellogg–Briand Pact compelling signatories to renounce war as a tool of foreign policy. In 1929, it signed up to the Court of International Justice, the first member of the Commonwealth to do so. The Free State could take these principled stands safe in the knowledge that they would not impact its own national security, which was then still entirely in the hands of Britain.

This activism and its success in registering the Treaty gave the Free State delegates confidence in international relations. The Free State successfully ran for membership of the League's ruling council in 1930 and took its place alongside Britain as an equal. By then it was also well aware of the limitations of what small nations could achieve within its structures. For example, in 1924, the Free State was in favour of financial sanctions against Italy when Benito Mussolini ordered the invasion of Corfu in revenge for Greek troops shooting dead Italian border guards. Instead, the League voted to force Greece to pay reparations. Irish doubts about this form of collective security would further solidify throughout the first half of the 1930s.[34]

Alongside its work within the League, the Department of External Affairs worked to build up bilateral relations with other non-commonwealth countries, including the United States in 1924 and France, Germany and the Vatican in 1929. It also sought to take part in international conferences, even when they had little to do with Irish interests. In 1927, it sent a delegation to the Naval Disarmament Conference in Geneva, at a time when the Free State still did not have a navy (there was some concern among officials however that taking part in the conference would draw attention to the Free State's position of enjoying the protection of the world's largest navy while doing nothing to pay for it).[35]

The Free State would not have been able to assert itself so much on the world stage without significant advancements within the Commonwealth system through a series of conferences and declarations. The Cumann na nGaedheal government was an active participant at these conferences, particularly the 1926 Imperial Conference at which Britain recognised dominions were equals in matters of foreign relations. These efforts would culminate with the Statute of Westminster of 1931, which defined the Commonwealth as a 'free association' of nations and prevented Britain from imposing its laws on dominions.

Despite the allusions in the 1922 constitution and occasional unconvincing assertions by the government, the Irish Free State was not neutral in the 1920s. The provisions of the Treaty meant it could not be. The Royal Navy controlled three Irish ports with the option to take over more if it saw fit. Dominion status meant that in any war, Ireland would automatically be on the British side. At the same time, the Free State government displayed little ambition in pursuing a neutrality policy. Its neglect of the Defence Forces showed it was happy to rely on British protection and its eagerness to join the League of Nations showed it did not see itself bound by the classical definition of neutrality. On the other hand, League membership demonstrated on the world stage the Free State's independence from Britain, while the government's often unrecognised achievements from the Commonwealth conferences put in place the foundation for de Valera to credibly declare neutrality at the start of World War II, something no other dominion did. But there was still a long road to travel to get to that point. For the time being, Ireland viewed its security as protected both by Britain and the novel concept of collective security. It would soon realise however these were not permanent solutions.

CHAPTER FIVE

THE TESTING TIME

We want to be neutral ...
Éamon de Valera (June 1936)[1]

On 26 September 1932, Éamon de Valera rose to address the
League of Nations Assembly in Geneva to a deafening silence.
Due to the diplomatic efforts of the previous Cumann na
nGaedheal government, Ireland held the presidency of the
League council that year and, as was tradition, the job of formally
opening the session fell to its representative. There had already been
a great deal of apprehension ahead of de Valera's speech. To most
delegates, this tall, awkward Irishman was an unknown quantity; de
Valera had only been elected as head of government that February.
They also worried that the former revolutionary, whose conversion
to constitutional politics was still a matter of debate in some circles,
would use the opportunity to embarrass one of the great powers, most
probably Britain. Even de Valera's officials were nervous; the Free State's
permanent representative to the League, Seán Lester, urged that the
speech be kept short, for de Valera's 'personal dignity'.[2] The speech
would indeed prove controversial, but the British delegates needn't have
worried: de Valera took aim instead at the entire League of Nations.

Refusing a speech prepared by League officials, he used the opportunity to highlight the organisation's mounting failures. At the front of

his mind was the recent invasion of Chinese Manchuria by Japan. De Valera, and many others, saw the League's weak response to the invasion (Japan was a permanent member of the League Council) as evidence it was biased towards powerful countries to the detriment of their weaker or smaller neighbours. Although the League issued various condemnations, the Japanese stayed in Manchuria, setting the stage for world war in the Pacific later that decade. 'The testing time has come,' de Valera told the delegates. It was time for the League to decide its purpose. Was it to be a talking shop or a genuine protector of international order?[3] It was not an academic question for the young Free State. Ireland, then as now, saw a rules-based international order as its best security guarantee.

When he sat down again a few minutes later, de Valera heard the same sound that had greeted him when he stood up: silence. At first, it seemed the speech had gone down like a lead balloon. For many delegates it had. But in private, other officials praised the Irishman's frankness. This was a man who was willing to call out the hypocrisy of the League without fear of upsetting the great powers. The reaction in the press was even more positive. A correspondent from the *London Daily Herald* called it 'the best speech I ever heard from a president of the League [...] That is not only my own judgement. It is the opinion of almost every League journalist with whom I have spoken.' The *New York Times* said the speech 'unquestionably made him the outstanding personality of this session'.[4] It was an appropriate start to what would be a tumultuous relationship between Ireland and the League from then on. It was a relationship that would end the following decade, with Lester, who had by then been made secretary-general of the organisation, trying to keep the lights on in its near-empty Geneva offices as war raged just across the border in France.

De Valera placed a major emphasis on international relations when he entered government in March 1932. He made himself his own minister for external affairs, putting him in charge of the crucial Anglo-Irish negotiations which followed. This would also make him a regular visitor to the League of Nations. But neutrality was not a priority for de Valera. Almost immediately after taking power, he embarked on a process of dismantling the Anglo-Irish Treaty that had been agreed upon a decade ago. These early efforts focused on issues such as removing the oath to the king and the position of governor general. There was no effort at that stage to regain the Treaty Ports, which were still one of the main obstacles to true Irish neutrality. For now, despite his frequent criticisms, de Valera believed Irish security was best protected by a strong, proactive League of Nations rather than pursuing a policy of permanent neutrality.

Neutrality and League of Nations membership were not easy bedfellows. In theory, the Covenant of the League of Nations could demand members go to war to punish an aggressor state.[5] The inherent weakness of the organisation meant this was always a remote possibility but there is some evidence Ireland would have supported military operations if they were approved by the League. In July 1936, de Valera told League delegates that economic and financial sanctions can only be effective if they are backed up by 'military measures'.[6] It is open to interpretation whether he meant this as an endorsement of military means or a commentary on the futility of financial sanctions, but there is other evidence that de Valera favoured a stronger, quasi-military role for the League.

In January 1935, the people of the Saar, a region on the border of France and Germany, were to vote on reunification with Germany (France had been given control over the territory 15 years previously as compensation following World War I). With the Nazi party in the ascendency in the Saar, there were fears the vote would be marred by violence. This led Britain to propose an international security force to keep the peace. The Free State government was interested in taking part, with one Irish official referring to it approvingly as an 'international police force'. League officials were told that, if invited to take part, the Defence Forces would provide between 240 and 400 soldiers (up to 7 per cent of the Army's strength) to help keep the peace during the vote.[7] In the end, the Irish contingent was not required but the episode demonstrated the Free State was willing to go beyond diplomacy in protecting the international order. This commitment is all the more impressive, considering Irish troops in the Saar would have been under the command of a British general.

Despite this episode, by 1935 the Free State was starting to have doubts about how much the League of Nations could protect it in the event of a major European war. De Valera's speeches were becoming more ominous about the League's future as it became increasingly clear its members were either unwilling or unable to push back against powerful aggressor countries.

The Abyssinia Crisis of 1935 would cement this view, not just for the Free State but for many other small nations. In October of that year, Mussolini ordered an invasion of Abyssinia (modern-day Ethiopia), prompting the League to impose limited sanctions on Italy. The Irish government fully supported these sanctions, despite opposition from some TDs who favoured supporting Catholic Italy. However, the already weak sanctions were soon undermined by Britain and France, who were willing to allow Italy to take Abyssinia in the vain hope it would prevent Mussolini from entering into an alliance with Adolf Hitler. Abyssinia fell in May 1936 and a disgusted de Valera stated the next month that the League 'does not command our confidence'.[8] He believed the Abyssinian crisis was the League's 'final test' and it had failed comprehensively.[9] 'We want to be neutral,' he told the Dáil that June.[10] After this, he also became a strong advocate of appeasing both Italy and, later, Germany, in the hope of avoiding war.

Also in June, de Valera tentatively raised the prospect of withdrawing from the organisation completely. But Ireland would remain a member, albeit a much less enthusiastic one. The League still offered a useful forum for international relations, which Ireland, with its tiny diplomatic corps, could not afford to do without. It would stay in the League right up to the League's dissolution in 1946, by which time Seán Lester – the unassuming Antrim diplomat who had been appointed Ireland's permanent representative at the start of the 1930s – was its secretary-general. Lester distinguished himself in service to the League: he was one of the first diplomats to highlight the Nazi persecution of the Jews and was responsible for keeping the beleaguered organisation alive throughout the war. This would later be of huge benefit to the United Nations, which inherited many of the League's institutions. But Lester would get little credit for his actions. His grandson and biographer Douglas Gageby later recalled that Lester barely got an invite to the founding UN conference in San Francisco in 1946.[11]

The Spanish Civil War, which started in 1936, provided an opportunity for Ireland to demonstrate to the world its newfound affinity for neutrality. It also highlighted the difficulties such a policy posed for decision-makers. Whoever said history is written by the winners has never studied Ireland's role in the bloody, three-year conflict. The Irishmen who travelled to Spain to join the doomed fight against General Francisco Franco are today remembered much more fondly than the much larger numbers who travelled to fight on the victorious fascist side. What is often forgotten is that Irish society then was overwhelmingly supportive of Franco's forces, whom they saw as resisting the godless communism of the Spanish republicans. This support raised serious problems for de Valera's neutrality policy. Such support wasn't limited to the Catholic Church and the Fine Gael opposition. It was also the view of most ordinary Irish people and even many members of Fianna Fáil. Reading his statements in the Dáil, it is reasonable to assume de Valera himself, whose faith touched on most aspects of his political life, was personally supportive of Franco's nationalists. Nevertheless, official Ireland would remain strictly impartial during the conflict. In fact, its neutrality would be far purer than the neutrality adopted during the subsequent world war. Despite the huge public support for the Spanish nationalists, de Valera resisted calls to cut ties with the republican government and recognise the fascist opposition while the result of the war was still in question. Irish officials would also try, largely in vain, to stop Irish people from travelling to fight for either side, something it did not do in World War II. It could reasonably be argued that the Spanish Civil War was the last time Ireland adopted a policy of true neutrality in a major European conflict.

The domestic opposition to de Valera's policy was significant. 'All who stand for the ancient faith and the traditions of Spain are behind the present revolt against the Marxist regime in Madrid,' the *Irish Independent* thundered in an editorial on 22 July 1936, five days after the war began. Throughout the first half of the war, the newspaper repeatedly allied with Fine Gael and called on de Valera to take sides against the Spanish republicans, mainly on religious grounds but also to combat the spread of communism. By August, it was demanding to know why de Valera hadn't cut ties with the republican government in Madrid. That same month, a large number of county councils adopted what had become known as the Clonmel Resolutions, which called on the government to sever diplomatic relations. Much of this organising was done by Patrick Belton, an independent TD who founded the Irish Christian Front (ICF) in support of the Spanish nationalists. He found a willing ally in Eoin O'Duffy, the former army and Garda chief who, until 1935, had led the fascist-leaning Army Comrades Association, or Blueshirts as they were more commonly known.

There were people in Ireland who supported the republicans. Most of these were not communists but rather people who were uncomfortable with a democratically elected government being overthrown in a military coup so close to home. But in the fevered atmosphere of the time, these people risked being labelled as Bolsheviks. There was a desperate fear in some sections of Irish society of the red menace. In truth, outside of some factions of the IRA, actual communists were very hard to find in Ireland. This lack of any genuine communist threat in Ireland to stir emotion meant de Valera's government was able to endure the criticism of neutrality. Despite mass rallies and fundraising efforts by Franco's Irish supporters, Ireland continued to recognise the republican government until Franco's final victory. De Valera successfully argued that breaking relations with the republican government would be a breach of diplomatic norms and would place Ireland in the same category as Mussolini's Italy and Hitler's Germany.

A further expression of neutrality came when Ireland joined the Non-Intervention Committee, which was established by Britain and France in 1936 to prevent the flow of materiel and volunteers to either side in Spain. As part of this effort, de Valera's government introduced legislation in February 1937 banning Irish people from travelling to Spain to fight. It passed, but only after a contentious three-day debate, during which Fine Gael TDs argued it would only help the republican side. To support the ban, another bill was passed contributing Irish officials to an international observer force that would monitor ships and ports for breaches. In total, 11 sea observers and 6 land observers were sent from Ireland. It was the first time the State had contributed to an international force of any kind, and it marked a major milestone for a country still trying to gain respect on the world stage. That it was done to protect Irish neutrality made it all the more significant.

But the impact of these measures was negligible. For one thing, most of the Irish people who had wanted to fight in Spain had already travelled: some 80 Irish republican volunteers, led by republican icon Frank Ryan, travelled to fight against Franco in December 1936, and around the same time, a much larger group, consisting of some 700 volunteers and led by O'Duffy, went to fight for the nationalists. Furthermore, the non-intervention measures received only lukewarm support from many European countries. Hitler, Mussolini and the Soviet Union ignored them completely while France was willing to turn a blind eye to the transfer of personnel and materiel over fears about upsetting Italy. Once again, de Valera had proof that international cooperation was only of limited use when the interests of great powers were at play.

As the war dragged on into the second half of 1937, Irish interest was waning and the febrile pro-Franco atmosphere was starting to subside. De Valera's policy of neutrality came to enjoy a good deal of public support, and even some of the most zealous anti-communists questioned the wisdom of further intervention, as reports on the increasing numbers of dead Irishmen appeared in the newspapers. O'Duffy's brigade arrived home in Dublin in June 1937, his men on the brink of mutiny following a disastrous campaign. The anti-Franco volunteers came home a year later after suffering many deaths and injuries in the fighting. In February 1939, along with the rest of Europe, the Irish government recognised Franco's government as legitimate. The war was essentially over and it was only a matter of time before the nationalists would control the entire territory. The Non-Intervention Committee held its last meeting in March 1939, having long ago ceased functioning in any real sense. De

Valera had weathered the storm. His stance during the Spanish Civil War has since been called 'a kind of a rehearsal' for World War II.[12] This is certainly true in at least one way. The war drove home to de Valera the complexities of neutrality; complexities the Free State would have to deal with a few years later. In stemming the flow of men and supplies to Spain, neutral states had aided the nationalist side, which had always been far better equipped than the republicans, so even while trying to remain strictly impartial, Ireland had helped one side. In the bloody but limited conflict in Spain, this did little to endanger Irish security, but in a war involving Ireland's neighbours, this could be fatal.

Of course, with the Free State still so tightly bound to London by the Anglo-Irish Treaty, all of this was largely academic. The treaty would have to be dismantled if neutrality was to mean anything. That's exactly what de Valera set his mind to in the latter half of the 1930s. The Constitutional Amendment and External Relations Acts of 1936 abolished the office of governor general and removed the king from any role in Irish internal affairs. The following year, the 1937 Imperial Conference helpfully decided that Commonwealth members could decide their own defence policy. No longer could Britain sign a dominion up to a war with the stroke of a pen, as it had done with Canada in 1914. All that remained was for the Free State to cement these freedoms in a new constitution. In 1937, Bunreacht na hÉireann made the country a republic in all but name, but it was accepted by the British as it was written in such a way that Westminster could still pretend to itself Ireland was a dominion. The constitution unambiguously stated that war of any kind could only be declared with the assent of the Dáil, but there was no mention, implied or otherwise, of neutrality in the text, despite the fact de Valera was, by then, firmly set on the policy. The taoiseach recognised that in such uncertain times, it was best to leave neutrality as elastic a term as possible.

This was impressive progress but the awkward matter of the Treaty Ports remained outstanding. In a major European war, any Irish claims to neutrality would be scarcely credible if some of its major ports were controlled by one of the belligerents. That situation changed on the evening of 11 July 1938 when, to the sound of 19 cannons firing across Cobh

Harbour, de Valera disembarked from a boat on Spike Island. He was there to oversee the (very slight) enlargement of the Irish Free State as Defence Forces troops took possession of the first of the Treaty Ports to be handed back by the British. The British soldiers had left by ferry earlier that day – de Valera had refused to set foot on the island until they were gone – and were well on their way home by the time the Tricolour was raised to the sound of thousands of people cheering on Cobh promenade. At the same time, soldiers in barracks across the Free State saluted the flag. Similar pageantry would play out later that year at Berehaven and Lough Swilly. These ceremonies were the culmination of a process that had begun six years previously with the outbreak of the Economic War between Britain and the Free State after Ireland had refused to pay the land annuities it owed Britain under the Treaty. The return of the Treaty Ports was one of the terms of the 1938 Anglo-Irish Agreement that brought the Economic War to an end. If Britain was to go to war in the next few years, as was widely expected, Ireland now had a realistic chance of staying out of it.

During the course of the secret negotiations aimed at ending the Economic War and clarifying Ireland's defence position, de Valera faced remarkably little difficulty in convincing Britain to return the Treaty Ports. The view of the British Admiralty had evolved. It believed that the ports would be useful for anti-submarine warfare, but were not essential. The British would also still have to worry about defending themselves from the landward side from possible IRA attacks in the event of war. Neville Chamberlain's government reasoned that giving up the ports was an acceptable price to pay for improved relations with Ireland. Unsurprisingly, given his role in negotiating the Treaty, Winston Churchill was one of the few MPs to oppose the decision. He noted that, under the new deal, Britain would not even be permitted to use the port facilities in the time of war. 'On the face of it, it seemed to have given everything away and received nothing in return, except the payment of £10,000,000,' he thundered.[13] Churchill's depth of feeling on the matter was to be expected. During an inspection visit to Cork in 1912, he called the Treaty Ports, in typically melodramatic terms, 'the sentinel towers of the defences of Western Europe'.[14] When Churchill became prime minister after the outbreak of World War II, the goal of taking back the ports became almost an obsession, but for the moment, London was happy to dispose of three expensive outposts which were of limited military use.

It's tempting here to conclude that the many failures of the League of Nations, combined with the success of the Free State's policy towards Spain and the reclamation of the Treaty Ports, meant de Valera had a newfound respect for the concept of neutrality. But this is not the case. He held the same realist view as he had during the War of Independence: Irish neutrality would always have to take account of British interests. Furthermore, he believed the entire concept was worth sacrificing if it meant the end of partition. On several occasions before World War II, de Valera made it clear he would be willing to enter a defensive alliance with Britain if it meant the return of the six counties. This went beyond merely assuring Britain the Free State would not allow itself to be used as a base for an attack (as he did on several occasions), during the negotiations preceding the 1938 agreement, de Valera spoke about joint British–Irish defence plans and interchangeable military equipment. There was even talk of a munitions factory being built in Ireland. In 1939, he told Chamberlain, 'in the event of war the attitude of Ireland would be very different' if it wasn't for partition.[15] It is no surprise then, that in 1940, Churchill, facing the very real prospect of a German invasion, believed de Valera would abandon neutrality if offered an end to partition.

By 1938, de Valera had put in place the political prerequisites for neutrality, but in practical terms Ireland remained entirely unable to defend that neutrality. Even the return of the Treaty Ports might not have been as beneficial as they'd earlier appeared. Defence Forces planner J.J. O'Connell (by then a colonel, having been demoted from General during the Army's post-Civil War reorganisation) wrote in 1938 that the return of the ports did not change the fact that the west coast of Ireland was strategically vital from a naval point of view and they still might draw Ireland into a war. Furthermore, the Defence Forces did not have either the expertise or resources to maintain the ports as viable coastal defence hubs. By one estimate, if Ireland was drawn into war, half the Defence

Forces would be required to operate and defend the ports.[16]

Back in 1936, Colonel Dan Bryan, the second in command of G2, the military intelligence branch, had written a document outlining exactly how ineffective the Defence Forces would be if the Free State was invaded. He had been prompted to write the memo in response to bluster from other Irish officers, buoyed up by the naive patriotism of the Economic War, that the Defence Forces could end partition through military means. This was 'utter insanity', Bryan wrote. The Free State was 'not relatively but absolutely disarmed' and the country could only fight a war against a reasonably powerful state for a very short time before it exhausted its resources. Bryan also noted that to be neutral, a state had to adhere to 'very onerous military and international obligations'. A failure to meet these obligations would give Britain the excuse to take what measures it thought necessary.[17] He was one of the few Irish officials at the time to recognise that neutrality during wartime obliged countries to defend that neutrality.

The Defence Forces Chief of Staff Lieutenant General Michael Brennan used Bryan's document when prevailing on the government to invest in the military ahead of the war, which he predicted would start in '1938/39' at the earliest. The Free State needed fighter planes, light bombers, anti-aircraft guns and, most importantly, soldiers, many more soldiers. Predictably, the pleas were entirely rejected by Minister for Finance Seán MacEntee. In a remarkable combination of optimism and pessimism, MacEntee reasoned that there probably wouldn't be any war and, even if there was, Ireland would be immediately overwhelmed if invaded.[18] From a military point of view, de Valera's 'we want to be neutral' policy was based on blind hope rather than adequate preparation.

This meant that on the eve of the war, Ireland had no navy, a tiny, ill-equipped air force, and just 20,000 troops. About half of these were members of the newly formed 'Volunteer Force', a reserve organisation with minimal training and even worse equipment than the permanent Defence Forces. The plan was, in the event of an invasion by Britain from Northern Ireland, the full-time soldiers would attempt to delay the advance to give the Volunteers time to mobilise. The entire Defence

Forces would then revert to the guerrilla tactics used in the War of Independence. There were some late attempts to better equip the military ahead of the war, but by the time the scale of the problem had been accepted it had become almost impossible to source supplies from Europe, and Britain was in no mood to assist what it saw as its disloyal former subjects. In 1939, military spending was increased to 10 per cent of the budget, more than double what it had been five years previously, but still woefully inadequate to address the problem.

As soon as war clouds began appearing on the horizon, Irish officials became aware of another weakness. Despite de Valera's stated goal of self-sufficiency, in 1939 Ireland remained highly dependent on Britain for vital supplies, including 100 per cent of its coal needs and 51 per cent of its cattle feed. This dependency was a weapon Britain would no doubt be willing to wield to influence Irish defence policy if it felt under threat. Perhaps even more concerning was, despite the impact of the Economic War, Britain still received a significant proportion of its food from Ireland. Germany could well take the view this made Ireland's neutrality meaningless. What's more, Ireland possessed no merchant marine, meaning it was unable to develop independent supply routes. This meant that when war started, Ireland was almost as unprepared economically as it was militarily.

Going into the war, neutrality was an overwhelmingly popular policy among the public. Some resisted the idea of aiding Britain in the war while partition existed, but most simply did not want to see their sons die in a conflict which seemingly had little to do with Ireland. But, popular as neutrality was, there was no guarantee Ireland would be able to maintain the position. The government's representative in London, John Dulanty, predicted Ireland would join the war within two weeks of it starting due to attacks on shipping.[19] This fear was evident when Germany's Ambassador to Ireland Eduard Hempel met de Valera on 31 August 1939, three days before war was declared. Germany demanded 'unimpeachable neutrality', Hempel said. De Valera replied that Ireland would observe neutrality equally towards both sides, but its dependence on trade with Britain meant it would have to show 'a certain consideration' for its nearest neighbour. Hempel came away from the meeting impressed with de Valera's sincere commitment to neutrality. The German representative also detected great fear on the Irish side.[20]

Events moved quickly in the 1930s. The decade marked the high point of Ireland's commitment to collective security. When de Valera had come to power as head of Fianna Fáil, he'd seen Ireland's interests as being best served by the structures of the League of Nations. Despite its imperfections, he believed the League would protect Ireland from the machinations of powerful states, including the one right next door. But by the latter half of the decade, the government had seen how the League had failed to protect countries like Abyssinia and it feared Ireland could suffer a similar fate. This is when it truly turned to a policy of neutrality, something it could only do because of de Valera's success in the Anglo-Irish negotiations.

But from the start, de Valera's commitment to neutrality was based on realism rather than idealism. Neutrality was a means to an end – or several ends, to be exact. The first was security: Ireland needed to rely on neutrality as it was entirely incapable of defending itself militarily. The second was avoiding another civil war: de Valera's statements from this period show he firmly believed that if Ireland joined Britain, it would enrage a certain section of the public to the extent that it could tear the country apart – 'no Irish leader will ever be able to get the Irish people to cooperate with Great Britain while partition remains,' he said in 1938, 'I wouldn't attempt it myself for I know I should fail.'[21] And the third was ending partition: before, during and after the war, de Valera was willing to bargain away neutrality if Britain offered to end partition under the right circumstances.

This realist approach to neutrality during the war meant de Valera was willing to stretch it to breaking point, and arguably beyond, to accommodate the interests of the Allies.

CHAPTER SIX

THE TRACKLESS DESERT

*Neutrality is not like a simple mathematical formula
which has only to be announced and demonstrated in
order to be believed and respected ... Instead of earning
the goodwill of both belligerents it is regarded by both with
hatred and contempt.*
Frank Aiken (January 1940)[1]

L ocked away in a glass cabinet in the corner of an old aircraft
hangar in Casement Aerodrome is perhaps the most unusual
ashtray in Ireland. It's made out of a large bomb intended to be
dropped from a B-17 aircraft. On the front is an engraving: a
map of Ireland inside a dotted red outline. The ashtray/munition was
presented to Defence Forces Chief of Staff Lieutenant General Daniel
McKenna by the US Eighth Air Force near the end of World War II in
recognition of the assistance the Defence Forces provided in the preparations for D-Day. On 11 May 1944, one month before that crucial day,
McKenna had personally arranged for his American counterparts to
fly around the coast of Ireland to gather navigational information that
would be vital for any Allied pilots who became lost during the invasion. Normally such assistance from a friendly nation would warrant
a medal or two. Indeed, after the war, McKenna and two other Irish
officers were put forward by the Pentagon for the Legion of Merit, for

'exceptionally meritorious and outstanding services to the US'. That was until someone from the US State Department wisely pointed out that giving medals to senior officers of an ostensibly neutral military might prove embarrassing for all concerned.[2] McKenna and his senior officers would have to make do with the ashtray, which remained in use in the chief of staff's office in McKee Barracks for decades before being taken, cigarette butts and all, to the Air Corps Museum in Casement.

It's an episode which neatly illustrates the thinness of Irish neutrality during World War II, or 'the Emergency' as it was euphemistically known in Ireland. The country's position during the conflict has been described as akin to a duck swimming across a pond: above the surface, it looked calm but below the waterline, it was strenuously and secretly exerting itself for the Allies. Much of this activity has been extensively documented. Ireland's World War II foreign policy is the one area of neutrality that has been well-covered by historians. Works such as *In Time of War* by renowned journalist Robert Fisk, along with countless memoirs and documentaries, mean most people are aware of the general outline of the 'certain consideration' de Valera showed the Allies. But most are probably unaware of just how extensive that cooperation was. It was a cooperation so broad that it wouldn't be covered by even the most flexible definition of neutrality, never mind the one laid out in the 1907 Hague Convention. In fact, 'non-belligerency' is perhaps a more accurate term than neutrality for Ireland's position during the conflict. From codebreaking to espionage to repatriating stranded pilots (sometimes along with their planes), Ireland was doing almost everything short of engaging in active combat to assist the Allies.

De Valera's approach was based on pragmatism rather than ideology. Irish assistance to the Allies and the strictness of its interpretation of neutrality ebbed and flowed during the war, depending on circumstances. When Britain appeared likely to lose the war, Irish assistance dropped off (although never ceased completely) and neutrality became more sacrosanct. When it became clear Germany would lose, Irish assistance increased. As always, for de Valera, neutrality was not an end but a means to an end. The end was to protect Ireland from threats, both external and internal; a goal the government believed could not be met with military means.

At the start of the conflict at least, the internal threats were considered greater than the external ones. De Valera believed if Ireland was to join the war on the Allied side it would revitalise the beleaguered IRA and may have even led to a civil war against those who believed Ireland had no business assisting its historic oppressors. Neutrality was the only policy that could unite the majority of Irish people. It's often forgotten how popular this policy was. All major parties, including Fine Gael, supported neutrality, and when one Fine Gael TD, James Dillon, criticised the policy in 1942, he was forced to resign from the party. Rallies in support of neutrality held in 1940 and attended by the main party leaders attracted thousands. There was no perception among the Irish public at the time that this was a crusade against the evils of fascism; rather, it seemed like just another great power clash that would see their sons, brother and fathers die on obscure battlefields in Europe. Hitler was seen by de Valera and the Irish public as a despot and a bully, but one in the same vein as Kaiser Wilhelm II, rather than the personification of evil he is regarded as today. The prevailing view was the same one expressed by Wolfe Tone 150 years earlier: Ireland had no obligation to fight alongside Britain and had little to gain by doing so.

For such a young state, and one that was technically still a dominion of the British Empire, neutrality was also 'the ultimate expression of independence'.[3] During this period, de Valera frequently noted that small states suffer disproportionately when they take part in great power wars as they have no influence on how they start, how they end or how they are run. By becoming the only dominion not to declare war alongside Britain, Ireland was not only avoiding this fate, but it was also sending a powerful message about how it saw its position in the world: as a truly sovereign nation charting its own course. And this time, thanks to the dismantling of the Anglo-Irish Treaty over the previous decade, and in particular the return of the Treaty Ports, it had a realistic prospect of remaining on the sidelines.

The same realpolitik that informed the public declaration of neutrality also influenced the decision to secretly assist Britain, and later America when it entered the war in 1941. The Irish government knew it faced a greater threat of invasion from Britain than it did from Germany. The only way of avoiding this was appeasing Britain to the greatest extent possible, short of joining the war or giving back the Treaty Ports. At several points, Churchill and his generals considered taking Ireland by force to deny it as a base for the Germans and to use its ports and airfields to protect Allied shipping in the Atlantic. Misled by rumours that German U-boats were being supplied by communities in the west of Ireland, Churchill (then First Lord of the Admiralty) even tasked General Bernard Montgomery with drawing up a plan to take back the Treaty Port of Cobh. Wise counsel from British advisers, who said that Irish neutrality was extremely partial towards Britain, played a major role in ensuring these plans never came to pass. De Valera maintained the same view he expressed in 1920, that if an independent Ireland were to survive, it had to ensure it could not be used as a base for attack against Britain.

In giving this secret assistance to Britain, Ireland could take some comfort in the vagueness of the established rules surrounding neutrality. Despite the importance of the decision, Ireland's declaration of neutrality was remarkably informal. As noted in a 1942 memo from Michael Rynne, legal adviser in the Department of External Affairs, there was no bill or instrument lodged in the Dáil, and the actual declaration took the form of statements de Valera had made. Irish ambassadors informed their host governments of the decision but usually only verbally. The only 'quasi-legal' proclamation was a written note sent to the secretary-general of the League of Nations after the start of the conflict that 'Ireland intends to maintain neutrality in the present war'.[4]

The lack of domestic law or formal declaration was not a problem, Rynne believed. Instead, in navigating what he called the 'trackless desert' of modern neutrality law, Ireland depended on common sense and previous international treaties such as the Hague Convention of 1907 on neutrality. The country had never signed the treaty but, he said, Irish neutrality 'would not survive one week' if it wasn't based on international conventions.[5] Thankfully, the Hague Convention was silent on many of the areas where Ireland was assisting the Allies, including through espionage and the sharing of weather reports. Other provisions, such as the use of railways or the provision of armaments to belligerents, had no practical application to Ireland. However, one part of the convention did apply to Ireland: Article 11, which obliges neutrals to detain any belligerent fighters it finds on their territory.

The difficulties neutral Ireland would face in dealing with stranded aircraft became evident just ten minutes after war was declared on 1 September 1939. As if on cue, and to the astonishment of locals, bad weather forced an RAF seaplane to land just off the coast of Skerries, County Dublin. Soon after, it was joined by another RAF seaplane which had also experienced difficulties, prompting rumours in Dublin that a British invasion force was just over the horizon. One of the pilots came to shore on a dingy to make a call in the local Garda station while the authorities debated what should be done – strictly speaking, the crew should be interned until the end of the war. In the end, both aircraft were allowed to take off. It became clear this was going to become a pattern when, two weeks later, de Valera met secretly with Britain's wartime representative to Ireland, John Maffey, for the first time. During the meeting, de Valera's phone rang with the news that another RAF seaplane had just come down, this one in Ventry Harbour, Kerry. 'There you are,' the taoiseach said to Maffey after hanging up. 'What am I to do?' To the relief of both men, another phone call followed a few minutes later with the news that the plane had taken off again, having been fixed up by a local mechanic.[6]

Over the course of the war, 223 Allied and Axis pilots crashed and died on Irish soil [or in Irish waters]. A reminder of them – a collection of twisted metal and wood gathered over the decades from hills and mountains around Ireland, most of it barely recognisable as having once formed part of aircraft – exists in Casement Aerodrome, in the same aircraft hangar that houses the US bomb ashtray. After the Ventry incident, and throughout the first half of the war, Ireland had decided it had little choice but to intern British pilots who crashed within its borders. Many of those were interned in the Curragh Camp, although some still managed to find their way across the border to Northern Ireland. That position changed in 1942 when, after America's entry into the war, a secret policy was adopted of letting all Allied aircrews escape to Northern Ireland.

This often went far beyond 'letting them' escape. Aircrews were often driven to the border in Defence Forces vehicles. On occasion, their aircraft were also repaired and sent back. When an American B-17 bomber came down in Sligo in December 1942, RAF mechanics were brought south to fix it. When an American P-51 fighter crashed a few days later, an Allied pilot was sent down to pick it up and fly it across the border. Another aircraft which could not be saved after crashing in Donegal was stripped of important parts and secret equipment by Allied personnel with the assistance of the Defence Forces. After an RAF seaplane crashed into a mountainside in Kerry in late 1943, one of the crew, a Limerick man, was allowed to visit home before being driven up north. This secret assistance to Allied aircrews sometimes went far beyond what would normally be expected from a friendly nation. When another B-17, this one carrying senior US General Jacob Devers, along with three other generals and 12 officers and enlisted men, crashed in Galway after becoming lost over the Atlantic, Irish officers brought them to a local hotel. There Devers was treated to an impromptu lunch in his honour before being brought to Northern Ireland with his crew. The aircraft, memorably named *Stinky*, was dismantled and sent over later.[7]

Irish authorities tried to cover up these blatant breaches of neutrality by claiming the crashed aircraft were on training or rescue missions and therefore not subject to the internment rules. Allied crews were instructed by their superiors to stick to this story if they happened to crash-land in Ireland. But it hardly mattered if they did. The first 34 US aircraft crew members to crash-land in Ireland failed to make the standard claim they were on 'non-operational' flights, yet all were released to Northern Ireland. On one occasion, when a crashed US pilot failed to stick to the agreed script, his Irish captors simply replaced his account with one that would justify his release.[8] Canada's representative to Ireland, John Kearney, observed at the time that the term non-operational flight 'has, sometimes, been stretched almost beyond recognition'.[9]

By contrast, all the surviving pilots and crews of the 18 German aircraft which crashed in Ireland were interned for the duration of the war, although many enjoyed considerable freedoms and mixed frequently with the local community. The logic of the Irish government was that German pilots flying so far from home could not realistically claim to be on training exercises and must therefore be engaged in active combat. News of the release of Allied airmen provoked a strong protest from Eduard Hempel in 1943 and he demanded the release of a number of German crew members by way of compensation. The government held firm, responding that the distinction between operational and non-operational flights was based on international law, a claim that was at least questionable.[10] Irish authorities meanwhile were supplying the Allies with valuable information on crashed German aircraft and crews, including on aircraft that had washed ashore. Additionally, Ireland agreed to return, or at least intern, any German who escaped to the south from a prisoner-of-war camp in Northern Ireland.[11]

Even when attempting to demonstrate strict neutrality, de Valera merely highlighted the thinness of the position. When the taoiseach met Maffey on the day the plane came down in Ventry, the main item on the agenda had been a document the Irish government had sent to London several days previously. Citing the Hague Convention, this aide-memoire – an informal diplomatic note – stated that no naval vessels belonging to any of the belligerents would be permitted to operate in Irish waters or ports. Though the document was merely spelling out the basic obligations of a neutral power, the British government was greatly disturbed. It had known for a long time Ireland would be neutral in the war, but it was not yet clear how strict that neutrality would be. This aide-memoire was a bad omen. While it applied to German ships as much as British, geography meant the restrictions would have a disproportionate impact on Royal Navy operations. Maffey pleaded with de Valera not to proceed with it. He was successful and de Valera agreed to temporarily hold up the order.

Part of the reason the aide-memoire so disturbed Britain was the view in London that free navigation of Irish waters would be vital in maintaining the Atlantic supply routes and keeping them safe from U-boat attack. This was a lesson Britain had learned during the previous world war when its people faced the very real prospect of starvation as a result of Germany's navy. Given such anxiety, it's perhaps not surprising that, from the earliest days of World War II, rumours spread like wildfire that not only were the Irish tolerating German submarines in their waters, they were sometimes supplying and refuelling them. These rumours persisted for decades after the war, despite scant supporting evidence. While there may have been isolated instances of fishermen selling supplies to surfaced U-boats, there is little to support the idea that crews were being sustained by coastal communities, much less that this was happening on any organised scale. In his work on the period, Robert Fisk records one coast-watching officer in Kerry as saying most of the submarines 'had been seen in pubs'. The British response to the rumours, however, went as far as to deploy submarines to secretly travel the coast of Ireland hunting for signs of U-boats and evidence of collusion. For months, they searched for breaches of Irish neutrality while simultaneously breaching Irish neutrality. These missions came up empty.[12]

But while rumours of widespread provisioning of German submarines were baseless, it was undeniable that U-boats were plying their deadly trade off the coast of Ireland and were sometimes operating well within Irish waters. In the first two weeks of the war alone, Britain lost 28 ships to U-boat attacks. In Churchill's eyes, those losses further justified his position that the Treaty Ports should be returned. He argued the ports would cut significant time off the journeys of British ships and serve as bases for anti-submarine aircraft. De Valera refused. To return the ports would amount to an immediate and public abandonment of neutrality and would open up those areas, particularly the town of Cobh, to German naval and possibly even air attacks. He also turned down the compromise idea of launching joint Irish–British maritime patrols. But de Valera knew something had to be done to calm British fears, lest London took matters into its own hands.

The solution was one of the more inventive ways Ireland bent the rules during the war without breaking them entirely. In 1939, the Defence Forces established the Coast Watching Service which comprised more than 80 lookout posts dotted around the country to watch for maritime activity and possible invasion. Early in the war, an order was given that any reports of submarine sightings should be broadcast on open channels, meaning anyone could listen in. Should it wish, Germany could listen in for reports of British vessels and vice versa. On the face of it, it was pure neutrality in action. But in reality, Germany's distance from Ireland meant the information was long out of date by the time it could be acted upon. It was much more useful for Britain, with its sub-hunting aircraft operating from Northern Ireland. Later in the war, Ireland dropped the pretence that this was a neutral action and the broadcasts of the locations of belligerent vessels were encoded with a British cypher, meaning only the Allies could monitor it. This had the effect of making the Coast Watching Service effectively an arm of British naval intelligence.[13]

That this was a deliberate way of assisting the Allies was demonstrated by a 'most secret' memo penned by Department of External Affairs Secretary-General Joseph Walshe in 1941. He listed the broadcasts as one of thirteen distinct ways Ireland had so far assisted the Allies. He also referenced what later became known as the Donegal Corridor, a 6km stretch of land in south Donegal which RAF aircraft based in Lough Erne in Northern Ireland were allowed to fly over in order to reach the Atlantic and protect shipping from U-boat attacks.[14] Technically, British aircraft were only supposed to cross Donegal when engaging in rescue missions but, as the Irish well knew, there was no practical way of monitoring this. The benefits of this were clear; the use of the corridor added 100km in range to the aircraft and Lough Erne sub-hunters sunk many German vessels during the war.

Other assistance in the maritime and air domains included granting Britain permission to station an armed rescue tugboat in Cobh and allowing a British naval attaché to travel around the country to carry out his own evaluation of the Coast Watching Service. Royal Navy ships were secretly allowed to 'pursue and attack U-boats' that entered Irish waters and Britain was allowed to set up radar stations in Cork and Donegal. Even the huge, white EIRE markings dotted around the coast which have become perhaps the most well-known symbol of Irish wartime neutrality were adapted specifically to aid Allied airmen. At first, the signs' only purpose was to alert both Allied and Axis airmen they were over neutral territory and that they shouldn't attack or try to land. But America later asked that numbers be added to each sign to help its pilots navigate. The details of the numbers were supplied only to the Allied side.[15]

Among the most blatant acts of assistance was when Britain was granted permission to permanently station a sub-hunting aircraft in Foynes, Limerick, ostensibly to test equipment but actually to aid in the search for U-boats.[16] Dublin also made a point of not objecting when the British turned Lough Foyle between Derry and Donegal into a flying boat base. Ownership of the Lough was contested at the time, and this tacit approval spared Britain a major diplomatic headache. All Ireland asked was that Britain not formally request the use of the Lough, which at least gave Dublin plausible deniability. Those are just a selection of the practical ways, small and large, in which Ireland assisted the Allies on the west coast. Britain may never have obtained the use of the Treaty Ports but it was not found wanting for much else.

Important as these measures were, they were eclipsed by the assistance Ireland supplied to the Allies in the intelligence and espionage sphere. This went well beyond just bending the rules of neutrality – in the words of one historian, Irish and British spies were 'running a joint intelligence operation'.[17] Few artefacts encapsulate this better than a children's copybook held in the manuscripts room of the National Library in Dublin. It forms part of the collection of papers of Richard Hayes, who happened to be the library's wartime director at the same time as he acted as the Defence Forces' chief code breaker. Inside the copybook is a baffling series of numbers and equations, part of Hayes' efforts to break some of the most important German codes of the war. With a tiny staff and a fraction of the resources of Britain's Bletchley Park, Hayes was given the task of decrypting secret radio communications emanating from the German legation in Dublin. He also interrogated captured

German spies as part of his code-breaking efforts. Needless to say, all of this intelligence was passed to the Allies.[18]

After Hayes broke a particularly important cypher being used by Hermann Goertz, a German spy parachuted into Ireland in 1941, a senior British intelligence officer was invited to Ireland to review his work. This brought cooperation between Ireland's military intelligence service, G2, and Britain's MI5 to new heights. Even after they broke the code, G2 allowed Goertz's messages to the German legation in Ireland to continue in the hope of learning more about his contacts. All of this was shared with the Allies, even when it implicated important Irish figures. Indeed, in one message Goertz revealed one of his contacts had been Defence Forces General Hugo McNeill, British intelligence later noted. MI5 said that Hayes' gifts for decryption 'amounted almost to genius.'[19] Unlike McKenna, Hayes did later get a medal. According to his daughter, it was given to him by Churchill after the war in utmost secrecy.[20]

Irish and Allied intelligence had enjoyed an extremely close working relationship, which dated from August 1938 when MI5's Cecil Liddell and G2's Colonel Liam Archer established an official liaison. Similarly, close relations were later established with America's Office of Strategic Services (OSS), the forerunner of the CIA. These were the foundations of an intelligence relationship which lasts to this day. As well as transmitting a huge amount of data on aircraft and ship sightings, information gathered by Irish diplomats in Axis-occupied countries was passed to America. Intelligence on German immigrants living in Ireland was also handed over and official communication lines from the German and Italian legations in Ireland were deliberately routed through Britain to make the interception of messages easier. This was so valuable to the Allies that when David Gray, America's prickly representative in Dublin, demanded the closure of the German legation in 1944, MI5 objected on the grounds that it would disrupt a vital stream of easily intercepted intelligence.[21]

German, British and American spies all operated in Ireland, but only the German ones were hunted by the Gardaí and Defence Forces. The vast majority of German spies were detained shortly after landing in Ireland, with Goertz being one of the few who managed to stay at large for any length of time before capture. Early in the war, Ireland protested to London after a number of British agents were detected operating on Irish soil but this died down as the conflict progressed. It's a testament to the effectiveness of Irish intelligence that, by the end of the war, G2 was aware of Britain's entire network of spies operating in Ireland. These agents were allowed to continue their work unimpeded and G2 never informed their British counterparts that their cover was blown.[22] American intelligence received even greater consideration, with OSS representative in Ireland Ervin Marlin commenting in 1943 they were receiving 'maximum cooperation' from the Irish. Another US spy, Martin Quigley, later wrote that the breadth of secret assistance to the Allies made the term neutrality a 'misnomer'.[23]

Intelligence on aircraft, spies and codes were all well and good but if the Allies wanted to take back Europe they also needed the weather on their side, and here Irish assistance again proved vital. Weather stations on the Irish west coast were particularly important in providing early warnings to the Allies of storm fronts that could make or break military operations. Throughout the war, there was a constant flow of accurate and timely weather reports from Irish stations to Britain. Air Corps aircraft were also deployed over the Atlantic to gather weather information for onward transmission to a base in Dunstable in the UK. Meanwhile, Germany's hapless spies in Ireland were reduced to using barometers in shop windows to take weather readings.[24] Undoubtedly, the most important of the Irish reports was taken by Maureen Flavin at Blacksod, County Mayo on 3 June 1944. Unbeknownst to Flavin, her report of a low-pressure system approaching over the Atlantic would cause US Supreme Commander Dwight D. Eisenhower to postpone the D-Day landings for a day, ensuring their success and saving the lives of many Allied soldiers. In June 2021, the US House of Representatives awarded Flavin with a medal for her contribution – she'd just had to wait 77 years for it.[25]

Both sides in the conflict had devised detailed plans for the invasion of Ireland. In Germany's case, it was 'Operation Green' and for Britain, it was 'Plan W'. The main difference was that the latter was drawn up with the enthusiastic cooperation of the Irish government. De Valera first asked Britain for help in the event of a German invasion in May 1940, leading to a series of top-secret meetings between political and military figures from both sides. The Irish conditions were clear from the start: as soon as Germany invaded it would request help from Britain, whose troops would immediately move south from Northern Ireland to reinforce the Defence Forces. But there could be no question of Britain moving before this point. Britain seems to have reluctantly accepted this condition, but there is evidence that if it did invade, it intended to take full advantage of the situation to seize the Treaty Ports for its own use. As Fisk has noted, any potential German invasion would surely occur on the south coast, yet Plan W devoted an entire British division to take the Treaty Port in Lough Swilly in north Donegal. Other parts of the plan referenced possible attacks from hostile Irish Army soldiers, indicating that perhaps the British envisaged the operation being implemented without the full support of the Irish authorities.[26]

This highlights a tension between Irish neutrality and assistance to the Allies that should not be overlooked. While the evidence that Ireland greatly assisted the Allies is overwhelming, this could at times be a very pragmatic and changeable type of assistance. For example, neutrality took on a decidedly stricter character around the time France fell to Germany in June 1940, when it was the popular opinion that Britain would lose the war. De Valera's strong preference was for an Allied victory, but he was prepared to adapt to circumstances should Germany win. It was in this context that Dublin officials sought assurances from Hempel in 1940 that Irish independence would be protected in a new Nazi-dominated European order. At one point de Valera even briefly considered the possibility of accepting weapons from Germany in order to fight off a potential British invasion.[27]

It is probably no coincidence that it was in September 1940, when British fortunes were at their lowest, that the Irish government decided to finally publish the aide-memoire banning British ships from its waters and ports. Around the same time, Irish authorities had also cracked down on private fundraising initiatives in Ireland for the British war effort. These moves did not go unnoticed by Maffey, who reported back to his superiors: 'You have no use in going to these people for certain things while they are convinced Germany have won the war.'[28] It was a point well illustrated by Ireland's decision to sabotage a trade deal on shipping and exports with Britain in November 1940. With northern France securely in German hands, the Irish government feared any visiting British commercial ships in its ports would be targeted for bombing.[29] In late 1941, before the tide of the war had definitively shifted in the Allies' favour, de Valera turned to his chief press adviser, Frank Gallagher, and remarked with a smile, 'I wish there was some way of knowing who will win this war. It would make decisions much easier.'[30] It was a throwaway comment, but it summed up a brutally pragmatic attitude to foreign policy, one which was at the centre of one of the most well-known episodes of Irish wartime foreign policy.

In June 1940, British officials offered de Valera a deal: Britain would make a declaration accepting 'in principle' a united Ireland, in return for Ireland allowing Royal Navy vessels in its ports and the stationing of British troops in certain key locations. In an impressive display of mental gymnastics, Britain argued Ireland could do this while still maintaining its neutrality. Further proposals and counterproposals followed, with de Valera at one point suggesting American instead of British ships might secure the ports. But the deal was doomed to fail, for several reasons. In practical terms, British forces in southern Ireland would mean an instant abandonment of neutrality. Furthermore, Britain was only promising a united Ireland in theory, the actual terms to be worked out after the war – the likelihood of Northern unionists happily going along with this was remote indeed. But above all, de Valera believed Germany would win the war, something that would render a deal with Britain moot. In such circumstances, if he did make such a deal it would destroy any chance of southern Ireland later retaining its independence in the new European order. Churchill's chief negotiator on the matter, Dominion Secretary Malcolm MacDonald, summed it up after the talks failed: 'I felt that one of the decisive influences on Mr de Valera's mind now is his view that we are likely to lose this war.'[31]

Irish assistance to the Allies never ceased, even in these darkest of days, but de Valera was adamant that there were certain lines he would never cross. These included returning the Treaty Ports and inviting British forces into Ireland in the absence of a German invasion. It was a position he maintained even when, from 1941, Churchill attempted to coerce Ireland into joining the Allies by denying it the use of Britain's commercial ships. These were effectively unannounced economic sanctions. Ireland's response was to set up its own civilian shipping service from scratch, Irish Shipping Limited. At sea, the flag of neutral Ireland often provided no protection. There were 40 attacks on Irish commercial ships during the war, from both Allied and Axis forces – 16 ships were lost and 149 sailors perished, almost a fifth of the company's total workforce.

To defend neutrality, de Valera was prepared to make these sorts of sacrifices on land as well. Just as preparations were made to resist a German invasion, Defence Forces officers planned for a British one that may come from Northern Ireland. The Army would form a line of resistance south of the border before eventually retreating into Dublin and making a final doomed stand in the south city centre around Dublin castle. As de Valera said in March 1941:

> Whoever comes first is our enemy ... If America comes first we are determined to shoot down the Americans. If Britain comes first we will shoot them down with greater relish. If the Germans come first we will shoot them also.[32]

They were not just empty words. On occasion, the Defence Forces' few anti-aircraft guns opened fire on both British and German aircraft in the first half of the war, shooting down at least one of each. It was a situation well summed up in January 1940 by Minister for Defence Coordination Frank Aiken. Modern neutrality is not a condition of peace with both sides, he said, 'but rather a condition of limited warfare with both.'[33]

However, the point should not be overstated: this strict interpretation of neutrality was the exception rather than the rule. And even when Germany was at the height of its victories in 1941, various branches of the State continued to provide vital assistance to Britain. Crucially, the government also continued to allow its citizens to travel in their tens of thousands to join the British war industry and its various military branches. Estimates of these numbers vary widely. According to one study, 70,000 southern Irish citizens served with British forces during the war. Another study states that over 3,600 were killed.[34] De Valera could have passed legislation to stop Irishmen joining up – after all, he did just that during the Spanish Civil War the previous decade – but this does not seem to have been contemplated, even in the darkest days of World War II.

The myth of Ireland's strict wartime neutrality endured for decades. This was partly due to the government's wartime censorship, a censorship so strict that a photograph in the newspaper of a government minister ice-skating was suppressed lest it tip off the belligerents about Irish weather conditions. This meant the actual assistance being provided to the Allies remained a closely guarded secret, with the files being hidden away for years afterwards. We may never know the full extent of this assistance. According to Fisk, after the war, the Irish government shredded about 70 tonnes of documents.[35]

The neutrality myth was cemented by de Valera's ill-judged visit to Hempel to pay his condolences on the death of Hitler in May 1945. His reasoning behind this has been debated ever since. Some saw it as de Valera's way of giving a subtle middle finger to Gray, America's representative in Ireland, a man who was generally disliked by official Ireland and who seems to have largely returned the sentiment. Others, such as Maffey, believed de Valera wanted to show he was not jumping on the Allied bandwagon now that it approached final victory in Europe. De Valera himself said he was simply abiding by standard diplomatic protocol. Whatever the reason, the visit allowed some Allied leaders to portray de Valera's neutrality as far less benign to the Allies than it really was.

This view was buttressed by the dramatic exchange of radio broadcasts between Churchill and de Valera following the declaration of victory. Instead of acknowledging Irish assistance, Churchill used his victory speech to shame Ireland for not returning the Treaty Ports and to laud Britain's 'restraint and poise' in not invading.[36] In his reply, de Valera also declined to mention Ireland's assistance, instead asking if Churchill 'could not find it in his heart to acknowledge that this small nation had stood alone, not for one year or two, but against aggression for several centuries and not surrendered her soul.'[37]

The true measure of Irish assistance can be found in the assessments of lower-ranked Allied officials after the war. James Russell Forgan, America's intelligence chief in Europe towards the end of the conflict later told historian T. Ryle Dwyer that Ireland acted 'almost as if they were our allies' in the area of intelligence, that 'they have never got the credit due to them'.[38] Forgan's boss, William 'Wild Bill' Donovan, the chief of the OSS, told President Roosevelt that Irish intelligence cooperation had been 'very full'.[39]

Perhaps the most remarkable assessment came from MI5, which concluded Ireland's pretend neutrality was of more use to Britain than if it had joined the war. Its logic was that if Ireland had joined with Britain, conscription would undoubtedly have been introduced, meaning some 300,000 Irishmen would have been guarding Ireland against an invasion which never came. This meant the number of Irishmen available to work in the British war industry and enlist in the British military would have been cut by half, severely hampering the war effort. Furthermore, MI5 said in its official wartime history the 300,000 soldiers guarding Ireland would have had to have been supplied with British weapons and air defences, which early in the war were extremely scarce. It's an interesting view and one which perhaps overly relies on hindsight, but it reflects the position of British intelligence that Irish neutrality was of an extremely partial nature.[40]

Even those bitterly opposed to Irish neutrality were later forced to admit it was beneficial. Viscount Cranborne, the 6th Marquess of Salisbury, whose anti-Irish prejudice was well-known, acknowledged at the end of the war that Ireland 'has been willing to accord us any facilities which would not be regarded as overtly prejudicing their attitude to neutrality.' Even Gray, the equally anti-Irish representative from America, conceded after the war that Irish cooperation 'went beyond what might reasonably be believed possible.'[41]

Was Ireland neutral during World War II? If neutrality can be claimed by not becoming actively involved in combat, then yes. But that's not the measure of neutrality. From the point of view of the Hague Convention, Ireland certainly did not abide by the obligations of neutral nations. It's also clear the broader definition of wartime neutrality, that of not providing assistance to either side, does not apply either.

Then again, it's important to note that Ireland was not all that unique in this regard. Switzerland and Sweden both declared neutrality while also displaying their own 'certain consideration' – in their cases to Germany. However, this assistance paled in comparison to the assistance given by Ireland to the Allies. Nevertheless, in the public mind, Ireland's position in World War II became the high watermark of its 'traditional neutrality'. What's rarely remembered is that, almost immediately after the war, the Government was willing to completely abandon it.

CHAPTER SEVEN

NICE KNOWING YOU

Whether or not we were neutral in the last war, there can never be any question again of this country being neutral in any future war ...
John Costello (1946)[1]

I n July 1948, in the middle of a contentious Dáil debate, Fine Gael Taoiseach John Costello made a cryptic but tantalising statement. TDs were told that, for the first time since 1922, the Irish government had 'some hope' of ending partition. Costello explained that he was basing this prediction on the belief that the interests of Britain, America and Western Europe would soon demand the unification of Ireland to 'face the menacing situation which will possibly develop in the new few years' – in other words, the Soviet Union.[2] It was a strangely optimistic statement. Ireland was still dealing with the fallout from World War II: living standards were falling, the country was beset by major strikes and rationing would continue for another three years.

Things weren't much better on the international stage. Despite its extensive assistance to the Allies during the war, the State found itself diplomatically isolated afterwards due to its claimed neutral stance. Its prized diplomatic relations with America were particularly strained and it was only with some reluctance on the part of the US State Department that Ireland was admitted to the multi-billion-dollar Marshall Plan, which was aimed at rebuilding Europe and warding off the threat of communism. In the famous (and somewhat melodramatic) words of historian F.S.L. Lyons, when it came to international relations, Irish people found themselves 'in Plato's cave, with their backs to the fire of life and deriving their only knowledge of what went on outside from the flickering shadows thrown on the wall before their eyes'.[3]

Although Ireland's diplomatic footprint had made some modest expansions since the 1930s – by 1948 it had diplomats accredited to 18 nation-states – much of the goodwill it had built up through its activity in the League of Nations had been erased by de Valera's policies during the war, particularly his decision to visit the German embassy to express his condolences on the death of Hitler. In 1946, Ireland's application for membership of the newly formed United Nations was vetoed by the Soviet Union, partly due to Irish neutrality during the war and partly because the Soviets assumed, quite reasonably, that Ireland would act as a US ally in the UN. At times it seemed the only other countries actively seeking relations with Ireland were those who had even poorer international reputations. In 1948, fascist Spain suggested a neutral, Catholic alliance of nations, involving itself, Ireland, Argentina and the dictatorship of Portugal. Mercifully for Ireland's international reputation, this proposal went nowhere. Joseph Walshe, Ireland's ambassador to the Vatican, believed the pope would prefer to see Ireland try to uphold Catholic principles alone, rather than allying with 'essentially undemocratic regimes'.[4]

There was little to indicate anyone outside Ireland cared much about partition when Costello made his cryptic remarks in the Dáil. The remarks themselves caused little stir at the time, and the taoiseach declined to elaborate further for fear of scuppering the government's plans. Costello's coyness is explained by the fact that he knew something most people did not. Three months previously, Britain's foreign secretary, Ernest Bevin, had cautiously informed Irish Minister for External Affairs Seán MacBride of plans to combat communism by establishing an international organisation that would lock Europe and America into a collective defence arrangement. Around the same time,

Ireland's ambassador in Canada, John Hearne, relayed information back to Dublin that America was considering establishing an alliance of 'Atlantic Nations', based on South America's 1947 Inter-American Treaty of Reciprocal Assistance – also known as the Rio Pact. Like the signatories of the Rio Pact, those involved in this Atlantic Nations alliance would adopt the principle that an attack on one north Atlantic country would be regarded as an attack on all.[5] The organisation would eventually become known as the North Atlantic Treaty Organisation, or NATO. Implicit in Bevin's disclosure to MacBride was the possibility that Ireland might be a founder member of such an organisation, despite its neutrality in the most recent conflict.

To Costello's Inter-Party Government, which had taken over from Fianna Fáil earlier in the year, this appeared to be the perfect opportunity to end partition. If Ireland was so strategically vital to NATO, surely Britain would be willing to give up the six counties to ensure its participation. And if Britain was reluctant, it would no doubt be convinced by America, which by the end of the war had entirely eclipsed it as a world power. That was the reasoning anyway. Ireland believed it had the perfect bargaining chip and it intended to use it. If its plan was successful, not only would the Inter-Party Government be responsible for banishing partition, but it would also restore Ireland's standing on the international stage and announce to the world the Irish were willing soldiers in the fight against godless communism. What's striking is that Ireland's repeatedly stated policy of neutrality barely featured in these calculations.

Joining NATO would have massive consequences. Unlike the League of Nations and its vague allusions to collective security, the military obligations of NATO were clear. Countries would be expected to defend the alliance both by adequately providing for their defence at home and by potentially contributing to foreign expeditions against an aggressor state. It is unclear whether the Inter-Party Government ever considered the implications of these obligations for the budget or the beleaguered Defence Forces, which after the war had been rapidly reduced to pre-1939 levels and had resumed its position as a distant policy afterthought.

One of the Inter-Party Government's first major defence decisions on taking office was to reduce army numbers by 1,000, bringing it down to just 8,000 full-time personnel. Fine Gael TD Éamonn Coogan even advocated abolishing the Army altogether and replacing it with an armed police force.

In some ways, there should be little surprise the government was so willing to abandon any pretence to neutrality in 1948. Fine Gael and its allies started speaking against neutrality almost as soon as the war ended. In 1946, TD John Dillon, who had resigned from Fine Gael due to its support for wartime neutrality but still voted with the party as an independent, began speaking in favour of joining a military alliance. By 1947, he was joined by Fine Gael leader, Richard Mulcahy, and Coogan, who advocated that Ireland take part in either a Western or a common-wealth alliance (it's not clear how this would fit in with his suggestion of abolishing the Defence Forces). Furthermore, as Europe divided itself into two camps after the end of the war, Fine Gael and Fianna Fáil made it clear they were very much in the anti-communist camp. Any alliance aimed at stopping its spread could only be a good thing. In July 1946, Costello, then in opposition, declared, 'whether or not we were neutral in the last war, there can never be any question again of this country being neutral in any future war'.[6]

But why was the government so confident NATO would bow to the will of impoverished, militarily insignificant Ireland, just to secure its membership? The answer is that MacBride and his colleagues over-estimated Ireland's strategic importance to the Western allies. This is somewhat understandable; in 1949, a Defence Forces military intelli-gence report noted that Ireland would be of vital interest to NATO in the event of the Cold War turning hot. If Russia overran continental Europe – something military planners considered a reasonable possibility in the late 1940s – Ireland would be vital as a last-ditch location from which to launch retaliatory air strikes.[7] It's true that both America and Britain attributed some strategic importance to Ireland. A CIA report from the time highlighted Ireland's strategic location on the air and sea routes to Western Europe and noted its flat terrain, which would allow for the rapid construction of airfields. These would be 'invaluable as bases for strategic bombers attacks as far east as the Ural Mountains.'[8] Furthermore, Ireland's lack of heavy industry was compensated for by its agricultural output and its 'potential manpower contribution' to a war.[9] The British also continued to regard Ireland as having military importance, with Chief of the Air Staff John Slessor pointing out in the early 1950s that there was a 'pretty nasty gap' in NATO's air defences over Irish skies.[10]

However, at the same time, the CIA was talking about using Irish airfields to drop bombs on the Ural Mountains, it was also pointing out to President Harry Truman that America could live with a neutral Ireland. The most recent war had shown the Allies as much. The priority for America was not to secure Ireland as a military ally (although that would be nice), it was to deny Ireland as a base for Russia in the event of war. Allowing Russia to take Ireland was a nightmare scenario as Irish territory could be used to outflank British defences and as a 'base for bombing North America'.[11] American intelligence reasoned that if a shooting war broke out, Ireland would quickly join the Allied side due to its strong anti-communist and pro-American ideology. Even de Valera would not remain neutral in a 'holy war' if he came back into power, the CIA reasoned.[12] A separate CIA report in 1949 concluded it was 'beyond question' that Ireland would fight back against the Soviets and that it 'requires no encouragement.'[13] There was no need for it to join a pre-emptive alliance. The Americans did view Ireland as a possible 'stepping stone', linking it logistically with its European allies, but it was not the only such stone: Norway, Greenland and Portugal could fill the role just as easily.[14] The following year, a National Security Council report reached the same conclusion: Irish participation in NATO would be good to have but by no means essential.

The Irish Government was aware of none of this. It was further encouraged to use partition as a bargaining chip by what it perceived as a softness on the part of the British Government to maintain control of the six counties. After all, hadn't Churchill been willing to offer the prospect of a united Ireland just a few years ago in return for Irish entry into

World War II? Now Churchill had been replaced by a Labour government, which in the eyes of Dublin, was even less committed to retaining control of the north. MacBride wrote in February 1949 that he believed the British government wanted to see partition ended but was reluctant to do anything about it for fear of drawing criticism from the Conservatives. Any such criticism, however, would likely be muted, he said: 'I believe any British government would be glad to see the problem solved.'[15] This was overly optimistic. While Labour might be glad to be rid of the north, it also believed ending partition in order to entice Ireland into NATO would result in civil war in Northern Ireland. Britain had no intention of relinquishing the north in such circumstances. Furthermore, military occupation of Northern Ireland was a key part of its NATO strategy. Giving control of the north to the Republic, with its minuscule Defence Forces, would open up a gap in British defences, regardless of whether Ireland joined NATO or not.[16]

Domestic considerations were also a factor in the Inter-Party Government's gambit. The government was made up of an unlikely coalition of Fine Gael, Labour and various smaller parties and independents, including the republican Clann na Poblachta, which was led by MacBride. Appearing weak on partition could have cost the support of MacBride's party, which had campaigned on the issue. This was something the government could ill afford if it wanted to keep de Valera from returning to power. At times, this prospect seemed to be more of a concern for them than an attack from the Soviets. The situation was made more precarious by de Valera's constant campaigning against partition during this period which included a speaking tour of America. It is reasonable to assume that if de Valera had not made partition such a live issue at the time, or if Fine Gael had enjoyed an outright majority, the Inter-Party Government would have been more amenable to joining NATO on a no-strings-attached basis.

As it was, the government could not afford to be outflanked on the issue of the north. This was reflected in MacBride's comments to US Secretary of State Dean Acheson in April 1949 that no Irish government would have lasted two months if it joined NATO while partition still existed. It was also the case that Inter-Party Government likely did not believe it had much to lose in trying to use NATO membership to end partition. Despite the gathering storm of the Cold War, the government considered a war in the near future highly unlikely. Ireland was 'facing a period of peace and not a period of war', a cabinet committee concluded shortly after Costello took power.[17]

In January 1949, America finally made the long-awaited offer to the Irish government to join the pact as a founding member and to help draft its treaty. The approach was made in the form of an aide-memoire delivered to Ireland's embassy in Washington. The note made it clear that members would be bound by a 'definite obligation' to contribute to collective defence during times of peace and war. It was not the case that any attack on a NATO member would trigger a military reprisal from all its allies. In certain cases, limited retaliation may be preferable. But it was obvious that each member state would be expected to assume onerous military obligations.[18] The Americans had good reason to believe the Irish government would be willing to sign up. The previous month, its representative in Dublin had relayed the view back home that important parts of Irish society were not supportive of neutrality in the current paranoid climate. It was also considered advantageous that the offer was coming from America and not from Britain, which might normally have been expected to take the lead in such matters.

When the aide-memoire arrived, the Irish plan was put into action. Over the course of a month, the government carefully crafted its own aide-memoire responding to the offer. This was delivered to the Americans on 8 February. Ireland, it said, was 'essentially a democratic and freedom-loving nation [...] deeply attached to the ideals of Christian civilisation and the democratic way of life.' It then went straight into the issue of partition. Ireland agreed with the general aim of the treaty, but it could not countenance entering into a military alliance with a country that occupied six of its counties 'against the will of the overwhelming majority of the Irish people'.[19]

The objections were not just a matter of principle. The government believed that while partition still existed, participation in NATO would likely lead to civil war in Ireland (in contrast to the British view that ending partition would lead to civil war). It contended that a united Ireland would also be a much more useful part of NATO from a military and economic point of view.[20] The intent of Dublin's response was not to shut the door on NATO membership. Rather, it was hoped it would start a process that would culminate in Britain ending partition in order to secure Ireland's participation in the alliance. The Irish suggested they were doing everyone a favour by finally bringing the issue out in the open:

> By offering their assistance and mediation, and by creating a situation wherein the problem could be discussed, the participating nations would help to end an undemocratic and dangerous situation, and in doing so would render an invaluable service by strengthening the internal harmony and cohesion of the community of states in the North Atlantic.[21]

The only indication that Washington ever seriously considered the Irish proposal is a request from Secretary of State Acheson for one of his diplomats to enquire with London what its attitude would be if America attempted to mediate in partition. The diplomat was instructed that if the British responded negatively, as was expected, he was to tell MacBride that America could not get involved. There is no response on record, but it is clear the Americans got the answer they expected. Around this time, a British diplomat in Washington sent a dispatch home noting that the Americans had so far shown no intention of letting Ireland use partition as a bargaining chip. Unbeknownst to Dublin, MacBride's plan had been doomed from the start: America had been warned well ahead of time that the Dublin government would likely try such a gambit if asked to join NATO. It was Britain who had suggested Ireland should be invited in the first place and that America should make the offer. Alongside this suggestion came the warning from Bevin that 'if the Irish raised partition as a barrier to joining the pact' they should be told it was beyond America's competence to discuss the issue.[22]

Relations between America and Britain were at a high point following their cooperation during the war and Washington was happy to take Bevin's advice and skirt the partition issue. However, it was not willing to give up just yet on the possibility of persuading Ireland to come into the pact on American terms. America's ambassador to Ireland, George Garrett, suggested it might be advantageous to use the influence of the Catholic Church to change MacBride's mind. MacBride was, after all, an ardent Catholic, and Archbishop John Charles McQuaid, the head of the Church in Ireland, was at the height of his influence. McQuaid had been a major influence in the drafting of the 1937 Constitution and frequently shaped government policy, including infamously seeing off the Mother and Child scheme. Furthermore, McQuaid and the Vatican were in favour of Ireland joining NATO, reasoning that it offered the best defence against communism. However, the archbishop discovered there were limits to his influence and that those limits appeared to lie in the area of Irish foreign policy. Despite his public friendship with MacBride, his appeals on the matter fell on deaf ears.

Ultimately, the Americans did not pursue the matter, a reflection of the fact that it did not need Irish membership all that much. Theodore Achilles, a senior US official instrumental in the foundation of NATO, put it most bluntly: he recalled that, when Ireland kept bringing up partition, 'we simply replied, in effect, that "it's been nice knowing you", and that was that.'[23] But MacBride kept trying to link partition with membership. He repeatedly suggested, and sometimes outright declared, that the only barrier to Ireland joining NATO was partition. Neutrality is not mentioned once in records of his statements on the matter. But America was not willing to jeopardise its relationship with Britain over the matter. It also knew that, owing to geographic, religious and political factors, Irish neutrality was more beneficial to America than it was to the Soviets.

MacBride was still pursuing the matter as late as March 1951, the final days of the Inter-Party Government. During a meeting with Acheson on 13 March, he said he still believed Britain would concede on partition if pressed by America. Acheson repeated that it was a matter between Ireland and Britain and no one else. MacBride raised it again ten days later, this time with Truman himself. He received the same answer. MacBride also raised the prospect of a bilateral defence arrangement between Ireland and America. This would not solve the partition issue but would help to repair diplomatic relations with Washington and would provide badly needed equipment and training for the Irish Defence Forces. As a consolation prize, it wasn't bad. And it had Garrett's support. Truman told MacBride to discuss the matter with Acheson.

Unbeknownst to MacBride, the US had already decided against such a course. The previous year, its National Security Council (NSC) rejected the idea of offering a bilateral treaty to Ireland on the basis that it would only encourage other would-be NATO members to seek such an arrangement instead. The NSC recommended a bilateral treaty should only be offered to Ireland in the case of 'extreme military necessity', and only after the possibility of NATO membership had been thoroughly explored and rejected. 'This necessity does not exist,' it concluded.[24] MacBride's strategy had failed completely. He was left to pursue the ending of partition in European forums, including the Council of Europe, which Ireland had joined as a founder member in 1949.

This approach of raising partition no matter the actual topic of discussion, which some historians have dubbed Ireland's 'sore thumb' strategy, not only failed to achieve its aim but also often frustrated other members of the council.[25] During one meeting, after Ireland raised the issue yet again, Council President Paul-Henri Spaak beat his desk with a ruler in exasperation. On another occasion, Spaak implored Irish representative Seán MacEntee, 'I beg you to keep to the matter at hand.'[26]

The Inter-Party Government lost power in June 1951, paving the way for the return of Fianna Fáil and de Valera as taoiseach. Regarding NATO, de Valera remained on the course set by MacBride, even after it started to financially impact Ireland. In October 1951, Truman signed the Mutual Security Act, which tied future Marshall Plan funds to a military alliance with America. In response, Frank Aiken, by then minister for external affairs, wrote to the US ambassador reiterating that Ireland would not join a military pact while deprived of national unity. A month later Marshall Aid was cut off. Ireland had benefited handsomely from the plan – Marshall Aid accounted for 50 per cent of State structural spending between 1948 and 1951 – and losing it was the price to pay for the partition strategy.

Forty-five years later, in 1996, the Irish government published a white paper on foreign policy titled *Challenges and Opportunities Abroad*, which reaffirmed Ireland's commitment to 'military neutrality'. It also claimed that Ireland's decision not to join NATO in 1948 was due to its desire to preserve that neutrality. The actions of the Inter-Party Government show this claim has little, if any, basis in truth. Ireland's refusal to join NATO was based solely on the issue of partition. Despite de Valera's policy stance during World War II, neutrality in the late '40s and early '50s was not a priority for Irish politicians in either of the main parties.

For example, in 1946 the Fianna Fáil government favoured applying for UN membership, despite the opinion from its attorney general, and future Irish president and chief justice, Cearbhall Ó Dálaigh, that it would obligate Ireland to engage in war if the Security Council called for it. Neutrality and UN membership may seem like easy bedfellows today but at its formation, there was significant confusion about countries' military obligations. In recommending membership to the Dáil, de Valera said that if the Security Council voted for war, Ireland must go to war: 'We must do so, even though we have no say in the decision to take such action, and the decision is one with which we disagree.'[27] The Dáil voted to apply for membership regardless.

The sidelining of neutrality was not particular to just the immediate post-war period. In 1959, the prospect of joining NATO was being re-examined and the head of the Department of External Affairs was tasked with drafting a memo on the pros and cons. He came out against membership for several reasons, including that it would oblige Ireland to increase defence spending and that it would put Ireland at risk of a long-range missile attack. Nowhere among his reasons was neutrality mentioned. Nor, for that matter, did he refer to partition. The government, it appears, was finally willing to abandon MacBride's strategy.

Along with de Valera's policies during World War II, the NATO episode has become part of the foundational myth of Irish neutrality, despite the two matters having little to do with each other at the time. At some point over the subsequent years, it became accepted wisdom among Irish public and political opinion that it was Ireland's commitment to peace that kept it out of the alliance. And, after a while, the legend became fact. 'Something happened sometime in the 1970s to make neutrality into moral principle,' said Rory Montgomery, former second secretary in the Department of Foreign Affairs.[28] Exactly what this something was is hard to pin down. Montgomery suggests it was the growth of the anti-nuclear weapons movement, combined with a growing number of left-wing politicians who took anti-American stances. Opposition to the war in Vietnam, and the USA's sometimes anti-democratic interventionist policy in South America also played a role. Whatever the reason, in the public mind, Ireland's practical objections to NATO became moral ones. The result was politicians became wary of even uttering the name NATO, lest they be accused of anti-neutrality.

CHAPTER EIGHT

COLD WARRIORS

We do not wish in the conflict between the free democracies
and the Communist empires to be thought of as neutral.
We are not neutral and do not wish to be regarded
as such ...
Seán Lemass (September 1962)[1]

For most of the 1980s, whenever a phone call was made from the embassy of the Soviet Union in Dublin, a tape recorder in an anonymous attic room of the GPO seven kilometres away would activate with a click. The gadget, which had been installed by the Garda Special Detective Unit, commonly known as the Special Branch, was attached to the telephone exchange located in the historical building on O'Connell Street. It was voice-activated, a relatively modern innovation for the time, and the recordings were captured on reel-to-reel tapes. These would be replaced frequently and listened to a few times a week by detectives. Not that there was much to listen to. Soviet diplomats, even the ones who weren't in the KGB, knew not to use the main phone line for anything sensitive. Sometimes detectives might hear something that would warrant transmission up to the Garda Commissioner or even the Minister for Justice. On very rare occasions, the information was juicy enough to warrant passing it on to one of Ireland's overseas intelligence partners. But for the most part, the recordings captured only the most mundane of embassy business.

However, surveillance of Soviet activities in Ireland went far beyond tapping their phone lines. Ken McCue, a Dublin left-wing activist who was a member of the Workers' Party in the 1980s, had regular meetings with a senior Soviet official who was a known KGB agent. McCue remembers the spy pointing out the two unmarked Garda cars that were invariably parked outside the embassy, a sprawling five-acre compound on Orwell Road in Rathgar. Each car faced a different direction so the gardaí could follow the KGB man no matter what route he took when driving out of the embassy. The agent would wave to his Garda followers before trying to lose them. The KGB man would often succeed, said McCue, 'because the guards were from the country and wouldn't know the area.'[2] There seemed to be little ill will between the spy and his pursuers. On one occasion, the KGB agent was attending a Workers' Party event in Nealon's pub on Capel Street. Unfamiliar with the north side, he got out of his car on the quays and asked the detectives following behind for directions. They happily led the Russian to his destination.

If neutrality is difficult to define in an actual war, it's even trickier when it comes to a cold war. But, if that definition includes not showing favour to either side, either from a diplomatic or security point of view, then Ireland does not come close to meeting the criteria during this period. Spy tales from the streets of Dublin illustrate that Ireland considered the Soviets an ideological, and potentially even a military enemy. For much of the period between the 1960s and late 1980s, the monitoring of Soviet agents was second in importance only to the monitoring of republican groups. This would continue on a smaller scale after the fall of the Soviet Union before ramping up again as Russia became more belligerent on the world stage. Today Russia is again one of the main targets of the Garda Crime and Security Branch and their colleagues in Defence Forces military intelligence.

During the Cold War, UK intelligence activities were also kept under observation, but to a far lesser extent, while the American CIA, when it showed interest in Ireland, was essentially allowed to do as it pleased. Diplomatically too, Ireland was firmly on the anti-Soviet side and almost always endeavoured to keep the Americans happy, even after Dublin and Moscow exchanged ambassadors in 1974. While Ireland cultivated a reputation at the UN as an independent voice, its voting record for much of the Cold War shows it sided with America more often than even some NATO members. According to Keatinge, when it came to Cold War-related topics, Ireland voted with the US at least three times as often as it voted against it.[3]

This stance wasn't much of a secret either: 'We do not wish in the conflict between the free democracies and the Communist empires to be thought of as neutral. We are not neutral and do not wish to be regarded as such,' Taoiseach Seán Lemass said in 1962.[4]

But Irish–Soviet relations didn't start out like this. In their younger, more idealistic days, revolutionary leaders in each country showed a certain affinity for each other. In 1920, during de Valera's fundraising tour of America, republican leaders agreed to advance a $20,000 loan to Russia's Bolshevik government in the hope the Soviets would recognise the Republic. This was secured against the Russian Crown Jewels, which were only returned in 1949 when the loan was belatedly paid back. Later, in the 1930s, de Valera was one of the few world leaders to support Russia's admission to the League of Nations, thereby tacitly recognising the legitimacy of the regime.

But Ireland's geographical position and, more importantly, its Catholic faith, meant it was always going to plant itself firmly in the anti-Soviet camp. Opposition to Soviet ideals was present throughout Irish society well before the Cold War. In 1977, Michael O'Riordan, founder of the Communist Party of Ireland, recalled seeing as a child in 1930s Cork, a touring photographic exhibition depicting 'the many horrors of life under "godless communism"'.[5] The exhibition saw full attendance for the duration of its stay. Decades later, Irish people were still praying at Mass for the redemption of Soviet souls. Relations weren't helped after World War II by the Soviets' repeated vetoing of Irish entry to the UN, ostensibly because of Irish neutrality in the war, but actually because it viewed Ireland as an American ally. When Ireland was finally permitted to join in 1955, Minister for External Affairs Liam Cosgrave declared the country's mission was to preserve Christian civilisation and help stop the spread of 'communist power and influence'.[6] Similar arguments were offered during discussions on joining NATO in the late 1940s.

Though still a relatively isolated state, official Ireland played a surprisingly large role in the events which came to define the early Cold War period. This role was not as a neutral peace broker, attempting to bring about détente between the two sides. Rather, Ireland had both feet firmly planted in the American camp. For example, in 1948 the Irish government cooperated in Operation Sandstone, a top-secret project by the British to map the coasts of Ireland and the UK in case the islands were overrun by the Soviets and had to be retaken by the US. Over seven years, British military personnel and equipment, accompanied by Defence Forces personnel, travelled the coasts of Ireland, photographing and mapping every part of it, before the data was sent across the Atlantic. The Irish and British went to great lengths to keep the operation secret, both to maintain Irish claims of neutrality and to prevent public backlash. British personnel wore civilian clothes at all times and equipment was painted in Irish Army colours. Attempts at secrecy were not always successful. Over the summer of 1951, traffic jams formed outside Bundoran, County Donegal, as curious onlookers gathered to observe a strange new aircraft operating off the beach. This was one of the first helicopters to fly over Ireland.[7]

This assistance was mirrored on the world stage. In October 1960, Frederick Boland, the first Irish ambassador to the UN, was one month into his term as President of the UN General Assembly, when Soviet leader Nikita Khrushchev, angry over accusations from the Philippines that his country had colonised Eastern Europe, started to furiously bang his shoe on his desk. Boland failed in his attempts to bring the session to order, culminating in the frustrated Irishman banging his gavel so hard that it broke in two. Boland's actions may have been rooted in frustration rather than any deeply held anti-Soviet sentiment (although he would later privately compare Khrushchev to Hitler), but Ireland's actions two years later, during the 1962 Cuban Missile Crisis, were unmistakably pro-American. After the Soviets began building up a nuclear weapons infrastructure in Cuba in 1962, America put a naval blockade around the island and asked Ireland, which was on the UN Security Council at the time, for help in ensuring the Soviets couldn't skirt it by air. According to declassified documents, Lemass readily agreed to authorise inspections of all Soviet and Czech aircraft flying through Shannon Airport for technical personnel and weapons. Furthermore, this data was passed on to the Americans, a practice which would continue for another eight years, long after the crisis had abated.[8]

Then, in 1964, came a remarkably frank memo from the Department of Defence to the government laying out what facilities Ireland might be compelled to provide NATO forces if war broke out, including facilities for nuclear weapons. In the secret communication, officials considered that Ireland was unlikely to be asked to host intercontinental ballistic missiles, as they could already be launched from the United States mainland, but may well be requested to accommodate nuclear-armed submarines in the 'many suitable locations' along the Irish coast. It was also likely the Americans would request that long-range nuclear bombers be based in Ireland, as well as more conventional military installations such as troop training facilities and air defence systems. Strangely, the Department of Defence seemed to consider it possible that Ireland could remain 'non-belligerent' in such a war while hosting these facilities, although in its memo it does concede that if word of the plans got out it would seriously damage Irish claims of neutrality.[9]

There were limits to Irish support for America however, and Ireland's reputation for independence at the UN, which began with the appointment of Frank Aiken as minister for external affairs in 1957, is not entirely unearned. For example, Aiken supported the admission of communist China to the organisation, leading to Ireland voting with the Soviets and against the US on the matter in 1957 (although Aiken would continue to strongly criticise China's human rights record). Twelve years later, in 1969, the Soviets supported Ireland's efforts to secure an international peacekeeping force for Northern Ireland following the beginning of the Troubles.[10] The UK was strongly of the view that this was an internal security matter and none of the UN's business and they were supported in this by the US. In the face of such opposition, and despite the support of the Soviet delegation, Ireland failed to progress the matter on the world stage. These were important exceptions to the general theme of Irish anti-Soviet sentiment at the UN, but they were few and far between.

Further evidence of Ireland's anti-Soviet stance can be seen in the complete lack of diplomatic ties between the two countries until 1974 The road to the opening of the Soviet embassy on Orwell Road was long and torturous, with the main obstacle being a fear among Irish officials that the country would be immediately infiltrated by spies. Irish worries about Soviet infiltration dated back to before the war. They were enunciated most clearly in a 1947 memo from Colonel Dan Bryan, who by then headed G2, as Defence Forces military intelligence was known. Bryan warned with remarkable confidence there were at least 1,000 people in Ireland so indoctrinated to communist ideas that they could form the nucleus of a Soviet 'fifth column'. The Soviets, he warned, could use Irish sympathisers for anti-British and anti-American propaganda or for sabotage or espionage against these countries.[11]

One fear was that members of the tiny Communist Party of Ireland (CPI), founded in 1933, would be recruited as agents by Soviet intelligence. As historian Eunan O'Halpin notes, the CPI, like most international communist parties, danced to Moscow's tune. But Irish officials also worried that less extreme left-wing parties – Bryan specifically cited Labour in his memo – were vulnerable to exploitation as well.[12] The slow but steady leftward shift of some sections of the IRA, regarded still as the greatest threat to national security, also caused anxiety. How well-founded were these early fears of Soviet espionage? It is hard to say. As O'Halpin notes, Joseph McCarthy, the rabidly anti-communist US senator was not completely off the mark when he alleged there was widespread communist infiltration of Western society. But there is little hard evidence of Russian spies on the streets of Dublin in the first three decades of the Cold War.[13]

There were suspicions of course. Soviet journalists came in for particular attention. In 1955, the Garda Special Branch was alarmed by the unannounced visit to Ireland of the London correspondent for the newspaper

Izvestia to attend a scientific conference. Irish intelligence officials suspected he was an agent of the MVD, a precursor to the KGB, who was
sent to make sure none of the visiting Soviet scientists went AWOL.
In the same year, in an incident still shrouded in mystery, a Russian
national suspected of links to Soviet intelligence was found dead, hanging in a Malahide hotel room. In 1964, the Gardaí warned government
officials about a senior Soviet intelligence agent named Zhiltsov, aka
Boris Skoridov, who was acting under the cover of a diplomat from the
London embassy, and who had been spotted acting suspiciously during a
visit to Ireland. Later, in 1970, Ireland got its first correspondent from the
Soviet state news agency TASS; according to officials, Yuri Vladimirovich
Ustimenko was a charming, urbane addition to the Dublin social scene,
but he didn't appear to do much journalism. British ambassador to
Ireland John Peck told his superiors that Ustimenko was widely referred
to as 'the KGB man'. Such were British suspicions that they requested that
the Irish authorities impose specific restrictions on the reporter, which
required him to give 48 hours' notice before crossing into Northern
Ireland. [14]

In light of these developments, by the early 1970s, the British were
increasingly worried about the possibility of the Soviet Union opening
an embassy in Dublin, a proposal that had long been under consideration in Ireland. Their main fear was that Soviet agents based in the Irish
embassy would be able to take advantage of the common travel area and
use Ireland as a back door to Britain. In 1971, the British government
ordered the expulsion of 105 diplomats suspected of being spies, a move
that crippled Soviet intelligence operations in Britain. Officials there were
worried that the KGB would use the new Dublin pipeline to replenish
their ranks. They were equally concerned that these agents would attempt
to further aggravate the security situation in Northern Ireland in the
wake of the Bloody Sunday massacre of January 1972.

British intelligence passed on secret briefings on Soviet activities
to their Irish counterparts, partly in the hope of dissuading the Fianna
Fáil government from deepening diplomatic ties with Moscow. British
Prime Minister Ted Heath went a step further in March 1972 when he

wrote a personal, secret note to Taoiseach Jack Lynch asking him to reconsider plans to allow a Soviet embassy to open in Dublin. His letter included a warning that the KGB planned to throw its lot in with the Official IRA, a Marxist group that had splintered from the IRA three years previously. The British believed the Soviet aim was to destabilise Northern Ireland to the extent that it would have to transfer troops from its army on the Rhine to maintain order there. This was already starting to happen. Instead of preparing to meet a feared Russian invasion of Western Europe, many British squaddies in Germany were undergoing riot control training ahead of being shipped to Northern Ireland. The British also believed the KGB was actively arming the Official IRA, a belief that would be vindicated decades later when it emerged the KGB had been arranging arms shipments through Irish Communist Party leader Michael O'Riordan.

By far the biggest shipment took place under what the KGB code-named Operation Splash, which had been personally authorised by KGB chief, and later leader of the Soviet Union, Yuri Andropov. In 1972, dozens of weapons and thousands of rounds of ammunition were transported to the Northern Ireland coast in a vessel disguised as a fishing trawler before being dumped overboard in waterproof wrapping. A fishing net marker allowed the Official IRA to later locate and raise the cache. A huge effort went into disguising the source of the weapons – the gun oil, for instance, had been from West Germany. That effort paid off: confirmation of Operation Splash only came in 1992 when a former Soviet spy fled to the UK with a bundle of KGB files.[15]

As well as British objections to plans for a Soviet Embassy in Dublin, Lynch also faced opposition to the plans from within his government. Some ministers were strongly in favour of exchanging diplomats as it would open another market for Ireland's newly outward-looking economy. But officials in the Departments of Justice and Defence were deeply concerned: 'The national interest must always supersede commercial considerations if the nation is to survive,' was the dark warning from Minister for Defence Jerry Cronin in a secret memo in September 1971. He argued an embassy would provide cover for intelligence agents targeting both Ireland and its friends and that Ireland already had its fair share of Marxists 'who would not hesitate to do the Soviet bidding'.[16]

The matter lay dormant until 1973 when Fine Gael returned to government and Garret FitzGerald was appointed minister for foreign affairs. FitzGerald was not a fan of the Soviet Union but he believed Ireland needed to take foreign relations more seriously now that it was a member of the EEC. Ireland was one of the few remaining countries not to have diplomatic relations with the Soviets and, FitzGerald believed, its anti-communist objections were irrational. Again, the Department of Defence, this time headed by Paddy Donegan, raised objections. Donegan believed the Soviets were more interested in espionage than trade and that the Irish security services did not have enough manpower to keep an eye on the number of embassy staff being proposed. The Soviets had proposed 22 Russians be accredited to the new Dublin embassy. Donegan estimated that when wives were included this would increase to 44, of which 30 would likely be involved in spying. In the end, his concerns were ignored. The Soviet embassy opened in Dublin in August 1974, two months after Ireland opened its embassy in Moscow. In the words of historian Michael Quinn, 'unspoken anti-communist bogies counted for little when faced with the promise of new markets for an expanding Irish economy.'[17]

Donegan's fears of espionage would turn out to be entirely justified. Before the opening of the embassy, the Soviet spying threat had been an abstract one, based on rumours and shadows. Afterwards, it crystallised into a real national security issue and a potential minefield for Ireland's relationships with Britain and the US. Over the following decades, the Orwell Road campus would be developed into a sophisticated intelligence hub equipped for a broad spectrum of Cold War espionage activities. KGB agents disguised as diplomats, drivers, and cleaners gathered intelligence, ran influence operations and occasionally engaged in blackmail. 'The joke was always that the chauffeur was more senior than the guy he was driving because he was of course a KGB operative,' said Irish historian Donnacha Ó Beacháin.[18]

Within the walls of the embassy, cipher clerks worked in back rooms to intercept signals, with much of their activity focused on gathering communications between Ireland and fellow EEC members. Ireland was seen as a weak link in Western security and Moscow was (and still is) eager for inside information on further European integration, or potential rifts between members that could be exploited. Ireland's underdeveloped security infrastructure meant the streets of Dublin also served as a convenient training ground for young agents. There was little chance of them being caught red-handed. If they were detected by Gardaí or military intelligence, the worst that usually happened was they would be quietly told their cover was blown and it was time to return home.

This does not mean Irish security services were indifferent to Soviet spying. There was a very real concern KGB agents were making contact with republican paramilitaries and infiltrating Britain through Northern Ireland. As a result, Soviet diplomats were subject to onerous restrictions that were not applied to diplomats from other countries. For example, if they wanted to travel more than 25 miles outside Dublin city centre they had to apply in triplicate to the Department of Foreign Affairs and provide their full itinerary and car registration details, to make the jobs of their Special Branch shadows that bit easier.

These measures stand in stark contrast to the counter-intelligence resources dedicated to spies from America and Britain. The Irish security services saw the CIA as a friend rather than an enemy. This is partic-ularly true in the case of Defence Forces military intelligence which considers the CIA relationship by far its most important. Since World War II, information has flown relatively freely from Ireland to America (although not necessarily vice versa). In 1955, Cosgrave, the minister for external affairs, had formalised relations with the CIA when he ordered G2 to pass on information to the agency's man in London.[19] CIA Director Alan Dulles had, since 1951, been making repeated requests to the Irish government to allow the agency to post a man in its Dublin embassy to liaise with G2, but the Irish authorities had always objected – passing information through the London embassy was seen as a compromise.

Four years later, in 1959, CIA officials from London briefed G2 offi-cers, saying that they believed the Soviets were using Ireland as a base for spying in Western Europe. Colonel Brendan Barry of G2 believed that if Ireland did not get its house in order, the CIA would have to set up its counter-espionage operation in the country to combat it. It is believed that when the Soviet embassy opened in 1974, the CIA assigned an agent to Dublin full-time to work closely with his Irish counterparts. This person was later withdrawn on the basis of being surplus to requirements: the Americans believed they were getting all the information they needed on Soviet activities from their Irish colleagues.

The relationship with British intelligence was more complex and ebbed and flowed depending on events in Northern Ireland. Nevertheless, the Gardaí generally enjoyed a good relationship with MI6; some in the Defence Forces regarded it on occasion as being too good. In December 1972, it was discovered that Detective Sergeant Patrick Crinnion, who worked in the Garda intelligence section (C3), had been passing secret documents to an MI6 agent named John Wyman. Both men were arrested in Dublin, causing huge embarrassment to both the British and Irish governments. The episode might have seriously imperilled relations between the two countries. However, according to declassified documents, the Irish government was more concerned that the incident would hand a propaganda victory to the IRA, rather than the fact its security apparatus had been so thoroughly infiltrated (it was strongly suspected Crinnion was not the only agent Wyman was running).[20] Ireland's ambassador in London, Dr Donal O'Sullivan, seemed eager to assure British officials their man would not be treated overly harshly by the justice system. The ambassador told one official a long sentence was unlikely, and there might not be any prison term at all.[21]

Both men were later tried before the non-jury Special Criminal Court with neither the press nor the public allowed to attend. More than a few eyebrows were raised when the most serious charge against the men, under the Official Secrets Act, was dropped after the attorney general refused to make crucial documents available to the court. They were later convicted on lesser charges and sentenced to time served, before being allowed to quietly leave the country, never to return. Needless to say, no British diplomats were expelled over the incident.[22]

Every so often, details of Soviet activity in Ireland would also become public, with the most sensational being the Lipasov affair in 1983. Ostensibly, Viktor Lipasov was the second secretary in the Soviet embassy, but he and his wife, Irina, were actually KGB agents tasked with gathering information about NATO forces. In a sting operation, arranged with the help of American intelligence, the pair were observed in Stillorgan Shopping Centre on Dublin's southside receiving classified information about the US military.[23]

Irina, who was the higher ranking of the pair, was also suspected of having travelled to Northern Ireland on several occasions to liaise with paramilitaries, and to London and northern England on intelligence-gathering missions. Jim O'Keeffe, a junior minister at the Department of Foreign Affairs, was ordered by Garret FitzGerald – who was, by then, taoiseach – to expel the couple for 'unacceptable activities', diplomatic code for espionage. The embassy's first secretary and press attaché, Gennadi Saline, who was out of the country at the time, was also told not to return.[24] It was the first time Ireland had expelled a diplomat, but it would not be the last. In the following decades, further expulsions of Soviet or Russian officials would take place in response to various international outrages. It is noteworthy that no British officials were expelled after the Crinnion affair. The Soviet Union/Russia is the only country Ireland has ever taken such action against.

There is some evidence the Lipasov expulsions were part of a wider attempt by FitzGerald's government to engage in some Cold War geopolitical games of its own. On 1 September 1983, ten days before the Lipasovs were expelled, the Soviets had shot down Korean Air Lines Flight 007 when it mistakenly entered Soviet airspace. All 269 passengers, including a US congressman, were killed, drawing a furious response from Washington and leading the Reagan administration to demand the Irish government end flights from Soviet airline Aeroflot to and from Shannon Airport. These flights were a valuable source of income for the region and the government refused America's request, adding to their frustration. It has been suggested that FitzGerald then expelled the Lipasovs to soothe Washington. FitzGerald doesn't go into detail in his biography but does say the expulsions may have incidentally calmed the Americans' anger.[25]

By that stage, Irish officials were getting rather skilled at placating Washington while maintaining a semi-plausible sheen of neutrality. This is partly due to the lessons learned in the wake of the Soviet invasion of Afghanistan in December 1979. Ireland had joined most Western nations in condemning the invasion. But it was faced with a dilemma when US President Jimmy Carter's administration asked it to join a boycott of the 1980 Moscow Olympics, due to take place that summer. In Ireland, there was little public support for such a boycott. Internally, Department of Foreign Affairs officials questioned why an Olympic boycott was justified now when there had been no similar calls following Britain and France's invasion of the Suez in 1956 or America's invasion of Vietnam in the 1960s. Further, Irish-Soviet trade links had by then become important enough to form part of the diplomatic arithmetic: a valuable deal had just been signed to sell the Soviets vast amounts of Irish butter, and the Soviet Union was judged to be a reliable source of oil.

As senior Irish official Noel Dorr noted at the time, Ireland had to choose between offending the Soviet Union 'or losing goodwill in the U.S. where our basic interests and shared values are much greater'.[26] In the end, Charles Haughey's Fianna Fáil government was able to keep the Americans happy while not entirely offending the Soviet Union: it declined to send any government representative to the games and advised the Olympic Committee of Ireland (OCI) not to send any athletes, in the knowledge that the committee was free to ignore such advice. As expected, the OCI sent an Irish team, which marched in the opening ceremony under the Olympic flag rather than the Tricolour to denote the lack of government support. Both the butter deal and American relations were saved and Ireland came home with three medals.

Despite positive relations between Ireland and the Soviet Union in the early days of the existence of both states, for the duration of the Cold War, Ireland remained firmly in the Western camp, and more specific- ally the American camp. There were exceptions, such as when Ireland attempted to reach an understanding with communist countries at the

UN, sometimes raising the ire of Washington. And events in Northern Ireland frequently caused tensions between Dublin and London. But on the global scale, Ireland was firmly on team NATO. Ireland's diplomatic relations with the Soviet Union began many years after that of most other European countries, including those who were NATO members: Switzerland, that archetype of neutrality, had established diplomatic relations in 1946, despite being accused by the Soviet Union, with some justification, of collaborating with the Nazis during the preceding war.

There were Irish attempts at maintaining a gloss of neutrality, such as the prevarication over the Olympic boycott or the reluctance to ban Soviet planes from Shannon. But the priority for foreign policy across multiple governments was keeping Washington happy rather than demonstrating Irish even-handedness. The Dublin government was well aware that this had not gone unnoticed in Moscow and that its claims to neutrality counted for little within the walls of the Kremlin. Throughout the Cold War, Irish preparations for war therefore proceeded on the basis that Dublin would be one of the cities to come under nuclear attack from the Soviet Union should such an attack come.[27]

CHAPTER NINE

LOCKED OUT

*I don't understand Ireland. You are not aligned, and you
are not aligned with the non-aligned ...*
Andrei Gromyko (1976)[1]

I n April 1953, the same month Dag Hammarskjöld was elected as
the UN's second secretary-general, an Austrian lawyer named Hans
Kelsen gave a speech at an otherwise anodyne political science conference, which caught the attention of Irish diplomats. Kelsen was
regarded as one of the greatest legal minds of the twentieth century, at
least when it came to international law. By the time he addressed the
UK's Political Studies Association, he was already long-established as a
giant of twentieth-century legal thinking. Kelsen was the main author
of the Austrian constitution of 1920 and a close associate of Sigmund
Freud in Vienna before being forced to flee for Switzerland after the
Nazi occupation. After the war, his legal writings formed part of the
basis for the Nuremberg trials and, much later, European integration.

So when, in 1953, he said neutrality was fundamentally incompatible
with membership in the United Nations, people – particularly people
in Iveagh House, the headquarters of the Irish Department of External
Affairs – paid attention. Neutrality mandated that nations maintain
'indiscriminate impartiality' towards all sides in a war, Kelsen said.[2] But
the United Nations is based on the idea of collective security; in other

words, if one country commits an 'act of aggression', all members will take action, in the form of diplomacy, sanctions or even military action, to suppress that aggression.[3] Therefore a country could not be both neutral and a member of the UN.

Ireland, under de Valera, had been an early applicant to the UN. Although scalded by the failure of the League of Nations to prevent war in the 1930s, the government was aware that, while great powers had the military might to do as they wished, small nations needed a rules-based order to survive and thrive. This was something acknowledged by de Valera as early as 1943 when Ireland was still publicly committed to wartime neutrality. The taoiseach told the Dáil that when a successor to the League of Nations emerges, 'there need be no doubt that this country will, as in the past, be prepared to take its full share in endeavouring to secure international peace and security'.[4]

The Dáil voted to apply for UN membership in July 1946 as the format of the new organisation was thrashed out in San Francisco. Despite its early application and de Valera's previous sentiments, neither the Irish government nor the opposition nor the general public was overly enthusiastic about membership. On the subject of partition, the UN was judged unlikely to be of much use. Another major concern was the advantage the great powers those on the victorious side in the recent war would hold over smaller nations. Under the UN Charter, the Security Council would consist of five permanent members – the US, the UK, France, China and the Soviet Union – and a rotating roster of ten non-permanent members. Each of the five permanent members would have a veto over any decision by the council, meaning they could prevent the UN from intervening in any area where their interests might be threatened.

Irish concerns about the veto appeared vindicated when the Soviet Union immediately deployed it to prevent Ireland from joining the UN due to the belief it would serve as just another US ally. The Soviets continued to block the Irish application for another nine years, during which time Irish suspicions about this seemingly exclusive club only increased. The Irish application had become a victim of the type of great power machinations the UN was supposed to avoid. As a result of this competition between East and West, the organisation seemed destined to be as useless as the League. Irish Government leaders and opposition members suggested on several occasions that the membership application should be withdrawn. In 1949, Minister for External Affairs Seán MacBride said, only half-jokingly, that he was very thankful the Irish application was still being vetoed as his department had enough work as it was. Asked for his view in 1952, de Valera, then back in power, said, 'The UN has shown itself an imperfect organisation; in fact it now consists of two blocs. I do not think that Ireland particularly wishes to enter the UN under such circumstances.'[5]

Kelsen's speech raised another issue about the Security Council. At first glance, the UN Charter appeared to give it the power to order member states to go to war 'to maintain or restore international peace and security'.[6] How could any country call itself neutral while subject to such a treaty? It was a concern already noted by the Department of External Affairs as early as 1945, when, on viewing the draft charter, the department's legal adviser Michael Rynne suggested it could cost Ireland its sovereignty as well as its national security. He even suggested the charter could compel Ireland to give over its ports and airbases to the great powers.[7] The Treaty Ports may become the Charter Ports. During their long wait for acceptance as UN members, Irish officials held two seemingly contradictory fears: that the UN Charter made the Security Council too powerful and that its veto powers made it too weak.

Kelsen's speech prompted Rynne's successor William Fay to write a rebuttal, which is today filed away in a dusty folder in the National Archives. But really, it wasn't much of a rebuttal. In fact, for the most part, Fay, a skilled diplomat and future ambassador to France and America, actually agreed with Kelsen. He argued that the founding UN documents made it clear that being neutral does not absolve a member from adhering to the charter. Relying heavily on Catholic theological thought, Fay concluded that 'even in the case of those small countries which have no military potential, the Security Council would call upon them and thereby oblige them to provide assistance'. But crucially, this could only happen if the Security Council worked as intended and by 1953 it was painfully clear the council, thoroughly riven by Cold War rivalries, was not working as intended. There was little prospect of such a divided council agreeing on military action of a type that could endanger Irish neutrality. If, for example, America proposed UN military intervention against a country in the Soviet sphere of influence it would surely be vetoed by Moscow, and vice versa. Therefore, Fay determined, Kelsen was wrong… sort of. As long as the UN remained divided, there would be no threat to neutrality: an Irish solution to an Irish problem.[8]

But what about the Korean War? The bloody and often forgotten conflict of 1950–3 involved UN troops, led by the US, intervening to stop communist forces from taking over the Korean peninsula. This was exactly the type of conflict Ireland was worried about. If it had been a UN member during this period, surely it would have been compelled to offer assistance? Not so, was the official conclusion. For one thing, the mechanism for gathering UN forces to fight in Korea was such that it was up to each country if it wanted to contribute or not. Furthermore, the sequence of events that led to the mission was a freak occurrence. At the time the resolution was voted on, the Soviet Union was boycotting the Security Council over the UN's refusal to recognise communist China. In any other circumstances, it would have immediately vetoed the Korea resolution. On realising their mistake, the Soviets had quickly retaken their seat at the table. They would not make the same mistake again, meaning aggressive UN military missions – known as peace enforcement missions or Chapter VII missions – remained off the table for the remainder of the Cold War. Instead, the UN would come to rely on less divisive means of solving problems, including diplomatic wrangling, economic sanctions and, crucially for Ireland, peacekeeping missions – or Chapter VI missions in UN terminology.

Despite Fay's conclusions, there were still some lingering fears about the impact on neutrality, right up to the point Ireland was finally admitted to the UN in 1955. After all, Switzerland was not joining precisely because it believed UN membership was incompatible with neutrality. Finances, as always, were also a concern: several department officials warned the costs of membership could be ruinous. But these were put to one side and the government took some comfort in the fact that Austria, a country with neutrality written into its constitution, was joining at the same time. Ireland was one of sixteen countries admitted on 14 December 1955, after the Soviet Union agreed to drop their veto in return for the admission of some of its allies. The young organisation was far from ideal, but, as Frederick Boland noted in September 1946 'with the rest of the world belonging to it, Ireland could scarcely afford to remain outside'.[9]

From the start, Ireland tried to ride two horses at the UN: neutrality (or at least the appearance of neutrality) and showing solidarity with America and the Christian West. This is reflected in the priorities set down for Ireland at the UN by Liam Cosgrave, who at that time was minister for external affairs in the Second Inter-Party government, which had taken power by the time Ireland was formally admitted. Ireland's UN mission would be to stay true to the UN Charter, avoid 'as far as possible' joining particular blocs or groups, preserve Christianity and resist the spread of communism. 'We belong to the great community of states, made up of the United States of America, Canada, and Western Europe,' Cosgrave added, in case he hadn't already made himself clear on the matter. It was Ireland's duty, he said 'to strengthen the influence of this group, to resist efforts aiming at its disintegration and to lend support and co-operation wherever possible to its individual members.'[10] As Keatinge put it, 'this is hardly the sort of statement an Austrian foreign minister would make'.[11]

Unsurprisingly, given Cosgrave's priority list, once Ireland took its seat, it voted almost without fail with the Western powers. This lasted for two years until 1957 when Fianna Fáil returned to power and, with them, Frank Aiken returned to the Department of External Affairs. Aiken involved himself intimately in UN affairs and, over the next 12 years, almost single-handedly forged Ireland's reputation as an independent voice on the world stage. During his maiden speech in the General Assembly, Aiken suggest a UN-supervised 'drawback plan', where every step American troops took out of Europe would be matched by the Soviets on their end, thus reducing the risk of World War III breaking out. Aiken also played a leading role in work on nuclear disarmament and was not afraid to get on the wrong side of the US, including on whether to discuss the admission of communist China.

However, there were limits to Ireland's willingness and ability to go it alone. Although Aiken favoured a UN discussion on the admission of China, he remained a staunch critic of the Peking regime and said it should only be granted membership if it introduced sweeping human rights reforms. When it came time to vote for the first time on admitting China, Ireland joined with the US in voting against it. Even during this heyday of Irish independence at the UN, it still voted with the US much more often than not.

Aiken's early position on China and his devotion to nuclear disarmament might have made Ireland the ideal candidate for what had become known as the Non-Aligned Movement (NAM), the bloc of nations that did not ally themselves with either side in the Cold War. With its anti-colonial ethos and commitment to remaining neutral in the Cold War, NAM was in many ways a perfect home for Ireland. But, despite Ireland's absence from NATO, the movement viewed the Irish as having two feet planted solidly in the Western camp and had little interest in inviting it to join. Ireland returned the sentiment and has never sought an invitation. This was the case even after other European neutrals established diplomatic links with NAM, which saw them invited to summit conferences. Even countries like Portugal, a NATO member, and Romania, a member of the Warsaw Pact, were invited to NAM conferences as guests. But not Ireland. During a visit to the Soviet Union in 1976, Garret FitzGerald, then minister for foreign affairs, tried to explain Ireland's version of neutrality to his counterpart Andrei Gromyko. 'I don't understand Ireland,' the confused Russian responded. 'You are not aligned, and you are not aligned with the non-aligned.'[12]

One area where Ireland's neutrality was recognised, however, was peacekeeping. Starting with its first UN mission as part of the United Nations Observation Group in Lebanon (UNOGIL) in 1958, which involved the deployment of some 50 Irish officers to monitor the armistice line between Israel and Lebanon, Ireland began developing a version of neutrality which is still recognisable today. The country would not be a member of a military alliance but would readily offer its troops to keep the peace around the world, sometimes with tragic consequences. That first mission in 1958 was a gentle introduction to peacekeeping and established the Defence Forces as a capable and professional (if often woefully ill-equipped) force.

The Irish soldiers' most valuable asset was their lack of colonial baggage. They were a professional, volunteer army whose presence in a country was typically viewed as uncontroversial by the great powers and by that country's inhabitants. It has often been said since that peacekeeping was also the saviour of the Defence Forces. It gave young soldiers a sense of mission, a few more pounds in their pocket and an opportunity to escape the monotony of garrison duties under grey Irish skies. In the words of John Duggan, the author of the most comprehensive history of the Defence Forces to date, it saved the post-war army from becoming a 'glorified gendarmerie'.[13]

If the unarmed UNOGIL served as a gentle introduction to peacekeeping, Ireland's participation in the Congo was a delayed baptism of fire. In 1960, the United Nations secretary-general asked Ireland to send a battalion to the former Belgium colony, which was verging on anarchy thanks to multiple internal crises. Soon, the first 60 Irishmen were on a US Air Force plane to the Congo. Within a year, a remarkable one-fifth of the Defence Forces were on peacekeeping duty in central Africa. From an Irish point of view, the Congo mission was like none before or since. As the conflict worsened, the peacekeepers' task evolved from keeping the peace to enforcing it and Irish troops frequently found themselves in combat situations. In total, 27 Irish soldiers died during the four-year mission, representing over 10 per cent of the mission's total casualty numbers.

But even after reports of UN casualties became a regular feature in Irish newspapers, there was little public backlash. Public commentary mourned the losses and celebrated the soldiers' bravery but hardly anyone questioned if a neutral country should be getting involved in bloody military operations thousands of miles away. This was the case even after the Niemba ambush on 8 November 1960, when nine Irish soldiers were killed in an ambush by Baluba tribesman in the Army's first battle since the end of the Civil War. Afterwards, there were questions about the preparedness of the Irish troops for such dangerous missions, particularly the lack of armoured cars, but not about whether they should be in the Congo in the first place. The soldiers were given state funerals, and thousands attended their processions through Dublin. The Niemba deaths, Eunan O'Halpin notes, 'were regarded not as a price too high but as an affirmation of Ireland's willingness as a neutral state to risk the lives of its soldiers in defence of peace rather than in prosecution of war'.[14]

Probably the most famous incident of the Congo campaign, and certainly the most talked about in recent years, was the battle at Jadotville, when, in September 1961, 155 Irish soldiers from 'A' Company fought off thousands of Katangese militiamen and Belgian mercenaries for four days before being captured. Precise casualty figures, along with many other details of the battle, have become muddied over the years, but most estimates suggest the Irish, thanks to their effective use of defensive positions, inflicted hundreds of deaths while not losing a single man themselves. It has been suggested that one of the reasons the remarkable accomplishment of 'A' Company was ignored at home for so long was a strange sense of embarrassment on the part of Irish people that purported peacekeepers had inflicted so many casualties. If this was the case, it is not reflected in the political or public discourse of the time.

The men of 'A' Company were jeered and derided, not for killing so many of their attackers, but for surrendering to them after they ran out of ammunition. Like after Niemba, few questioned if a neutral army should be taking part in such missions at all. Rather, the Congo mission marked the start of a long and unbroken tradition of Irish involvement in peacekeeping. To date, Irish troops have completed nearly 75,000 individual peacekeeping tours and 88 men have died in the process, including Private Sean Rooney who was gunned down in Lebanon in December 2022. Few missions have been as bloody as the Congo but that's because, with its aggressive mandate to prevent the secession of the province of Katanga, it was an outlier in UN peacekeeping during the Cold War. For the most part, Fay's 1953 memo had been borne out and the Cold War deadlock meant the prospect of Ireland being forced to join a UN-mandated war, similar to the Korean War, did not arise. The use of the veto by Security Council members, or, more commonly, the mere threat of the veto, meant aggressive UN missions simply did not get authorised.

To date, the veto has been used 266 times at the Security Council. Each of the permanent five members has deployed it to varying degrees to protect their own interests, but by far the biggest users are the US (82 times) and the Soviet Union/ Russia (122 times).[15] The outsized impact of the veto on the work of the Security Council was recognised at an early stage and there have been various attempts to dilute its power over the years. Most notable was the Uniting for Peace resolution in 1950, which stated if a resolution was vetoed by the council, it could be taken up by the UN General Assembly, meaning in theory UN missions could be launched even if the Security Council was at loggerheads.

Uniting for Peace was spearheaded in the General Assembly by the US, which was growing increasingly frustrated with Soviet abuse of the veto. This was just four years after the Americans threatened to tear up the UN Charter if the veto was not included as part of Security Council procedures. By the 1970s, the US had come to love the veto again as the influx of newly decolonised countries into the UN meant it was no longer guaranteed to win council votes. It increasingly fell back on the mechanism to protect its interests and soon rivalled the Soviet Union in its prolific veto use. On paper, the Uniting for Peace resolution appeared to solve the problem of powerful states preventing morally justified UN interventions. However, over the years it has proven to be something of a dead letter. The General Assembly has intervened following council vetoes in less than 5 per cent of cases and its use has never led to the establishment of a peacekeeping force, a reflection of smaller countries' unwillingness to upset their more powerful neighbours. It turned out the great powers didn't need a veto to control the agenda; economic and political pressure could work just as well.

This meant that UN interventions during the Cold War were almost entirely of a peacekeeping nature, rather than more aggressive peace enforcement missions, which would invariably be vetoed if proposed. That situation changed drastically with the dissolution of the Soviet Union in 1991, which marked the beginning of a period of détente between the US and a weakened Russia. Suddenly, it was possible to get support for aggressive UN mandates under Chapter VII of the Charter. Definitions of peace enforcement missions vary but their main distinguishing factor is the enforcers are not wanted in the country by at least one side in the conflict. According to a US Army definition, peace enforcers 'are active fighters who must impose a cease-fire that is opposed by one or both combatants; in the process, the neutrality that distinguishes peacekeepers will most likely be lost.'[16]

Despite the obvious implications for neutrality, Ireland was not found wanting in this new world order. In 1993, the Fianna Fáil government introduced legislation to allow the Defence Forces to take part in peace enforcement missions, with the intention of immediately sending troops to Somalia, as part of the United Nations Operation in Somalia II (UNOSOM II), to enforce a ceasefire in the country's civil war. 'Neutrality has gone,' declared Proinsias De Rossa of Democratic Left during a Dáil debate on the matter.[17] Nevertheless, the legislation passed with ease and an Irish transport company, supported by the Army Ranger Wing (ARW) – the Defence Forces' special forces unit – was dispatched to Somalia. The realities of this new type of UN mission quickly became apparent when Irish vehicles came under attack from armed militias as they ferried supplies between Mogadishu and the French Brigade in Baidoa, requiring soldiers to respond with sometimes deadly force.

Further missions followed where Irish troops were compelled to use aggressive force, and Irish special forces soldiers found a new role in acting as pathfinders for UN troops in dangerous environments. In 2009, the ARW was among the over 400 Irish troops deployed as part of the EUFOR/MINURCAT peace enforcement mission in Chad and the Central Africa Republic. It was a more complex, more dangerous mission than the usual Irish deployments, and at one point, according to its commander, Brigadier General David Dignam, Irish troops 'had to interpose themselves between Djabal refugee camp, and armed groups are fighting within two kilometres of the camp. And effectively, they said, we're about to stand here, we're going to protect the people in this camp, if needs to be with our lives.'[18]

Not all of these missions started as peace enforcement missions. Some have been traditional Chapter VI missions, where Irish troops have had to use force to protect civilians or other peacekeepers. In 1999, ARW troops were tasked with clearing the jungle of paramilitary forces threatening local villages in East Timor; while in 2014, Irish troops stationed in the Golan Heights took part in a daring rescue of 32 Filipino peacekeepers who had been captured by an Islamist group. In 2004, an ARW unit serving as part of the United Nations Mission in Liberia (UNMIL), rescued 37 civilians being held in a shipping container by armed rebels.

Violence during UN missions is nothing new; for example, in 1980, Irish troops in Lebanon were involved in the Battle of At Tiri after they came under attack from an Israeli-backed militia. But by the 1990s, the use of force was increasingly becoming a key part of some missions, rather than a side effect of self-defence. That process is ongoing. According to Defence Forces Major General Maureen O'Brien, who serves as the deputy military adviser at UN Headquarters in New York, the UN is moving away from 'the traditional missions where you are trying to place yourself between two forces and you are trying to keep them apart' and towards more challenging missions with 'more robust rules of engagement'. Such roles require 'more positive action,' she added.[19] As was the case after Niemba, this process has been occurring with little to no debate in Ireland about what it means for neutrality. Despite the growing challenges, the government remains completely committed to peacekeeping, including these new more dangerous variants, as do the majority of the Irish public, at least for now.

But the Defence Forces' future ability to take part in UN missions, be they in peacekeeping, peace enforcement or peacebuilding, is now in question thanks to a uniquely Irish device called the triple lock. Under the triple lock, no armed contingent of more than 12 Defence Forces soldiers can be sent on a peacekeeping mission without approval from the government, the Dáil, and a UN resolution. Its foundation was the Defence Amendment Act of 1960, but it wasn't until the early 2000s that the mechanism started becoming known as the triple lock. The term was devised around then by civil servants as a rhetorical device to assuage public fears Ireland might be drawn into an EU common defence agreement on a par with NATO. In 2001, Ireland rejected by referendum the Treaty of Nice on further EU integration, partly on the basis of these fears, and the government began talking up the triple lock to ensure the treaty would pass the next time around. It worked and, given a second chance, Irish people approved the Treaty of Nice in 2002. The triple lock has since become part of the DNA of modern Irish neutrality, a curious thing since the concept is mentioned nowhere in legislation.

The triple lock means Ireland will not be bounced into any EU military adventures as the Union becomes more integrated. But it also gives each of the five permanent members of the UN Security Council a veto over major areas of Irish foreign policy. It didn't take long for this to become apparent. In 2003, the EU planned to send peacekeepers to the Former Yugoslavian Republic of Macedonia (FYROM) to replace the previous UN mission there, which had come to an end when China vetoed the mission's renewal at the Security Council in revenge for FYROM recognising Taiwan. Ireland was eager to take part in the new EU mission but was legally unable to without explicit UN authorisation. The UN had 'welcomed' the mission but, in the view of the attorney general, this did not constitute a mandate. As a result, Ireland was forced to sit out the EU's first peacekeeping mission.

Changes to the law in 2006 mean a situation similar to the FYROM incident is unlikely to reoccur: missions can now be sanctioned on the back of a UN endorsement of any kind, rather than an explicit mandate. However, a newly belligerent Russia and generally increased tensions on the world stage suggest we are entering another era of veto abuse at the Security Council. This was shown most clearly on 28 February 2022 when, two days after its military launched a full-scale invasion of Ukraine, Russia vetoed a Security Council resolution calling on it to withdraw its forces. Presently, it seems certain any potential EU or

UN peacekeeping initiative in Ukraine would receive similar treatment, meaning Ireland would not be able to take part, even if every other Security Council member besides Russia was in favour.

Following the Nice referendums, successive Irish governments remained solidly behind the triple lock system. The 2013 Green Paper on Defence stated it reflects the central importance of the UN in granting legitimacy to foreign deployments. This was confirmed in the 2015 White Paper on Defence, which remains Ireland's de facto national defence policy. But since the invasion of Ukraine, cracks have started to appear in this position. In March 2022, then Tánaiste Leo Varadkar suggested Fine Gael should come out against the triple lock to differentiate itself from its coalition partner Fianna Fáil.[20] Not to be outdone, after taking over the foreign affairs brief in December 2022, Fianna Fáil's Micheál Martin said the triple lock should be reviewed given recent world events. In particular, the increased deployment of mercenaries by the Kremlin to developing parts of the world means Russia 'may not want peacekeeping in certain locations anymore' and may exploit the triple lock towards this end, Martin said.[21]

Privately, many more ministers and TDs have expressed unease with the restrictions the triple lock may place on Ireland in aiding its European neighbours in the face of an increasingly aggressive Russia. Several alternatives have been proposed with varying chances of success. These include lobbying internationally for the abolition of the Security Council veto, replacing the requirement in Irish law for a UN resolution with a requirement for one by the EU Council, or simply dispensing with the triple lock requirement altogether. To date, a consensus has yet to be built around any single option, though a change to Irish policy seems a far less daunting task than wholescale reform of the Security Council.

While government objections to the triple lock have only manifested since the invasion of Ukraine, the system has long been viewed with disdain by Irish diplomats who consider it a danger to Irish freedom of action. At the time of its formulation in the early 2000s, at least one senior official in the Department of Foreign Affairs (DFA) wrote a memo advising against making it a core part of Irish policy on neutrality.

'For twenty years getting a Security Council resolution was doable. Now the dynamic has changed. That means it's increasingly unlikely that we're going to see easy agreement on UN peacekeeping missions,' one retired senior DFA official said, before pointing out there hasn't been a new UN peacekeeping mission authorised in over five years.[22] In this former diplomat's view, Ireland's proficiency in peacekeeping 'is a card of diminishing value'. Rory Montgomery, the Department's former second secretary, goes further, calling the triple lock an 'illogical and immoral' abrogation of responsibility.[23]

Given Ireland's long and eager service to the UN, it's strange to imagine today that membership was once considered incompatible with neutrality. This was a view held not just by renowned international jurists but by Irish politicians and diplomats. Nevertheless, Ireland ploughed ahead with membership and, once admitted, found the UN the perfect forum for a small nation wishing to make itself heard on the world stage. The UN was, in many ways, where the modern Irish conception of neutrality was forged; where it defined itself as a country happy to get involved in another nation's affairs, but only if sanctioned by a higher power, i.e. the Security Council.

As the decades passed, Irish neutrality changed with the UN, rather than the other way around. When it became clear neutrality was no defence against peacekeepers coming home in coffins, Ireland did not object. When the UN wanted Irish soldiers to enforce the peace, rather than just keep it, Ireland went along. And when it became desirable for the EU to become a subcontractor for UN peacekeeping, Ireland went along with that too.

Now, with the return of great power politics and the renewed abuse of the Security Council veto, Ireland faces a new challenge that it may not be so happy to accept: the prospect that Moscow or Beijing could dictate when and where Irish peacekeepers can deploy, even in the face of overwhelming moral arguments in favour of action. If, at its core, Irish neutrality is based on not having to dance to the tune of the powerful nations, it's difficult to imagine a greater contradiction.

CHAPTER TEN

WEAPONISED NEUTRALITY

*Ireland is not afraid ... to reassert our traditional
policy of neutrality.*
Charles Haughey (1982)[1]

On the morning of 4 May 1982, on the southeast of the Falkland Islands, HMS *Sheffield* was struck by an Argentinian Exocet missile, leading to the loss of 20 crew members. The ship later sank, handing Argentina one of its few military successes in the short, grubby war over some desolate islands in the south Atlantic. That same morning, some 10,000km away at the UN Security Council in New York, an entirely different type of conflict was taking place, which thrust the issue of Irish neutrality back into the spotlight and resulted in damage to the relationship between Ireland and Britain that would take years to repair. The genesis of this crisis occurred three weeks previously when Charles Haughey, just two months into his second term as taoiseach, declared that, due to Ireland's 'traditional policy of neutrality',[2] it was withdrawing from economic sanctions that had been levied against Argentina by the EEC over the invasion of the Falklands. Britain was furious. It saw no link between neutrality and the issue of sanctions. Prime Minister Margaret Thatcher and her government were further enraged by an Irish call for a ceasefire that did not demand the withdrawal of Argentinian forces from the islands.

To understand why Haughey's announcement caught the world by surprise, it's necessary to consider the state of Irish neutrality in the early 1980s and the taoiseach's attitude towards it. Despite seeing himself as a statesman in the vein of his party's founder, Éamon de Valera, Haughey had no great attachment to the idea of a neutral Ireland. 'Ideologically and politically, Ireland was not neutral,' Haughey had told his West German counterpart Chancellor Helmut Schmidt the previous year,[3] echoing the sentiments of his Fianna Fáil predecessor Jack Lynch, who told the Dáil in 1969 'we have no traditional policy of neutrality in this country'.[4] Haughey also made it clear that Ireland would play its part in defending the European Community as it became further integrated. 'This is accepted by the Irish public,' he told Schmidt. He was, at least in the view of those around him, also willing to sign Ireland up to NATO if it might end partition.[5]

Michael Lillis, an Irish diplomat who played a key role in the Anglo-Irish talks of the 1980s, said of Haughey:

> There is, in my mind, no doubt that Charles Haughey was actually prepared to make a move on neutrality and even on NATO. This was certainly discussed among Irish officials, and was seen by Charles Haughey himself as being a useful inducement to Thatcher.

Despite this, Lillis said he has never found a record of Haughey or other officials putting neutrality on the table during their talks with Thatcher. 'That doesn't mean it doesn't exist', he added.[6]

Certainly, Haughey's successor Garret FitzGerald believed that, following the famous Anglo-Irish summit of 1980, Mr Haughey privately proposed to Thatcher some sort of Anglo-Irish cooperation on defence. Haughey always denied this, and Thatcher later appeared to pour cold water on the idea when she said in 1981 that 'if Ireland wished to discuss defence it would presumably do so with a much wider group of nations'.[7] Whether or not the proposal happened, Lillis is of the view that neutrality had little value as a bargaining chip when it came to Northern Ireland.

He developed a very close relationship with senior British diplomat David Goodall during the long and torturous negotiations preceding the Anglo-Irish Agreement. After Lillis asked outright about the potential value of Ireland dropping neutrality, Goodall replied 'it wouldn't matter at all and wouldn't have the slightest value.' Lillis said he is 'completely convinced' this was a genuinely held view'.[8]

Haughey was ambivalent towards neutrality. So when he invoked it during the Falklands crisis, it took those around him completely by surprise. This was especially so because, in the recent past, neutrality was not seen as a bar to imposing sanctions on rogue states. In 1979, during his first term as taoiseach, Haughey had apparently no problem in signing Ireland up to sanctions against Iran in response to the hostage-taking of US diplomats following the Islamic revolution. Ireland also joined in American-led sanctions against the Soviet Union after it invaded Afghanistan in 1979.

When Argentinian forces, under the leadership of despot General Leopoldo Galtieri, first landed on the Falkland Islands on 2 April 1982, Ireland was initially highly supportive of Britain while also keen, in its role as a newly elected non-permanent member of the Security Council, to play a proactive role in bringing the crisis to an end. Ireland joined with the other Security Council members in approving Britain's Resolution 502, which condemned the invasion and called on the Argentinians to immediately withdraw. Thatcher was thrilled with the Irish support. She wrote to Haughey saying she was 'deeply grateful' and asked for his further support in persuading other members of the EEC to impose sanctions on Argentina. She received a positive response from Dublin.[9]

In private, Irish officials, along with US President Ronald Reagan and many politicians in Thatcher's party, thought her decision to immediately dispatch a massive naval force to win back the desolate, economically useless rock, was ill-advised. Nevertheless, on 16 April, Ireland joined with the other eight members of the EEC in banning all imports from Argentina until at least 17 May 1982. This was after the Department of Foreign Affairs said publicly that joining sanctions had no implications whatsoever for Irish neutrality.

Over the following weeks, as the British task force steamed the thousands of miles across the ocean to confront the Argentinians, the Irish diplomatic team, led by its Ambassador to the UN Noel Dorr, attempted to craft a deal which might avert the need for further conflict. Dorr said:

> Ireland had friendly relations with both countries, and a temporary seat on the Council. So, in the Permanent Mission in New York we felt that, in line with Ireland's long-standing approach in international relations, we ought to help, if we could, to avert an even wider conflict.[10]

Dorr and his colleagues prepared an internal report outlining a plan where Argentina would withdraw and a small UN force would establish a temporary administration while negotiations resumed on the islands' future. Irish diplomats quietly floated these ideas in London and Buenos Aires.

Then, on 4 May, Dorr and his colleagues learned through a press release they had not been consulted on, that Ireland was to take an entirely different tack. This followed a meeting earlier that day between Haughey and his most senior colleagues in the taoiseach's palatial Abbeville home in Kinsealy during which the taoiseach announced Ireland would no longer support EEC sanctions against Argentina (it was not clear Ireland could legally unilaterally withdraw from EEC sanctions in such a fashion, but the war ended before this could be clarified). Thatcher and her cabinet were livid. The wording of the statement appeared to imply both sides were equally to blame for the crisis and it made no reference to the resolution of the previous month calling on Argentina to withdraw.

Haughey's announcement had followed the sinking of the Argentinian cruiser *General Belgrano* by a Royal Navy submarine on 2 May. The news of the sinking and the subsequent loss of 323 lives was met with revulsion in Ireland and it was widely, but erroneously, viewed as a war crime. The *Belgrano*'s captain survived, and later said it was 'absolutely not a war crime. It was an act of war, lamentably legal'.[11]

Nevertheless, whatever public sympathy in Ireland for the British position, and there wasn't much, quickly evaporated. Haughey's Minister for Defence Paddy Power was probably speaking for most Irish people when he said at a Fianna Fáil Parliamentary Party meeting that 'obviously Britain themselves are very much the aggressors now'.[12] This further enraged the British, and Haughey summoned Power to his office afterwards to ask him to withdraw the remark. Power refused and, perhaps sensing the public mood, Haughey did not pursue the matter.

In explaining his decision to withdraw support for sanctions, Haughey claimed sanctions were designed to prevent military action, not support it. Therefore, after the sinking of the *Belgrano,* they were no longer compatible with neutrality. But this ignores the fact that an effective state of war had existed between Britain and Argentina from the moment the British task force had departed for the Falklands a full month earlier, almost two weeks before Ireland imposed sanctions. The battle for the Falklands would not start in earnest until 21 May, when British forces landed on the islands but military operations to retake the nearby South Georgia island, which had also been invaded by Argentina, had been ongoing since 21 April.

Haughey seems to have been entirely alone in his interpretation of neutrality, and various senior advisers tried to change his mind. Political director in the Department for Foreign Affairs Paddy McKernan argued strongly that the move would damage Ireland's standing in the EEC (which it had just joined a decade earlier), while the secretary to the government, Dermot Nally, advised it would do major harm to Anglo-Irish relations. Officials from the Irish embassy in London had already warned against such a move, citing the fever-pitch of jingoism in British society since the start of the war and the resultant impact this might have on the large Irish community there.

Haughey was not for turning however, and Dorr and his colleagues in New York were forced to implement the instructions and call for a meeting of the Security Council. Irish diplomats in Europe faced the even more embarrassing task of lobbying other EEC members to also withdraw from sanctions. The Irish call on 4 May for a Security Council meeting could scarcely have come at a worse time. Frantic efforts led by UN Secretary-General Javier Pérez de Cuéllar to bring about a ceasefire had been ongoing in the background, and both sides were due to come back a day later with their responses to his proposals. There was a real danger the Irish efforts could throw a spanner in the works.

In the end, the Irish endeavours had little impact on the conflict, good or bad. When a meeting finally did take place on 25 May, Ireland proposed calling for a 72-hour truce between the sides. The other members rejected this as pointless since the British forces had already landed on the islands. The resolution that did pass was effectively a restatement of the previous resolutions calling for a ceasefire along with Argentinian withdrawal and was so toothless that even the British felt they could not vote against it. On 14 June, the British accepted the formal surrender of all Argentinian forces, saving further diplomatic embarrassment for Haughey. About 1,100 people were killed on both sides, including two Irish men.

In contrast to the frustration of his senior advisers, the Irish public's reaction to Haughey's decision to invoke neutrality was overwhelmingly positive. The taoiseach received a large number of letters welcoming his stance, and that support was reflected in newspaper editorials which typically referred to the Falklands as the Malvinas, the Argentinian name for the islands. In the minds of some, there was a parallel between the British occupation of the Falklands and its occupation of Northern Ireland: 'I'm no fan of the Argentine generals,' an unnamed Dublin newspaper editor told the *New York Times* correspondent in Ireland at the time, 'But "Brits out!" was the rallying cry that we grew up with here, and it is hard to ignore no matter what corner of the world we hear it from.'[13]

On closer inspection, though, the Falklands and the six counties could scarcely be more different. While the islands may have been 14,000km from the UK, they were also 1,500km from Argentina. The island was discovered by either the British or Portuguese in the early 1500s, before being settled first by the French, then the British and then the Spanish. All had abandoned the island by 1828, the same year a small Argentinian settlement was established there. It was destroyed by the US Navy shortly afterwards following accusations of piracy. It was then that the British settlement, which remains on the island to this day, was established. At the time of the invasion, none of the 1,500 inhabitants was Argentinian nor had any wish to be.

The British reaction to Ireland's position during the conflict was as bad as the embassy in London had predicted. 'As we stand at the brink of a shooting war, the Irish stab us in the back,' read one editorial in the *Sun* newspaper, one of many similar articles collected in Irish Department of Foreign Affairs files.'[14] One Irish diplomat told Dublin that the embassy 'had received more letters on the government's stand on the Falklands than we had on any other single issue for a long time'.[15] These included many people who said they were going to cut business links with Ireland or cancel their holidays there. The Irish Exporters Association (IEA) told Haughey that the trade 'backlash' in the UK because of Ireland's policy was 'the most severe since at least 1969'.[16] Even Guinness considered cutting ties with Ireland: Edward Guinness told the Irish embassy that it might be forced to start emphasising the fact that Guinness was a British company headquartered in London, given the backlash from the British public. It even prepared promotional material to this effect.[17]

Dorr once called the matter, 'the greatest single controversy in Anglo-Irish relations for a generation'.[18] At first glance, this seems like hyperbole, but archival documents released years later show just how badly the British took Haughey's decision. The senior British diplomat David Goodall later wrote:

> the anti-British stance adopted by the Haughey government during the Falklands crisis had come not just as an affront, but as a stab in the back at a time when she was under great personal strain and needing the support of all her European allies.[19]

He noted that even Thatcher's perennial rival, President of France François Mitterrand, had stood by the British. The French provided London with details of the missiles it had previously sold Argentina and had lobbied Ireland to change its stance. Thatcher herself was so furious she asked if it would be possible to withdraw voting rights from

Irish citizens living in Britain and to introduce a trade boycott of Irish goods. Thankfully for Ireland, both proposals never got off the ground.

So why did Haughey decide so suddenly to withdraw from sanctions? Was it a genuinely held commitment to the 'traditional policy of neutrality'? 'Neutrality implies standing off completely. But if you engage in very assertive calls for sanctions on one of the belligerents, then it's very hard to square that with the older concept of neutrality,' Dorr said.[20] There is some international precedent for this. Following Italy's invasion of Ethiopia in 1935, Switzerland, despite being a League of Nations member, refused to join in League sanctions against the aggressors. Ireland on the other hand was an enthusiastic supporter of those sanctions. The Swiss also refused on principle to sign up to sanctions against the white supremacist regime of Southern Rhodesia, although it did implement its own trade restrictions with the country.

But Ireland is not Switzerland. For one thing, unlike Switzerland, it was a member of the UN at the time of the Falklands War and thus a supporter of the idea of collective security. From a moral point of view, it could be said that in refusing to support sanctions, it was giving tacit support to Galtieri's brutal regime, which at the time was involved in a campaign of terror against its own people. Furthermore, Haughey's own Department of Foreign Affairs had said sanctions had nothing to do with neutrality. 'If anyone else was in power they never would have stopped supporting the sanctions' said Haughey biographer Stephen Kelly. 'You have to remember, everyone in the Department of Foreign Affairs ... were adamantly in support of sanctions.'[21]

It is interesting to compare Haughey's approach in 1982 to that of the Irish government in the spring of 2022 when it gave full-throated support to sanctions against Russia following its full-scale invasion of Ukraine. From the start, Ireland was not just a supporter of EU sanctions, it was one of the leading voices in lobbying for even harsher economic measures against Russia. This was the case even as Ukrainians fiercely battled the invaders using Western military aid, including aid from Ireland. In the eyes of this Irish government, sanctions were very much compatible with military measures. This is not a new position. In 2001, Ireland, while again on the Security Council, also supported sanctions against Afghanistan following the September 11 attacks and continued to support them in the run-up to the US-led invasion in December.

It's difficult then to accept that Haughey was simply upholding a grand tradition of neutrality. More plausible explanations for his actions can be found elsewhere, most of them relating to Anglo-Irish relations. 'There were multiple motives,' Dorr said. Things had gone 'fairly sour' between Haughey and Thatcher in the run-up to the conflict, he recalled.[22] This was due in part to the taoiseach's belief that Thatcher's hard-line policy towards the IRA was increasing support for Sinn Féin at the expense of Fianna Fáil. There was also a need to shore up support from Fianna Fáil's republican wing, led by Éamon de Valera's granddaughter Síle de Valera, who had been loudly proclaiming that the sanctions breached Irish neutrality. This was certainly the British interpretation. Declassified documents show British officials attributed Haughey's actions to the 'Anglophobia of the green fringe of Irish politics' and believed he used neutrality 'as a cloak to an anti-British attitude, [which] might be useful in domestic political terms.'[23]

Personal animosity may also have played a role in Haughey's decision-making. Thatcher had humiliated the taoiseach by not allowing him to play an honest broker role in the hunger strikes and by publicly rubbishing his interpretation of progress in Anglo-Irish negotiations over the future of Northern Ireland. If Haughey had intended to send a message that he wouldn't be messed around on Northern Ireland, it backfired. After the Falklands, Downing Street instructed its Northern Ireland Office to 'go slow' on any progress in intergovernmental negotiations 'and to avoid doing anything that looks remotely like a favour to the Irish'.[24]

Ever the diplomat, Dorr has always shied away from criticising Haughey's approach, even well into retirement. The furthest he will go is to say his actions were 'maladroit, to put it mildly'. But at the time, the New York team were duty-bound to implement it. 'We were stuck with this. It was an instruction from the government.'[25]

Whatever Haughey's motivations at the time, it seems safe to assume a commitment to neutrality was not high on the list. However, Ireland's poorly defined version of the concept allowed him to weaponise it to pursue his aims. The only result was to needlessly damage Ireland's standing in Europe and set back the delicate relationships it had built at great expense with its closest neighbour at a critical time for the country.

CHAPTER ELEVEN

THE 'DREADED N-WORD'

*I see no valid argument in terms of national interest as to
why we should ... become more neutral than the neutrals
themselves ...*
Bertie Ahern (1999)[1]

ieutenant Colonel Ray Lane was enjoying a pint in a pub in
Dundalk in 2007 when he got the call from a senior Army officer
telling him he was going to Afghanistan. The British Army, which
made up a large part of the International Security Assistance
Force (ISAF) in Afghanistan, was pulling its bomb disposal team out
of Kabul to support its beleaguered forces in Kandahar. A replacement was needed and the British recommended to ISAF leadership
that the Irish Defence Forces, and Lane specifically, be considered for
the job. The Dublin man, who was already internationally regarded
as an expert in improvised explosives, was initially reluctant to take
the assignment but was swayed by the fact that ISAF was under the
command of NATO, not the UN (although it did have a UN mandate).
'As an officer coming up through the Defence Forces, I was always very
anxious to get involved with NATO. I was sick of the United Nations.
I wasted years of my life in the UN,' the now-retired officer said. It's a
common sentiment among Irish soldiers who have served abroad that
peacekeeping missions under EU or NATO banners are better run,

better equipped and more impactful than UN-run missions.

Lane decided to take up the role and four days after he'd got the call he landed in Kabul to take over as Chief Operations Officer of ISAF's Counter-IED (improvised explosive device) programme. At the time, the coalition forces were losing 20–25 people a week to IEDs. Lane's goal was to reduce this number, by implementing the skills he had learned during the Troubles in Ireland. Instead of constantly reacting to events, Lane and his team started forensically analysing Taliban bombs to determine where they were being made and how they could be mitigated. He spearheaded three operations to educate military personnel on IEDs and made sure the IED issue was factored into military decision-making at the highest level. The exercises were called Saoirse Nua, which, as Lane put it, 'really annoyed the Brits'. He was also involved in the more aggressive side of the response; helping to track down and kill Taliban bombers. This included assisting US forces in directing airstrikes against targets responsible for IED attacks.[2]

Lane has some hair-raising stories from his time with ISAF. These do not sit easily alongside the image typically presented to the public of the blue-helmeted Irish peacekeeper who builds orphanages and plays football with the local children. But Irish forces have been operating under NATO commands since 1997 and undergoing military assessments by the organisation for almost as long. In the view of most military officials, these experiences have been nothing but positive. NATO ensures the Defence Forces adhere to a strict array of standards under the Operational Capability Concept (OCC) – a subprogramme of the NATO Partnership for Peace (PfP) programme which Ireland signed up to in 1999 – and regularly conducts evaluations of the Defence Forces' artillery, naval, armoured and special forces capabilities.

One of the people responsible for making sure the Irish military meets NATO's high standards is Commandant Daire Roache, a staff officer with the Defence Forces training directorate. As part of his role, Roache also evaluates other PfP members, including Ukraine, where he conducted an evaluation shortly before Russia's full-scale invasion of the country in February 2022.

For Roache, participation in the OCC has benefited the Defence Forces 'massively'.[3] He gave one example:

> After going through the first OCC evaluation, the 1st Armoured Cavalry Squadron were hands down the most tactically proficient unit in the Defence Forces. It reinforces the things we think we're good at and reminds us of the things we need to work on.[4]

A more public example of the benefits of the OCC is the impact it has had on Ukraine's military. When Ukraine entered the OCC programme, following Russia's initial invasion of its western territory in 2014, the Ukrainian military had been in disarray, yet the strides it has made in its command and control abilities can be seen in how it responded to the Russian invasion in 2022. 'Now I've been very, very fortunate to watch them develop to a point when I have been genuinely impressed,' said Roache. 'The OCC process, and the exposure to NATO standards, is one of two reasons the Ukrainians are currently sticking it to a military many multiples of their own size,' said Roache. 'The other reason is the incredibly sophisticated weaponry delivered by the West.'[5]

Ireland is also moving towards greater cooperation with NATO in more subtle areas. It is already a member of the NATO Co-operative Cyber Defence Centre of Excellence in Tallinn, Estonia where a Defence Forces officer is permanently seconded; and it is currently in the process of joining the Helsinki-based European Centre of Excellence for Countering Hybrid Threats (Hybrid CoE), which is run by NATO and the EU. Ireland pays over €100,000 a year for access to NATO's battlefield intelligence system and regularly sends troops to NATO training centres around Europe. This is in addition to bilateral training arrangements with other NATO countries such as the UK and US. The scope of cooperation is expanding gradually in ways that typically receive little publicity. For example, Ireland recently signed up to NATO's Malware Information Sharing Platform, which allows for the sharing of details of cyberattacks in real time between member states. As David Brück, director of the international security policy unit in the Department of

Foreign Affairs, told a conference in 2022: 'I think one of the things that we certainly are very open to looking at is if our partnership with NATO can be used to look at other things, including capacity building around cyber and hybrid threats in the future.'[6]

Given the breadth of this cooperation, the suspicion among pro-neutrality campaigners that Ireland is on an inexorable path to full NATO membership is understandable. Peace campaigners and politicians on both the left and right argue recent governments have been eager to sign Ireland up to the alliance. How this aligns with the same government's unwillingness to adequately fund the Defence Forces is as yet unclear, but the argument continues to find favour with a large segment of the public that views any association with NATO as suspect. In reality, this distrust of NATO is shared by both the large and small mainstream parties and, to a lesser extent, the civil service. Former and current defence and foreign affairs officials have ample anecdotes demonstrating this suspicion but perhaps none are as illustrative as the time the US embassy organised a NATO symposium in the Grand Hotel in Malahide in 1996. The event was held in Ireland for geographic convenience. But NATO leaders were also trying to coax Ireland into the PfP programme, and so the main Irish political parties were invited to send observers to the event. Most responded they would be happy to attend, and places were set for the politicians around the lunch table. But on the eve of the conference, an *Irish Times* article appeared describing who would be in attendance. According to one Irish official, 'None of the Irish politicians ended up showing up.'[7] (In fact, one party did: the Progressive Democrats, who, unlike every other party, were vocal supporters of NATO cooperation.)

The long, arduous road towards Ireland's eventual membership of PfP during the 1990s demonstrates the reluctance of Irish politicians to give any ammunition to those who might accuse them of eroding 'Ireland's traditional policy of neutrality'. PfP was established in 1994 as a direct response to the end of the Cold War and the break-up of the Soviet Union. After regaining their independence, a number of Eastern European countries had become members of the North Atlantic Cooperation Council, a forum for liaising with NATO members. But these countries wanted full membership, something America was reluctant to allow in the short term given the sensitive geopolitical situation. So PfP was devised as a halfway house. It put in place a structure for cooperation between NATO and former Warsaw Pact countries and prepared those countries' militaries for eventual membership. PfP members cooperate with NATO in a range of areas including peacekeeping, search and rescue and humanitarian responses. Partner nations also commit to sharing information on outside threats and improving the ability of their militaries to work alongside alliance members. Crucially, membership places no military obligations on partner countries, including in the area of collective defence, and all parts of it are optional. Each partner country's interpretation of PfP is unique; some sign up just for peacekeeping cooperation while others try to cooperate with the alliance in every way possible. One NATO spokesman, speaking to the *Irish Times* in 1996, helpfully compared it to a Chinese takeaway menu: 'there are dozens of choices and you need only take the bits you want.'[8]

Most partner countries view membership as uncontroversial. Even Russia agreed to join up on its formation in 1994. It saw PfP as a way of improving the security situation in Europe while limiting the spread of NATO. Neutral Finland and Sweden signed up at the same time in 1994 and were joined two years later by Switzerland, a country that would not become a member of the UN until 2002 due to concerns about the impact on its neutrality. But the situation was different in Ireland, where PfP membership was framed as the first step towards joining NATO and the abandonment of neutrality. Its most vocal opponents were left-wing parties, but Fianna Fáil was also opposed to the move for much of the 1990s. PfP's amorphous nature allowed its Irish critics to claim it was whatever they wanted it to be. With an apparently straight face, Sinn Féin's newspaper *An Phoblacht* called PfP 'a standing army dominated by the United States'.[9] Among some left-wing and republican figures, any Irish move to join would only justify their suspicions that the Department of Foreign Affairs was scheming behind the scenes to force Ireland into NATO.

These conspiracy theories were nothing new – in 1983, the Irish National Liberation Army blew up a radar station on Mount Gabriel

in west Cork because they believed it was a NATO facility – and sometimes they were shared by people who should have known better. In 1981,
former Minister for External Affairs Seán MacBride, who was once willing to sign Ireland up to NATO if not for partition, claimed civil servants
were misleading their political bosses with the aim of getting Ireland to
join a common defence alliance.[10] At the same time, similar conspiracy
theories were being spread on the other side of the Irish Sea by Ulster
Unionist politician Enoch Powell who claimed, without evidence, that
the British foreign office planned to reunite Ireland under Dublin control
in order to persuade the Irish to join NATO. Opponents of PfP could
also reasonably point to comments from the likes of US President Bill
Clinton, who said in 1994 that the partnership was a 'track that will lead
to NATO membership'.[11] Even the official invitation to join PfP made a
similar point, stating: 'active participation in the Partnership for Peace
will play an important role in the evolutionary process of the expansion
of NATO'.[12] However, despite these ill-judged comments, it was clear at
the time that many new PfP members had no intention of eventually
joining NATO, certainly not Switzerland or Austria.

By 1996, Ireland, Tajikistan and Malta were the only members of the
Organization for Security and Co-operation in Europe (OSCE) – the
broadest of broad churches – that remained outside PfP (Malta joined
in 1995, left in 1996 and rejoined in 2008). Pressure was building, including, perhaps surprisingly, from the public. In October 1996, the *Irish
Times* published a poll showing 77 per cent of people were in favour
of PfP participation. This did not mean there was a swing in opinion
towards joining NATO – 69 per cent of those polled said Ireland's policy
of neutrality should be maintained – but the majority of people realised NATO membership and PfP membership were two vastly different
things. Pressure was also coming from another sector, albeit one that
was easier to ignore. The Defence Forces General Staff was concerned
that without PfP, Ireland would fall behind in military developments, to
the extent it would no longer be capable of contributing to peacekeeping missions. Post-Cold War NATO was increasingly being used as a
subcontractor by the UN for peacekeeping missions. Once given a UN

mandate, NATO missions could be put together far more quickly than a UN contingent and were generally better trained and equipped. Crucially for the UN, countries taking part in NATO-led missions paid their own way, unlike in UN missions where countries' costs were mostly covered by UN Headquarters. The view among Irish generals was that if Ireland wanted to maintain its position as a preferred provider of peacekeepers, it needed to join PfP.

The Fine Gael–Labour coalition under Taoiseach John Bruton tentatively signalled support for PfP membership in a white paper on foreign policy, released in March 1996, which promised to 'explore the matter further'. This non-committal statement received a strong reaction in the Dáil, most notably from Fianna Fáil's Ray Burke, who accused the government of 'tinkering with neutrality'.[13] Other neutral countries had indeed joined PfP, he conceded, but their geopolitical positions were entirely different to Ireland's; in other words, they were much closer to Russia. Nevertheless, foreign affairs officials continued to push behind the scenes for PfP and were hopeful of getting the government to make a decision before the Dáil broke ahead of the June 1997 general election. But they were disappointed. While Fine Gael was willing to sign up, opposition from its Labour coalition partner meant the decision would be left to the next government.

Cabinet did take one important step, however. It agreed, for the first time, to commit troops to a UN-mandated but NATO-led mission. A military police company comprising 51 Defence Forces members deployed to the Stabilisation Force in Bosnia and Herzegovina (SFOR) in 1996 to help keep the peace following the Bosnian War, which had ended two years previously. The decision to take part in SFOR was not arrived at easily and the process demonstrated the government's continued nervousness about anything bearing the name NATO. Before any decision was taken, army officers and Department of Foreign Affairs staff were flown by NATO to the mission area to determine what contribution, if any, Ireland could make. They were told the mission had enough combat troops but needed police units. They also needed cooks as the US soldiers were unhappy with the food being cooked by the Turkish chefs. SFOR was the perfect tasking for a small army with no NATO experience. A lightly armed Irish contingent would keep order in the mission area but would not be involved in combat operations. They even agreed to bring a few cooks in return for the US agreeing to provide fuel for Irish vehicles.

But the mission, including the financial costs involved, still had to be approved by the Dáil, a potentially tricky proposition in the shadow of a general election. 'You wouldn't believe the shenanigans that went on', recalled one official involved in the preparations.[14] A document was drawn up for presentation to the Dáil outlining the financial agreement between the government and the secretary-general of NATO. One official in the Department of Defence asked if the cover page of the agreement could say the 'secretary-general of the UN' instead of NATO. A Department of Foreign Affairs official rebuffed them, saying it had nothing to do with the United Nations and to say that it did could open them to allegations of misleading the Dáil. In the end, a compromise was worked out where the cover page mentioned a 'secretary-general' without saying what exactly they were secretary-general of. The hope was that some TDs would fail to read the document fully and assume it was a UN mission. This odd omission was noticed only by Progressive Democrat leader Des O'Malley, who commented TDs 'were almost not allowed to use the dreaded N-word' (the N-word, in this case, being NATO).[15] Foreign Affairs officials breathed a sigh of relief when the Dáil approved the mission later that day.

The Defence Forces' participation in SFOR further highlighted its need for structured cooperation, and training with modern militaries and the question of PfP membership fell to the new Fianna Fáil–Progressive Democrats government led by Taoiseach Bertie Ahern, which took up office in June 1997. Although by then Ahern and many of his colleagues viewed PfP membership as relatively uncontroversial, the government was stymied from the start by a passage in its election manifesto, inserted by Ray Burke, opposing PfP and promising a referendum before any decision to become a member. The uniqueness of Ireland's absence from the programme was driven home when Ahern started to visit other EU leaders. Across the continent, officials expressed their confusion about

Ireland's reluctance to join. On the journey home on the government jet from an official visit to the Austrian chancellor in 1998, Ahern requested a briefing on PfP. Having been informed of the benefits and potential political risks, the taoiseach made a tentative decision to join.

Advice was obtained from Attorney General David Byrne that a referendum was not required and the Dáil approved a motion to apply for membership in January 1999 with the final decision announced that May. The conversion of Fianna Fáil was complete, with Ahern stating he saw no reason why Ireland should 'become more neutral than the neutrals themselves.'[16] At the same time, an explanatory guide was published for the public which emphasised that PfP would not involve any collective defence commitments; that other neutral states had joined; and that it would greatly benefit the Defence Forces. It spoke of Ireland's 'Atlantic heritage' and deep ties with the US and Canada and even cited President John F. Kennedy's view that Ireland was 'a maker and shaper of world peace'.[17]

It also took the highly unusual step of including the legal advice of Attorney General Byrne, detailing his view that a referendum was unnecessary. Polling suggests the public would have been in favour of PfP if a referendum was held. However, officials wondered whether a referendum could be held on something that was clearly not a constitutional issue. Curiously, the booklet also stated that a referendum would be required on any future decision to become a full NATO member. Twenty-three years later, in June 2022, when NATO membership was again a hot topic in the wake of Russia's invasion of Ukraine, Taoiseach Micheál Martin contradicted this view. He said he believed a referendum would not be required as it would be a policy decision of the government. Martin backtracked somewhat a short time later, and said that, while it was not legally necessary, 'in reality one would have to consult the people'.[18]

On 1 December 1999, Ireland officially became the 28th country to sign up to PfP when Minister for Foreign Affairs David Andrews signed the accession documents at NATO headquarters in Brussels. NATO officials expected the Dublin government to invite NATO Secretary-General Lord Robertson on an official visit to Ireland in return, as was tradition for new PfP members. But no invitation was forthcoming. The government had no desire to give more ammunition to NATO's opponents. Officials were also surprised when, instead of appointing an ambassador to NATO like every other PfP country, Ireland appointed a 'liaison'. The government 'simply couldn't swallow the idea of having an ambassador to NATO,' said one Irish official. 'It was absurd.'[19]

The Defence Forces have benefited hugely from PfP. Some long-serving officers credit the programme as being vital to the modernisation of the Army and its ability to serve in complex missions alongside advanced militaries under both NATO and EU banners. After the SFOR mission was wound down, Ireland contributed troops to its successor, the European Union Force in Bosnia and Herzegovina (EUFOR), which was led by the EU, and to the Kosovo Force (KFOR), which was a more challenging mission that continues today under NATO leadership. Just under 200 Defence Forces troops served with ISAF in Afghanistan between 2001 and 2014 in a wide variety of roles. One of those was Vice Admiral Mark Mellett, who was involved in security for the country's first democratic elections and who went on to become the Defence Forces' chief of staff before retiring in 2021. For him, one of the main benefits of PfP is the focus on improving interoperability with friendly nations. 'There is no point in us marching to a different tune,' said Mellett. If, for example, Ireland contributes troops to a training or peacekeeping mission relating to the war in Ukraine, the Defence Forces will be required to work closely with militaries from many other countries. This is not something which can be done on the fly. As Mellett put it, 'When that happens your troops are at risk and the people you are there to protect are in jeopardy.'

Mellett echoed Roache's opinion that the external evaluation provided by PfP subprogrammes, such as the OCC, is also vital: 'It's very hard when you're a small military to judge yourself on how good or bad you are doing.' To illustrate the importance of outside review, Mellett described an internal Defence Forces evaluation exercise, where Naval Service ships were tasked with intercepting an enemy threatening Irish sovereignty. The task failed so comprehensively that the naval commander in question wondered if the exercise had been sabotaged. As

Mellett put it: 'In my view failures give you the best learnings in terms of progress. But it's very hard to overcome that groupthink when it's your own side that's the adjudicator of capability.'[20]

Another key PfP programme for the Defence Forces has been the Planning and Review Process (PARP) in which the Department of Defence signed up to various military goals set by NATO, ranging from simple to complex. A relatively simple (and as yet uncompleted) goal may be outfitting every soldier with a first-aid kit and training them in its use. A complex goal might be upgrading the ability of the Defence Forces to protect itself against chemical, biological, radiological and nuclear attacks, or upgrading its cyber defence capabilities. According to the Department of Defence, since 1999 Ireland has completed 25 PARP goals out of 40. 'That's not a bad figure,' observes Commandant Roache.[21]

Over 20 years of experience has shown, in Ireland's case at least, that the PfP is not a waiting room for NATO. In truth, despite the benefits extolled by officers such as Mellett and Roache, many defence experts believe successive Irish governments have failed to take full advantage of the programme, due to fears it would create an impression they are interested in NATO membership. One retired Department of Foreign Affairs official has pointed to the Irish practice of usually only sending civil servants, and not ministers, to the Euro-Atlantic Partnership Council (EAPC), which oversees relations between NATO members and PfP countries.[22] The Defence Forces could also do a lot more to cooperate with others in the maritime sphere, an area particularly important to Ireland given the huge portion of the Atlantic Ocean that falls under its responsibility.

Even if Ireland was on the path to NATO membership, the question must be asked, does NATO want Ireland? The answer to this seems to be an unambiguous yes. Despite being seen as even less strategically important to the alliance today than it was in the late 1940s, Secretary-General Jens Stoltenberg believes that Ireland would be welcome in the alliance, diplomatically adding that 'it's always something they will do by their own free will.'[23] Any decision would also first have to be ratified by NATO's 32 other members. 'And again,' said Stoltenberg, 'it's a sovereign Irish decision. NATO will never put any pressure on any country to join the alliance.' On PfP, Stoltenberg said that the programme remains valuable but that NATO will always look for ways to strengthen its partnerships, 'including the partnership we have with Ireland'.[24] The secretary-general was likely referring to a desire by NATO officials to see Ireland move from OCC Level 1 to the next stage of cooperation, OCC Level 2. As Roache put it, 'Level 1 is about one thing and one thing only: interoperability. Level 2 is about operational capability.' But, at this stage, the Defence Forces and Department of Defence have 'no particular ambition' to move to Level 2.[25]

If Ireland wanted to join NATO, it would, at an absolute minimum, have to undergo a radical programme of investment and restructuring that is likely much more ambitious than the investment programme announced by Minister for Defence Simon Coveney in 2022. Signing up to OCC Level 2 would be only the start. For example, one of the many failings identified by the Commission on the Defence Forces – which began work in January 2021 at the behest of Minister for Defence Simon Coveney and issued its damning final report in February 2022 – was that Defence Forces battalions 'do not align to NATO standards, are understaffed and under-resourced. In these circumstances, the Commission believes that there is an urgent need to restructure the Army into a more agile and flexible force structure that can meet current and future operational taskings.'[26] NATO requires countries to spend 2 per cent of GDP on defence. In 2021, Ireland spent 0.2 per cent, the lowest in Europe. Even if the recently announced investment programme is delivered by the promised date of 2028, defence spending will still be just a fraction of NATO requirements.

Irish public opinion also remains strongly opposed to NATO membership. Russia's invasion of Ukraine, which saw support for membership of the alliance skyrocket in Finland and Sweden, did little to change this. A *Sunday Independent* poll taken in March 2022 showed 37 per cent of Irish people favouring NATO membership, up just three points since before the invasion.[27] A Behaviour & Attitudes poll published the following month showed just 29 per cent in support.[28] One notable exception was a study by Behaviourwise – 'a behavioural science and insight consultancy' – that was conducted over the summer of 2022. It found people were more likely to prefer NATO membership after being read a short paragraph highlighting potential military threats, the poor state of Ireland's Defence Forces and moves by other Western countries to improve their security. Fifty-six per cent of people who were read this passage, afterwards said Ireland should join NATO compared to 49 per cent of people who didn't hear it.[29] The results suggest that Irish opinions towards NATO may not be as immutable as they once appeared.

However, it takes more than one poll to change policy and, despite the claims of opposition politicians and peace campaigners, there remains little political appetite for joining NATO. Recent polling suggests that if Ireland has to join a military alliance, the public would much prefer it to be under an EU banner than a NATO one.

Even the military men who sing the praises of PfP participation are sceptical of full membership. 'Don't get me wrong, I enjoyed my time with NATO. I learned loads,' said Lane of his time with ISAF. 'But I did come home saying "we don't need to be part of this game".' For Mellett, a debate on joining NATO would be premature at a time when the focus needs to be on improving Irish security: 'I think it's too early for that,' he said. 'I think if we actually start raising that flag, we will find that it will be polarising.'

All this means that in most of the ways that matter, Ireland is not in the waiting room for NATO. It's barely in the car park.

CHAPTER TWELVE

JUST ANOTHER RICH WHITE WESTERN COUNTRY?

There was, of course, a smugness about the State's
abstention from the most titanic battle of the century.
Robert Fisk (1999)[1]

O n 23 May 1945, two weeks after VE Day, one of the subjects up
for discussion in the Dáil was whether Phoenix Park should be
planted with potatoes. The purpose was not to help with food
shortages in Ireland, severe though they were. It was to feed
the desperate people of Europe whose countries had been devastated by
six years of war. In response to suggestions from the floor, Minister for
Agriculture Dr James Ryan said that planting the park wouldn't work
as it was too late in the season and anyway, there wasn't enough space.
The possibility of using the Curragh was ruled out for similar reasons.
It wasn't that the government didn't take the problem seriously; it had
made the provision of aid to Europe a post-war priority and was urging
farmers to cultivate all available land for crops for the purpose. This
aid was badly needed. The newly formed United Nations Relief and
Rehabilitation Administration (UNRRA) predicted that 140 million
Europeans would soon not have enough food to allow them to work
or stave off disease.

Ireland was already active in providing aid to victims of the conflict well before the war ended. As early as 1942, it was offering to send food to Belgium and Greece. The next year, the government sent £200,000 in aid to alleviate famine in Europe and India. Many of these efforts were stymied by logistical issues, including difficulty in getting permission from Britain to transport aid by ship. But with the final defeat of Germany in sight, the floodgates opened. On 25 April 1945, two weeks before the end of the war in Europe, an Irish government committee decided to make £3 million available for European aid. A few days after VE Day, Taoiseach Éamon de Valera broadcast an appeal for Irish growers to increase food production:

> We have been spared what so many nations have had to undergo, and there lies upon us, accordingly, a duty, within our limited power, to assist in succouring those who have been less fortunate than we have been.[2]

Over the next few years, the aid to Germany continued to flow 'in astonishing amounts and with great speed', according to historian Cathy Molohan.[3] It came not just from the government but from the people who, despite dealing with rationing and widespread deprivation themselves, donated vast sums to aid efforts. Irish people gave nearly $2 million in food and clothing to Germany in the month of December 1947 alone. And assistance went far beyond donations. For example, Ireland contributed resources and medical personnel to establish a temporary hospital in France and, under the Operation Shamrock scheme, almost 500 German children were taken in by Irish families. One of the children later wrote, 'As we got off the boat ... the pier was lined with tables, covered with white sheets, and lots of Red Cross nurses standing behind serving out cocoa and bread with lots of butter on.'[4]

Crucially, Irish aid did not discriminate between the war's winners and losers. The victorious Allies were slow to devote resources to assist civilians in the occupied zone: the first American aid package didn't reach Germany until 14 months after its surrender and shipments didn't start in earnest until 1947 while UNRRA was initially only permitted to assist populations in liberated territories and was forbidden to assist civilians in Germany. But Irish aid was distributed across the occupied zones, including in the parts of Germany occupied by the Soviets. Donations coming from Irish Catholic organisations chiefly went to other Catholics, but government aid did not discriminate based on religion or any other factor. Irish officials even arranged for the provision of kosher food following a request from the chief rabbi of Palestine. All of this was crucial in filling the two-year gap between the end of the war and the US finally turning its attention to starvation in the occupied zones.

The undiscriminating nature of Irish post-war aid is arguably the moral high point of Irish neutrality. Official documents show that the government philosophy was 'needy people in all four zones benefit equally without consideration either of their political belief or religious faith'.[5] Inevitably, Irish willingness to help the starving citizens of both the war's winners and losers reignited wartime suspicions among the Allies that Ireland harboured pro-Axis sympathies. There were some very minor justifications for these suspicions in that one of the groups involved in trying to evacuate German children to Ireland, Save the German Children, had members with decidedly pro-German and anti-British attitudes (it also excluded Jewish children from its relief efforts). But the Irish government sidestepped the organisation and brought German children to Ireland through the Red Cross. The overwhelming majority of Irish aid was provided on the simple basis that civilians shouldn't have to face starvation because they were on the wrong side of the conflict.

It's remarkable how little this massive Irish aid effort is mentioned today. Indeed, there would likely be no discussion at all if it wasn't for the studies of a handful of historians like Molohan and Mervyn O'Driscoll, whose research is the source of much of the above information. Why were the Irish government and people so generous in helping the people of Europe, when they faced so much hardship at home and when they had no hand in the destruction of the continent? Was it perhaps guilt over their neutral stance in the war? That's probably going too far, but it is certain that part of the government's motivation was to mitigate Allied propaganda about Ireland's wartime neutrality. Irish officials ensured food shipments were branded with a shamrock and stated clearly that they were from Ireland. The provision of aid was vital in countering the impression that 'we were concerned only about ourselves and were enjoying higher standards of living than in any other part of Europe,' one official said.[6]

O'Driscoll suggests post-war aid might have been 'a therapeutic neutrality performative act that would differentiate Ireland from the belligerents and retrospectively legitimise its neutrality on humanitarian grounds'. The cultural memory of Ireland's famine might also have played a role. After all, 1945 was the 100-year anniversary of the beginning of the famine and, given the enormous shadow it continued to cast over the national psyche, Irish people were unsure how to commemorate it. According to O'Driscoll, 'Irish aid to war-torn Europe was a form of famine commemoration, and it appears that many saw it in this light.'[7]

Whatever the reason, Ireland's post-war relief effort formed the foundation of a new conception of Irish neutrality, that of 'positive neutrality' (or 'active neutrality', as it's often termed). This was a neutrality that was not isolationist. On the contrary, Ireland would use its neutrality to improve the state of the world through conflict resolution, disarmament, peacekeeping and development programmes and would be a friend to people everywhere, no matter their government or their ideology. O'Driscoll writes this 'emerging construct of positive neutrality' served as a reassurance to the Irish people that their stance in the war was a moral one and one worth pursuing in the future.[8]

In the 70 years since, the Irish policy of neutrality has come to be viewed (not always accurately) as one involving a proactive foreign policy that favours the underdog and resists bowing to the demands of the great powers. It's a definition that has maintained widespread support over the years. A 2001 study by the Economic and Social Research Institute found 40 per cent of people considered Irish neutrality to be an 'active' neutrality that 'embodies characteristics such as peace promotion, nonaggression, the primacy of the UN and the confinement of state military activity to UN peacekeeping'.[9] This definition is favoured by those across the political spectrum. Sinn Féin's 2020 manifesto pledged commitment to a policy of positive neutrality, including involvement in peacekeeping and sending Irish ships back to the Mediterranean to rescue migrants. The Green Party used similar language while sharing Sinn Féin antipathy towards militaristic international cooperation, such as the EU's Permanent Structured Cooperation (PESCO). Labour's manifesto was broadly the same, although it didn't mention PESCO or PfP at all. People Before Profit–Solidarity's 2020 manifesto didn't mention neutrality, positive or otherwise, at all but its statements since then suggest a commitment to such a definition.

The 2020 Programme for Government for the coalition of Fine Gael, Fianna Fáil and the Green Party, talks of 'active military neutrality and participative multilateralism through the UN and EU'.[10] Similar language is used throughout the 2015 White Paper on Defence and its 2019 update. Like definitions of neutrality, definitions of positive neutrality vary significantly depending on who you ask. Left-wing politicians might characterise it as standing up to the great powers and avoiding their influence, while those in the centre or on the right tend to emphasise the need to work alongside these powers and the institutions they dominate in order to get things done. But almost everyone agrees on the basic principle that Irish neutrality should be used for the general betterment of the world. In other words: neutrality should be a means to an end rather than an end in itself.

When people talk of a heyday of Irish positive neutrality, Frank Aiken is invariably one of the figures mentioned. Even among the left-wing neutrality activists, the name of this conservative, dyed-in-the-wool Fianna Fáil man is spoken with a sort of reverence in the context of his work in the United Nations between 1957 and 1961. This conveniently ignores that the delegation he led voted with the United States significantly more than even some NATO members. Nevertheless, his work on disarmament and peacebuilding during this period deserves all the praise it receives. 'For four years, they pressed neutrality as a virtue rather than a vice and, at the same time; transformed it from a policy of isolationism into a positive instrument of internationalism and peacebuilding,' wrote Trinity College international relations expert Bill McSweeney in 1986.[11] The capstone of this policy was undoubtedly Aiken's efforts on nuclear non-proliferation.

The idea of non-proliferation was a new one for the international community. Certainly, there had been previous attempts in places like Geneva and the Hague to ban or reduce the use of chemical agents or fragmenting ammunition as weapons of war. But never before had there been an attempt to convince countries to voluntarily desist from developing weapons that their neighbours were allowed to possess. On paper, the idea must have appeared almost ludicrous to some: why should some countries be allowed nuclear weapons and others not? It's hardly surprising then that the road to a non-proliferation treaty was a long and tortuous one. Aiken began the journey in 1958 when, shortly after his appointment for the second time as minister for external affairs, he submitted a draft resolution to the UN General Assembly calling for the creation of a committee to research and report back on the dangers posed by the spread of nuclear weapons. Even this modest step ran into immediate difficulties. The Americans were against it as they worried it would curtail their plans to place nuclear weapons in Europe, and some non-nuclear countries worried about creating a system where large countries would be legally allowed to have weapons in perpetuity while smaller countries had to give up all ambitions in the area. One of the few UN members to show any enthusiasm for Aiken's proposal was the Soviet Union, recalls veteran Irish diplomat Noel Dorr.[12] Around this time, Soviet leader Nikita Khrushchev made a separate proposal for the 'general and complete disarmament'[13] of all the world's militaries, a proposal rejected by the West as a Soviet PR exercise.

Aiken's proposals were far more limited and, thus, far more credible. By 1958, the nuclear club had grown to include the US, the Soviet Union and the UK, with France, Israel and China knocking at the door. The Irish intention was to stop the club from getting any bigger, and only once that was done, to consider how it may be abolished altogether. Aiken told the UN that nuclear-armed states 'should hold the keys of the stores' and assume responsibility for preventing the spread of weapons to other countries.[14] His initial suggestions for research into nuclear proliferation were rejected but he tried again in 1959. By this time the mood music had changed slightly, and he received support for a proposal for the consideration of an international agreement allowing for a system of 'inspection and control' to combat the spread of nuclear weapons.[15] This was the genesis of what would become the Treaty on the Non-Proliferation of Nuclear Weapons (NPT).

Ireland made further progress towards a treaty over the next two years through the introduction of resolutions with increasingly strong language. This culminated in the Irish resolution introduced in November 1961, which called for an international treaty banning the provision of nuclear technology or blueprints to nations without nuclear weapons, as well as preventing such countries from manufacturing or trying to acquire the weapons themselves. Dorr said that all of this took place against a backdrop of constant Irish lobbying, which even involved the writing of an article, under Aiken's name, for the *Bulletin of Atomic Scientists*; assumedly the only time an ex-IRA chief of staff has written for that august publication. But international treaties are a slow process, even when they're backed by unanimous votes, as Aiken's proposal was. It took another seven years for the NPT to be ready for signature. The final version had three pillars, one focused on the safe use of nuclear energy, one on non-proliferation, and one on eventual disarmament. By the time it was presented for signature simultaneously in London, Moscow and Washington in July 1968, Ireland's reputation as a strong voice in the UN for disarmament was secure. In recognition of Irish efforts, Aiken was invited to come to Moscow to be the first person to sign the NPT. The next day, Ireland also became the first country to formally ratify the agreement.

Today, 190 countries have ratified the NPT, more than any other arms control treaty in history. But, despite Irish efforts, the treaty can only be judged, at most, a qualified success. Since the NPT came into force in 1970, three new countries have joined the nuclear club: India, Pakistan and North Korea, while Israel is widely believed to also possess nuclear weapons. And, although the total number of nuclear weapons possessed by the US and Russia has declined significantly, each still possesses enough firepower to destroy the world several times over. Since the invasion of Ukraine in 2022, Russian officials have made several thinly veiled threats about using nuclear weapons. The deal brokered between Iran and the West to prevent Tehran from developing weapons remains in limbo after Donald Trump reneged on it in 2018, and North Korea is becoming increasingly brazen about testing ballistic missiles in the vicinity of Japan. The end goal envisioned by the Irish delegation of total nuclear disarmament seems further away than ever.

It could be worse, of course. It's impossible to say how many more nuclear-armed states may exist today were it not for the NPT – at the time it was signed some predicted there would be 30 nuclear powers within a few decades. This is why the NPT is still regarded as the crowning achievement of Irish foreign policy and a shining example of the benefits of positive neutrality. Neutral countries tend to focus their diplomatic capital on arms control, said Keatinge, as it makes their own position 'less precarious'. The fewer nukes that exist, the less of a chance there is that one will hit Ireland, accidentally or on purpose.[16] It's an area of diplomacy where Ireland's neutrality – in other words, its non-membership of NATO – was crucially important. One retired Department of Foreign Affairs official who has been closely involved with nuclear disarmament efforts over the years said that it would not have been credible for a NATO member who enjoyed the protection of America's 'nuclear umbrella' to take the lead on the NPT: 'They couldn't do it, but we could.'[17]

Another retired diplomat said that Ireland's realist approach to negotiations was of great benefit: 'They never said anything that would upset the Americans or the Russians too much. No one wanted proliferation and the Irish were able to build on that to win other concessions in the area of disarmament.'[18]

Just as neutrality allowed Ireland to donate aid to all areas of Europe after the war, it was also vital in giving Ireland the credibility to kickstart the flawed but enduring nuclear non-proliferation process. But does that link between neutrality and international altruism continue today? Is there any reason a country has to be neutral to be a good global citizen? In other words, is positive neutrality, in the words of one serving diplomat, 'a bit of a farce which lets us feel good about ourselves'?[19] First, there's the fact that the majority of Ireland's positive neutrality plays out within the confines of the UN, a body which, as noted previously, is arguably incompatible with neutrality. But, given that modern definitions of neutrality are generally accepted as compatible with UN membership, let's put that to one side and instead look at peacekeeping. This is perhaps the most visible and commonly cited example of Ireland's positive neutrality. Even the most vocal opponents of anything resembling Irish militarism typically carve out an exception for Defence Forces peacekeepers. But, in the view of many Irish diplomatic and military officials, there is no intrinsic connection between being neutral and being a good peacekeeper.

'It's a myth ... that somehow neutrality is linked to our role in UN peacekeeping,' said one former Irish diplomat, who was heavily involved with the work of the UN Security Council during Ireland's first term in 1981–2. 'There was never any link made between the two during my time.' In that diplomat's view, modern peacekeeping is the product of the minds of three UN diplomats, none of them Irish – Ralph Bunche from the US, Lester Pearson from Canada, and Brian Urquhart from the UK – and Ireland became involved in peacekeeping in the late 1950s because 'it wanted to be active in that space'. The diplomat also said that Ireland was viewed as a desirable supplier of peacekeepers because it had a small but professional army, was considered as having 'clean hands' when it came to colonialism and because it was a 'middle power' – in other words, a nation that was not a great power but still has a reasonable influence on the world stage – and that 'the neutrality thing was never mentioned'.[20] Indeed, the first modern, armed peacekeeping mission, the United Nations Emergency Force (which was deployed to the border of Egypt and Israel in 1956 after the Suez Crisis), was made up of troops from Brazil, Canada, Colombia, Denmark, Finland, India, Indonesia, Norway, Sweden and Yugoslavia. It's a list that contained only two neutral countries, neither of which was Ireland.

Brigadier General Ger Buckley currently serves as Ireland's military representative to the EU, but one of his many previous appointments was with the United Nations Interim Force In Lebanon (UNIFIL), Ireland's largest and longest-running peacekeeping commitment. When it comes to on-the-ground peacekeeping, Buckley said that neutrality doesn't hurt, 'but I think it is overstated'. His experience while in Lebanon was that the average Israeli or Lebanese person would shrug their shoulders if asked what they thought of Irish neutrality. The General said that, during his time in Lebanon, Irish troops were seen as

> no different to the Spanish, the Italians or the Slovenians [...] You'll notice I didn't mention the French there. They would probably be viewed differently because they have a colonial legacy in the area. To me, that is the big differentiator on the ground.[21]

Ireland's history as a colonised nation, and as one that did not colonise others, is a far greater factor in peacekeeping and international diplomacy than neutrality. 'You have to tell people we are neutral,' said Dan Mulhall, Ireland's former ambassador to the US. In contrast, everyone is familiar with Ireland's struggle to free itself from its colonial master: 'It's our story that gives us credibility in the developing world because we are seen as a non-imperial power,' said Mulhall. 'That's more important than the neutrality.' Of course, this ignores the fact that Irish functionaries and soldiers were often the vanguard of British colonialism, but, as the ambassador said, 'it's the perception that matters. We didn't have the same failings as our European neighbours.'[22]

The generosity of Ireland in international aid, particularly to Africa, is another oft-cited example of its positive neutrality. But there again, Ireland may not be as unique as it likes to think. The development aid budget of the Irish government – €967 million in 2021 – appears large, but it is only slightly above the average contribution by members of the Development Assistance Committee, a group of 24 wealthy countries that coordinates international aid efforts. According to the Organisation for Economic Co-operation and Development (OECD), Ireland committed 0.315 per cent of gross national income (GNI) to overseas development aid in 2021, making it the 17th most generous contributor. It's notable that the list of the top ten contributors contained just two neutral countries, Sweden and Switzerland. In that year, Sweden was the only neutral country to meet the UN's goal of committing 0.7 per cent of GNI to development aid. The Irish government has committed to reaching the 0.7 per cent goal by 2030 and, in 2022, committed a record €1.04 billion in aid. However, ministers concede this goal will be dependent on future economic growth. Like other countries, Ireland drastically cut its development aid budget during the last recession.

Eight of the nine largest beneficiaries of Irish aid are African countries, a reflection of the great need of developing countries on the continent and, perhaps, of a genuine felt connection between Ireland and poorer African nations. According to one former diplomat who worked in the area of development aid, this also has little to do with neutrality. If there is a connection between Ireland and Africa, it's down to the work of Irish missionaries there over many decades: 'The old joke about African revolutionary leaders is that they were educated by Irish and imprisoned by the British.'[23] As it did with European post-war aid, 'folk memory' of the famine may also account for the large amount of money sent to African countries facing starvation in recent decades. Neutrality, it seems, barely features. Certainly, to the citizens of African nations, neutrality has never been something specifically associated with Ireland. A 1979 poll of both the Organization of African Unity (OAU) and the Arab League found none of them identified Ireland as neutral. By comparison, one-third identified Austria as such.[24]

The history of the twentieth century has shown that a neutral country can play a positive role as an honest broker between belligerents, or as a mutually acceptable location for international dialogue. There's a reason why Switzerland was selected as the headquarters of the League of Nations and why today it hosts the headquarters of 23 international organisations (as well as 250 non-governmental organisations). Vienna in neutral Austria is not far behind: it hosts many UN agencies as well as the headquarters of the OSCE and the Organization of the Petroleum Exporting Countries (OPEC). Swiss diplomats have been at the heart of many sensitive international negotiations, from bringing the Iran hostage crisis to a conclusion in 1981 to attempting to secure a lasting peace in Mozambique in 2019. So, why hasn't Ireland been able to do similar? One reason is geography: a country at the northwest extremity of Europe is simply not a particularly convenient meeting place for diplomats. The other is wealth. For most of the twentieth century, Ireland did not have the infrastructure to host major international organisations or conventions. At the same time, its foreign diplomatic presence was too small and thinly spread to make much of an impression globally. And, unlike Switzerland, Ireland was seen as too firmly rooted in the Western camp to be a credible Cold War mediator.

Conversely, it was seen as too anti-Israeli, or at least too pro-Palestinian, to be considered as a mediator for the conflict in that region. 'We would never have even been in the running,' said one veteran diplomat. 'The Israelis would never have worn it.'[25] Instead, it was Oslo, in non-neutral Norway that was chosen to host secret talks between Israel and the Palestinian Liberation Organisation, which resulted in the Oslo Accords of 1993. The process illustrated that neutrality is not a prerequisite to be considered a peace broker, in the same way that it's not necessary to be a peacekeeper or a generous supplier of international aid.

The Irish government had hoped to use its experience in conflict resolution in Northern Ireland – which culminated in the 1998 Good Friday Agreement – to establish itself as a mediator on the world stage. In 2006, then Minister for Foreign Affairs Dermot Ahern said historically, the first phase of Irish foreign policy focused on securing sovereignty and international recognition, the second on peace and prosperity at home, and that the third will be based on 'active neutrality'.[26] To this end, his department established a Conflict Analysis and Resolution Unit to share the lessons learned during the Northern Ireland peace process. Since then, the unit has done some valuable work, including supporting peace efforts in the Balkans, Afghanistan and Moldova. But it has yet to see any of the headline-grabbing successes enjoyed by the Swiss or Norwegians. 'I don't think it made much headway around the world,' said one former department official. 'All conflict and post-conflict situations are different.'[27]

Even in the area of nuclear disarmament, which was once regarded as the best example of Ireland's positive foreign policy, neutrality seems to be less important than it once was. According to the late political scientist Richard Sinnott, after joining the EU, Ireland's approach to nuclear weapons became less strident and more incremental.[28] Despite being heavily involved in the process of renewing the NPT and in building support for a Comprehensive Test Ban Treaty (CTBT) on nuclear weapons, Irish contributions on the issue in the UN in the 1990s seem almost meek in comparison to those of Aiken and his colleagues in the 1950s. At times, statements from Irish representatives seemed specifically designed not to upset our nuclear-armed European neighbours. 'We realise that some of the nuclear weapons states continue to believe that a CTB would adversely affect their national security interests. We understand and respect such views,' said Minister for Foreign Affairs Gerry Collins during a UN debate in 1991.[29] Of course, there's nothing wrong with incrementalism, providing it works. It worked for the CTBT only to a point: the treaty was adopted by the General Assembly but has yet to enter into force as not enough nuclear powers have ratified it.

Irish diplomats continue to be highly active in the area of non-proliferation, but they do so in concert with many other countries, most of them non-neutrals. Ireland was one of the 'Core Group' of countries involved in initiating the Treaty on the Prohibition of Nuclear Weapons (TPNW), which was signed in 2017 and entered into force in 2021. The TPNW strengthens the commitments of the NPT and binds nuclear-armed states to a time-limited framework for permanent disarmament. No NATO states or existing nuclear states have signed the treaty but that does not mean it is a preserve of neutral countries. The other members of the Core Group include the decidedly non-neutral countries of Brazil, Mexico, Nigeria and South Africa. Aside from Ireland, the only other avowedly neutral member is Austria.

Positive neutrality is often also mentioned in the context of Ireland's work on non-nuclear disarmament, especially regarding cluster bombs. At its launch in September 2022, the Irish Neutrality League – which has been formed to counter what it says is a concerted attack on Irish neutrality by the government – said Ireland's role 'in negotiating the global ban on cluster munitions' was 'overwhelmingly linked to its neutrality and opposition to empire.'[30] Cluster bombs are a particularly nasty type of weapon. Fired from artillery pieces or dropped from aircraft, the canisters fragment into many smaller 'bomblets' which disperse across a wide area. They are excellent at two things: destroying large concentrations of infantry, and killing innocent people, particularly children, who later pick up the bomblets, which failed to detonate on impact (according to the UN, up to 40 per cent of the cluster bomblets dropped by Israel during the 2006 Lebanon War failed to explode initially).[31] Buoyed by the success of the 1997 Ottawa Convention limiting the use of landmines, diplomats from various countries saw cluster munitions as the next viable target for a weapons ban treaty. When efforts towards a ban hit a brick wall in the UN Conference on Disarmament, some of these countries, including Ireland, Norway, Australia, Austria and New Zealand, decided to pursue a treaty through other means.

The process started in Oslo, Norway in 2007. One year later, in May 2008, Ireland hosted a diplomatic conference on cluster munitions in Dublin Castle to negotiate a workable treaty. Over the course of ten days, representatives from 111 participating states, 21 observer states and 300 NGOs took part. Defence Forces ordnance experts, who had first-hand experience dealing with Israeli cluster munitions in Lebanon, were on hand to provide expert advice, and the Irish government paid the expenses of poorer countries so they could attend. 'Along with climate issues, arms control is one of the few areas where classical diplomacy, with big conferences and people getting in and out, still works,' said Rory Montgomery, the former second secretary-general at the Department of Foreign Affairs, who played a key role in the process. 'We had people basically camped in Dublin for a fortnight. That was planned.'[32]

Negotiations were not straightforward. Even countries in favour of a ban were worried that a treaty could prevent them from fighting alongside allies who still used cluster bombs. Others were concerned the definition of a cluster bomb was too broad. But Montgomery said that the NGOs in attendance were helpful in exerting some moral pressure on the holdouts, and the outcome was a comprehensive treaty, the Convention on Cluster Munitions (CCM), which banned the weapons. The CCM was powerful. Ben Tonra of UCD noted, 'It was only the seventh time that a weapon has been prohibited outright.'[33] Ratifying states could not use, produce, retain or transfer cluster munitions. There were no exceptions and no transition period. Since then, 110 countries have signed up. Unfortunately, and unsurprisingly, these do not include the US, Russia, China or Israel, the very states most likely to use cluster bombs.[34]

Nevertheless, the convention established an international norm against the use of these weapons, which, to Montgomery, was a significant achievement: 'We were never unrealistic about the extent of buy-in. But we thought that drawing up a set of standards would form a kind of benchmark of what was and wasn't acceptable.'[35] Another former diplomat involved in the process recalled that the skill, patience and 'force of personality' of some of the people in the Department of Foreign Affairs was crucial in getting the treaty across the line. But, for a small nation, that only goes so far. 'Small nations will always be pushed around to an extent by bigger powers,' the official said, and recalled an occasion where Ireland was pushing for India's agreement on a specific point, 'only to be told by America to back off, that India wouldn't have it.'[36]

Both diplomats agree Ireland made a valuable contribution to the cluster munitions ban. Both also believe neutrality played little to no role in this. 'I'd be sceptical, to be honest,' said Montgomery. 'Look at the Norwegians. They were extremely involved in this, to the extent that the final treaty was signed in Oslo in 2008. They're not neutral.' Neither were many of the other countries involved in the process. To Montgomery, neutrality does not necessarily make Ireland a better citizen of the world:

> There's a view that somehow being neutral gives us greater moral authority, that somehow what we say about matters like human rights should be taken more seriously ... my personal view for what it's worth is the arguments for positive neutrality are more or less bogus.

According to him, developing countries view Ireland not as virtuously neutral but as simply 'another rich white Western country' and that the moral authority of non-neutral countries like Denmark or Norway in areas of development or disarmament is in no way compromised by the fact they are NATO members.[37]

In the unlikely event Ireland does join NATO, there would be little to stop it from leading the way in disarmament, peacekeeping or international development. It would also not be precluded from challenging the foreign policies of the US. For as long as NATO has existed, its members have criticised US policy. In 1983, France offered minesweepers to Nicaragua to remove mines planted in its ports by the CIA. Spain had long been a critic of US policy in South America and voted to censure it in the UN after its 1989 invasion of Panama, a vote from which Ireland abstained. Both Spain and France refused to help in any way with the US bombing of Libya in 1986.[38] More recently, France and Germany coordinated in their efforts to oppose the 2003 invasion of Iraq. History shows NATO membership does not prevent a country from taking an anti-war stance.

Former Minister for Foreign Affairs Simon Coveney has said that non-membership of NATO can be valuable in international negotiations, 'without being pivotal' and that 'it allows us to speak to people in perhaps a more open way because we're seen as more neutral in the context of geopolitical tensions.' But Coveney also said that there is a tendency to overstate the importance of neutrality in Ireland's dealings on the world stage – 'Let's not exaggerate our own influence and importance there' – and that Finland and Sweden are no less likely to contribute towards disarmament and peacekeeping now they are joining NATO. Joining the Alliance was simply a means of protecting their citizens and sovereignty in the response to Russia's invasion of Ukraine. 'We shouldn't necessarily confuse being part of a defence pact or alliance with being less interested in peacekeeping,' said Coveney.[39]

Ireland's little-celebrated post-war European aid programme and the strenuous efforts towards nuclear non-proliferation in the 1950s and 1960s show that, at least at one point, there was a link between neutrality and a positive foreign policy. But it is not at all clear this link exists today. The fact that the two have become so interlinked in the public mind may be down to what historian Ronan Fanning called the 'emotional self-satisfaction, not to say smugness' of Irish neutrality.[40] Irish diplomats, military officers and even a recent minister for foreign affairs are remarkably consistent in the view that, despite some overlaps, being neutral and maintaining a foreign positive policy are two separate things. Just look at countries like Norway and its role as a peace broker, or Canada with its pioneering work in peacekeeping.

The Good Country Index – which uses many metrics to measure the altruism of a country, including UN activity and peacekeeper numbers – lists Morocco, as the greatest contributor to 'international peace and security'. You have to scroll down the list to number 22 to see Ireland's name.[41] Not a bad showing by any means, but behind many other non-neutral nations.

There's little to suggest Ireland is going to join NATO any time soon, but if it does, it would be no barrier to continuing or even scaling up its work in areas such as peacekeeping or disarmament.

CHAPTER THIRTEEN

NEUTRALITY ON TRIAL

We developed this rather contorted logic that the essence of
Irish neutrality was being able to make your own decisions.
And this was us making our own decisions ...
Rory Montgomery (2022)[1]

Edward Horgan, a former Defence Forces officer from County Kerry, isn't quite sure how many times he's been arrested at Shannon Airport, but he thinks it's about ten. This includes the time he was detained while trying to perform a citizen's arrest of US President George W. Bush. It was during a massive protest around Shannon Airport against Bush's visit to Ireland in June 2004, three years into the War on Terror. The visit was facilitated by perhaps the largest security operation in the history of the State to that point, involving 2,000 soldiers and 4,000 gardaí. Snipers and Scorpion tanks were stationed around the exclusion zone while Irish Naval Service vessels patrolled the coastline. This is what faced Horgan and three others as they approached the airport in his small boat to arrest the president. 'It was basically a protest type of arrest,' he said. 'We never expected to successfully arrest him.'

He was correct. After managing to get past a Garda boat patrol on the estuary, they were spotted by the Naval Service. An Air Corps helicopter appeared overhead, and two inflatable boats were launched from naval vessels to pursue and board them. Horgan and the others were arrested and taken to the shore before being brought before the courts that evening to face charges of breaching the exclusion zone. One year and several hearings later, the group were acquitted on all charges. 'It was intended to publicise the fact that George Bush wasn't welcome, and the visit of the US president was in breach of Irish neutrality. In that we did succeed.'

All of Horgan's arrests are related to his driving passion, protesting the US military's use of Shannon Airport. He is one of dozens of people arrested – Horgan estimated there have been at least 38 prosecutions – for protesting at the airport since the start of America's wars in the Middle East in 2001. It's a remarkably diverse group, which includes young peace activists, artists, members of the Dáil and, more recently, two US Army veterans in their 80s.[2]

The many criminal trials which followed created headaches for the Irish government, while the surprisingly high acquittal rate caused frustration for US diplomatic officials. Horgan has been prosecuted seven times for protesting at Shannon and has been convicted just once. Even on that occasion, in January 2023, the most serious charge against him was dropped and his punishment was a simple fine. The judge even took time to praise his 'upstanding character, composure and dignity'.[3] The message from the former Army Commandant and his fellow activists is simple: Ireland cannot call itself neutral, under any reasonable definition of the term, while permitting the US military to use Shannon to ferry troops to its military operations in the Middle East. Since 2001, around three million troops have transited through Shannon Airport on their way to or from overseas US military bases. Most of these have carried weapons of some sort, while some of the aircraft have been used in the illegal rendition of prisoners for the purpose of torture. The controversy surrounding the airport has, more than any issue since World War II, caused Irish society to question what it means to be neutral in a complex, interconnected world. It has also demonstrated that, in the eyes of Irish government leaders, Irish neutrality takes second place to economic interests.

It should be no surprise Shannon Airport has come to symbolise our strange version of neutrality: it has long been a player in the story of Ireland's relationship with its larger neighbours. During World War II, it was a desolate air base from which Irish Air Corps pilots flew sorties over the Atlantic to gather meteorological information that was then transmitted to the Allied forces. Later, when it became a civilian airport, Irish officials promised America it could have unimpeded use of Shannon should a third world war break out. Shannon was also used extensively by the Soviet airline Aeroflot, a source of considerable concern for the Americans during the Cold War. And as well as serving as a gateway between east and west, Shannon was the site of the world's first duty-free, Europe's first pre-clearance facility for the US, and an alternative landing site for the space shuttle.

Its association with the US military in particular dates back to well before the War on Terror. The US was first granted permission to use the airport in limited circumstances shortly after the end of World War II, and in 1958 it was granted blanket permission to overfly Ireland to save fuel as it transported troops and cargo to European bases (on the understanding that permission would lapse in the event of a 'serious deterioration in the international situation'). Permission had been granted by the departments of foreign affairs and transport, on the stated criteria that aircraft were not to be part of training manoeuvres nor en route to military exercises, and that their presence was in 'no way prejudicial to the security or safety of the State'.[4] Landings continued over the following decades, the numbers ebbing and flowing depending on the international situation.

Such permission was granted even when the US was at war, seemingly in direct contravention of the government's early stipulations and the 1907 Hague Convention which states neutral countries cannot allow belligerent troops to transit through their territory. Shannon was used as a stop-over during the first Gulf War in 1990 when a US-led alliance forced Iraq to end its invasion of Kuwait. There was some opposition to this practice, led by the Workers Party, on the grounds that, under the Constitution, Irish participation in war required Dáil approval. But the Fine Gael government maintained providing airport facilities did not amount to participation in the war. Minister for Foreign Affairs Gerry Collins also pointed out that neutral Austria was also providing refuelling facilities. In any event, the issue was not a major concern for the public, in part because the invasion had a UN mandate. One of the few opinion polls on the issue showed 54 per cent of the public was in favour of the US use of Shannon.[5] Not that a UN mandate was essential for American use of Shannon: the US continued to use the airport during the bombing of Kosovo by NATO forces in 1999, an operation that lacked UN support. Again, this passed by with minimal public controversy, at least compared with what was to follow.

The events of 11 September 2001 were met with an outpouring of grief and sympathy in Ireland. As well as announcing a national day of mourning, Minister for Foreign Affairs Brian Cowen, along with leaders from 39 other countries, quickly offered the US the use of Shannon to assist in the build-up of military forces for the invasion of Afghanistan. There was some muted criticism in the Dáil that its members had not been consulted ahead of the offer, but opinion polling shows the public mood was supportive. The government justified the offer on the basis of UN Security Council Resolution 1368, which had been passed the day after the attacks and which called on all countries to assist in bringing the organisers of the attacks to justice. Some peace campaigners, including the Peace and Neutrality Alliance (PANA), argued that the resolution did not justify the invasion of a sovereign country, Afghanistan, but they spoke for the minority.

By early 2003, as American forces were preparing to invade Iraq based on what turned out to be faulty intelligence – that Iraq possessed weapons of mass destruction – the public mood had shifted dramatically. PANA helped organise a march in Dublin on 15 February to protest both the looming war and the use of Shannon by the US military to prosecute it. Organiser and PANA Chairperson Roger Cole predicted that 25,000 people would turn up, a massive increase on previous anti-war marches, which typically attracted about 1,000 people. The Garda estimated there would be around 20,000 attendees. Both estimates were wildly off. Between 80,000 and 100,000 protesters took to the streets of Dublin that day. 'I didn't see it coming. It was a major, major event and a very good indication of the public view,' said Cole.[6] Meanwhile, an opinion published in the *Irish Times* the same day showed the number of people who approved of the US use of Shannon had dropped to 36 per cent.[7]

This created a major headache for the Irish government and officials in the Department of Foreign Affairs. Unlike with Afghanistan or the first Gulf War, it could not credibly be argued there was a UN resolution authorising an invasion of Iraq. The US and UK governments claimed Security Council Resolution 1441 – which had passed the previous year and threatened 'serious consequences' if Iraq did not comply with weapons inspections – provided a mandate for invasion. Most international law experts, as well as the UN secretary-general and other Western governments, argued this was not the case and that a further resolution was required to mandate military action. At the time of proposing Resolution 1441, the Bush and Blair administrations had stressed any further action would require another Security Council resolution. However, when it became clear France would veto any military action, they abandoned the diplomatic route and invaded without any further resolution. In the eyes of the Irish public, a UN resolution was crucial in justifying the war and Ireland's support for it. Just 21 per cent of Irish people approved of allowing the US to continue to use Shannon if it invaded Iraq without UN support. However, many people (49 per cent according to the opinion poll) believed the use of Shannon should be withdrawn even if a resolution was passed by the Security Council.[8]

Regardless, like Cowen did two years previously, Taoiseach Bertie Ahern announced there was unlikely to be any change to Irish policy, resolution or not. Speaking in Washington on 14 March 2003, after presenting the traditional St Patrick's Day bowl of shamrock to President Bush, Ahern said Ireland would not get involved in the war without a UN resolution, but suggested US use of Shannon would continue. Ireland would be alone in the free world if it withdrew landing rights from the US, the taoiseach claimed.[9] This was not quite true. While

NATO countries such as France and Germany, both trenchant opponents of an invasion of Iraq, continued to allow the US to use their airspace, several other European countries made it clear the Americans were not welcome. Neutral Austria specifically ruled out US landings or over-flights connected with the Iraq war in the absence of a UN mandate, a reversal of its position during the invasion of Afghanistan. Finland and Sweden, both also neutral, sent similar signals. Even Slovenia, which at the time was about to join NATO, requested the US not use its airspace in the event of war.

Back in Ireland, political opposition to the US use of Shannon continued to grow. The matter was the subject of a heated Dáil debate on 20 March, the day the invasion started. This time it was the turn of Fine Gael, then in opposition, to take up the role of defender of Irish neutrality. Party leader Enda Kenny argued that Ireland could not defend the primacy of the UN while allowing the US to use Shannon to prosecute a war of 'doubtful legitimacy'.[10] Even some government backbenchers expressed unease. Seán Haughey – son of Charles Haughey, who himself had an ambivalent attitude towards neutrality – took the view that the moral thing to do would be to withdraw landing facilities. However, he said he 'reluctantly' accepted this was not in the national interest.[11] The government won the day but not by much. Its motion to continue 'the long-standing arrangements for the overflight and landing of United States military aircraft' passed by 77 to 60.[12]

For Rory Montgomery, the issue of Shannon dominated his time as political director in the Department of Foreign Affairs. In March 2003 he was tasked with helping the government explain how Ireland could claim to be neutral while helping a foreign military force fight a legally questionable war with no UN mandate. 'We developed this rather con-torted logic that the essence of Irish neutrality was being able to make your own decisions,' said Montgomery. 'And this was us making our own decisions.'[13] This position was spelt out by Cowen in the Dáil as the matter was debated: 'The core of our neutrality ... lies in independence of judgement – in being able to make up our own minds about what is right for Ireland. That is the question facing all of us.'[14] It was a uniquely Irish definition of neutrality, untethered to international law or precedent. 'I always thought, to be honest, we had stretched the concept of neutrality to the limit,' said Montgomery.[15]

Diplomats involved with the decision at the time say the government's decision to continue US use of Shannon was based solely on practical interests, rather than any support for the war or kinship with the US. It was most concerned about endangering US investment in Ireland. Such was the perceived feeling in the US at the time that Irish officials believed withdrawing the use of Shannon would be seen by US government officials and investors as disloyalty. This became the primary defence of the government's decision over the following years and was supported by Garret FitzGerald, by then in retirement, who said that Republicans in the US would be emotionally influenced by any withdrawal of the use of Shannon[16]; and by US Ambassador to Ireland James Kenny, who warned after the start of the war that closing the airport to the US would not end the Iraq war but would end thousands of Irish jobs.[17]

There were also government fears for the future of Shannon and the surrounding regions. The use of the airport by the US military and its contractors made up a significant portion of its income. This would only grow as the war went on. By 2005, the stopovers were generating €37 million a year for the airport, and when the recession hit in 2009, the US military became vital to the airport's continued survival. Set against this, however, was the cost to the Irish taxpayer of providing security at the airport, against both terrorist threats and the anti-war protesters who became adept at disrupting airport operations. In the three-year period starting in 2006, just under €10 million was spent on security by the Irish government. Furthermore, Ireland waived tens of millions in air traffic control fees for US military aircraft.

After the start of the war, with little hope of achieving their aims in the political sphere, peace activists turned to the courts in the hope of halting the US use of Shannon. Horgan, the Army Commandant turned peace activist, lodged a case before the High Court that was heard over four days in early April 2003, while the US invasion was still ongoing, and as more and more troops were being moved through the airport. As neutrality is mentioned nowhere in the Constitution or Irish law, Horgan and his legal team had to take a subtle approach. First, they deployed Article 28.3 of the Constitution, which states: 'War shall not be declared and the State shall not participate in any war save with the assent of Dáil Éireann.' By allowing the US to land and overfly its territory, Ireland was participating in a war without the approval of the Dáil, Horgan argued. He also relied on the 1907 Hague Convention, which sets out the conditions for neutral countries and states they may not allow belligerent troops and arms to transit through their territory. Ireland was obliged by Article 29 of the Constitution to adhere to international law and to adhere 'to the principle of the pacific settlement of international disputes', Horgan submitted.

The State defended its position on several fronts, including by claiming Ireland has the right to operate a 'qualified neutrality', where it shows what de Valera once called a 'certain consideration' to one side or another in a war. This is what Ireland had done during World War II when it allowed Allied aircraft to refuel on its territory and granted passage to British vessels on their way to destroy German submarines. Furthermore, Article 29 was not prescriptive regarding Ireland's commitment to pacifism. Rather it was something to aspire to. Most importantly, it argued, Horgan had no standing to challenge the government on Article 29, as it did not impact his personal rights, and the court had extremely limited scope to intervene in government decisions when it came to international relations.

For the first time since independence, the meaning of Irish neutrality had come before the courts. If Horgan was successful, Irish governments would no longer be able to adapt neutrality to suit their needs but would be bound to the definition spelt out in the Hague Convention. And Shannon would immediately be out of bounds for US troops, at the very least pending a UN resolution. When they first read the final judgment of Mr Justice Nicolas Kearns, which was delivered on 28 April 2003, Horgan and his team must have assumed they had won. An international legal concept of neutrality does exist, Kearns ruled, even if it is not defined in Irish law. And neutral countries may not allow the transit of belligerent troops through their territory, even if they claim to only operate a 'qualified neutrality', he wrote.[18] But that's where the good news ended for the plaintiffs.

These questions of neutrality and international law were largely academic, as Kearns ruled the court could not intervene on alleged breaches of Article 28.3 and effectively reverse a decision of the Dáil, without proof of 'quite exceptional circumstances'. Regarding Article 29, which compelled Ireland to adhere to international law and the pacific resolution of international disputes, Kearns ruled it was also not a matter for the courts as the Article had no implications for Horgan's personal rights. In short, Horgan had won the moral argument – a High Court judge had ruled Ireland was in breach of neutrality according to international law – but he had lost the legal one, which, in this case, was the only one that mattered.

Stopovers in Shannon continued unabated. The next year, 159,000 US troops, armed and in uniform, travelled through the airport. That doubled to 341,000 the following year. Since 2001, around three million US troops have passed through the airport. There was one small consolation for Horgan: Kearns ruled that he was entitled to half his legal costs, amounting to some €50,000, as he had raised an issue of 'significant public importance'.[19]

The passage of UN Resolution 1483 in May 2003, and Resolution 1500 the following August, eased any lingering legal worries within the Irish government about the legality of the US use of Shannon. The resolutions recognised the UK and the US as occupying powers under international law and set up an assistance mission in Iraq. But the debate in Ireland over Shannon refused to go away. Every few months a new controversy raised its head, mostly regarding the passage of US weapons through the airport. Troops were permitted by the Irish government to carry their personnel weapons, but the transport of more substantial munitions was banned, in theory at least, unless a specific exemption was granted. Multiple breaches of these rules have come to light over the years. For example, in 2006 the government said it was 'dissatisfied' after learning US-made Apache attack helicopters had been transported through

Shannon.[20] In 2013, a transport aircraft armed with a 30mm cannon was spotted at the airport, something the US government later blamed on an administrative error.[21] Since the Irish government, as a matter of policy, does not carry out routine inspections of US aircraft, it's reasonable to assume there have been many more incidents that have gone undetected.

Then there's the role of Shannon in extraordinary rendition – the practice of transporting terrorist suspects to non-US territory, beyond the protections of US law, where they can be tortured and interrogated. In December 2005, then Minister for Foreign Affairs Dermot Ahern emphatically denied Irish airspace had been used by the US for such purposes, citing assurances he had received from US Secretary of State Condoleezza Rice. 'We will investigate any hard evidence that is brought to us, but to date, no such evidence has been brought to us concerning the use of Shannon in any shape or form,' Ahern told the Dáil.[22] Evidence would come the following year in the form of an Amnesty International report, which stated CIA aircraft known to be involved in extraordinary rendition had repeatedly used Shannon. This was backed up by a Council of Europe report two months later which said Ireland was one of 14 European states colluding in the practice. Multiple other reports followed from NGOs, such as the Open Society Foundation and the Rendition Project, saying the same thing.

In public, the government stuck by its position that no prisoners had been transported through the airport. It is correct to say no concrete evidence has emerged of prisoners passing through Ireland, but there is ample evidence that CIA flights travelling to and from rendition missions have refuelled at Shannon. Even if there were no prisoners on board, Shannon played a vital logistical role in what was plainly an extremely serious breach of domestic and international law, as well as basic morality. The founder of the Rendition Project, Dr Sam Raphael, compared Ireland's role to 'helping a bank robber on the way to a bank robbery'.[23] There is also no way of knowing for sure if prisoners passed through the airport because, as with the transport of weapons, Irish authorities did not carry out routine inspections. Instead, they relied on the assurances of US officials. 'I looked at the great President Bush and I said to him, you know, "I want to be sure to be sure," and he assured me,' Taoiseach Bertie Ahern said when asked about these assurances.[24] CIA pilots interviewed by rendition researchers have spoken about the lax conditions at Shannon. 'No one would check the manifest or look onboard the plane,' Steve Kostas, an investigator with the anti-torture NGO Reprieve, told the *Irish Times* in December 2014.[25]

In private, Irish officials were becoming increasingly anxious about these flights. The leaking of hundreds of thousands of US diplomatic cables by Wikileaks in 2010 gives a fascinating behind-the-scenes look. Dermot Ahern believed he had 'put his neck on the chopping block [and] would pay a severe price if it turned out that rendition flights had entered Ireland or if one was discovered in the future.' This was how US Ambassador Thomas Foley summarised the situation in a cable to Washington in December 2007 after meeting with the Irish minister for foreign affairs.[26] Ahern had fretted to the ambassador that Fine Gael and Labour would make hay out of the latest demand from the Irish Human Rights Commission, which called on Irish authorities to regularly inspect US aircraft. 'It was an endless debate which caused huge nervousness to Dermot Ahern and others,' said Montgomery.[27]

However, the Irish government repeatedly assured their US counterparts of their continued support. After a separate meeting in 2006, US officials noted with satisfaction that failures by the US government to notify Ireland of the transport of military equipment through Shannon were met with understanding. US Ambassador James Kenny also used the meeting to voice his concern over the case of the Shannon Five, a group of peace protesters charged with damaging a US transport aircraft. According to the cable, Montgomery, who attended the meeting, had assured Kenny the verdict was 'bizarre'. The US considered taking a civil action against the acquitted protesters but this came to nothing.[28] Years later, Montgomery said the jury verdict was an 'indication of public opinion'. He told the Americans as much, while also stressing the independence of the judiciary and saying that 'all sorts of weird and wonderful things happen in our lower courts'.[29]

The months following the US invasion of Iraq in March 2003 marked a low point of Irish pretences to neutrality. As Kearns noted in the Horgan judgment, there is no version of neutrality that permits countries to abandon it over economic concerns. This is the case even for the 'qualified neutrality' to which the Irish government claimed to adhere. This lack of principle seems to have at times been acknowledged by Irish leaders: US use of Shannon is 'good for business', Minister for Transport Martin Cullen said in 2005; while in 2003, Taoiseach Bertie Ahern argued the US and UK 'are our biggest trading partners' while defending the use of Shannon. Former Taoiseach Garret FitzGerald was perhaps most honest when he said in an interview in 2003 that foreign policy was about the interests of the State rather than 'ideals or values'.[30]

The status of neutrality in the period before and after the invasion of Iraq is less clear-cut from a legal point of view. UN resolutions for the invasion of Afghanistan and the reconstruction of Iraq post-August 2003, means Ireland can at least claim to have the backing of Security Council mandates in allowing US troops to transit through its territory during those periods. However, the continuing refusal of the government in the years since to inspect US aircraft, despite many recorded breaches of Irish law regarding extraordinary rendition and the transport of weapons, continues to ignore the spirit of neutrality and, at times, basic human rights.

This has not gone unnoticed by the Irish public. Since March 2003, opinion polls have consistently shown strong opposition to the US use of Shannon. One of the most recent of these, carried out by RED C in 2016, found 60 per cent of people opposed the US use of the airport.[31] These attitudes are entirely understandable given the many abuses and missteps by the US military in Iraq and Afghanistan, even when UN mandates existed.

Yet government policy has remained largely unchanged. This was the case even when the parties switched places. When the Fine Gael/Labour coalition entered government in 2011, it promised to 'enforce the prohibition on the use of Irish airspace, airports and related facilities for purposes not in line with the dictates of international law'.[32] But no additional restrictions were imposed on the US, and there was no increase in inspections. Since then, governments have continued to rely on US assurances. Sinn Féin, by far the most popular party in the State in 2023, has indicated it will completely end the use of Shannon by the US military once in power. Whether that promise survives contact with the realities of government will likely be one of the first major tests of its principles.

CHAPTER FOURTEEN

THE GAMBLE

It is a gamble, if you like, on peace ...
T.K. Whitaker (1973)[1]

Imagine a large aircraft, say a Boeing 747 cargo plane, travelling from New York to Dublin. It shows up on Irish air traffic control screens but it has deviated from its flight path and is failing to respond to radio communications. As nervous air traffic control operators use alternative frequencies to attempt to make contact with the aircraft, the dot representing its position suddenly disappears from their screens. Someone, accidentally or on purpose, has turned off the aircraft's transponder rendering it invisible to civilian air traffic. An air traffic controller picks up the dedicated line connecting them to Air Corps headquarters in Casement Aerodrome and alerts it to the situation. Despite its transponder being turned off, Air Corps personnel are able to pick up the plane's position on military radar. As they watch the Boeing get closer to Dublin, a decision is made to send up two fighter jets from the Air Corps' Quick Reaction Alert (QRA) to try to communicate with its pilots. When they near, the QRA jets try to talk to the Boeing on short-range frequencies but receive no reply. One jet moves alongside the aircraft to visually inspect the cockpit. Sure enough, the pilot is spotted at the controls. But there's no sign of the first officer or flight engineer and there are what looks like bloodstains on the cockpit glass.

Following procedure, the Air Corps pilot pulls in front of the Boeing and rocks his wings back and forth, signalling it to follow. But there's still no response. The situation is relayed back to the ground and then up the chain of command. Orders are given to evacuate Leinster House and Áras an Uachtaráin, but there is no time to issue a more general warning. It's coming up to Christmas and the city centre is packed, as is Croke Park which is hosting a concert. The taoiseach is alerted, along with the minister for defence. At the same time, Garda Headquarters delivers a message relayed by the NYPD: before take-off, the Boeing pilot posted a suicide message to social media, but there's no further detail of his intentions. The senior leaders agree they have no choice. A message no pilot ever wants to hear is sent over the radio, and two minutes later a missile strikes the jet, blowing off a wing and sending it down over the plains of Kildare.

If that sounds like something only likely to happen in the pages of a Tom Clancy thriller, that's because it is. Everything after the aircraft disappearing from air traffic control screens is not only fictional, it's impossible. Despite being responsible for one of the busiest flight corridors on earth, Ireland, alone among EU countries, has no military primary radar, meaning once an aircraft decides it does not want to be seen, it becomes completely invisible. Even if the Defence Forces could somehow locate the Boeing, it has no combat aircraft capable of reaching its cruising height of 35,000 feet, much less matching its cruising speed of 900km per hour. The Air Corps' eight Pilatus PC-9m propeller-driven aircraft, the closest thing it has to combat aircraft, have a top speed of less than 600km per hour and a service ceiling of 25,000 feet. The Defence Forces have a meagre supply of surface-to-air missiles, but these have a ceiling of no more than 10,000 feet. The military would be unable to either locate the aircraft or catch up to it to determine the cause of its communications problems.

Globally, communication failures, usually caused by a pilot forgetting to switch to the correct frequency, occur from time to time and are mostly resolved without interceptor jets being scrambled. Suicidal pilots are thankfully rarer still but are by no means unheard of; since 2010, there have been 14 recorded incidents worldwide, including the crash of

Germanwings Flight 9525 in March 2015 in France which killed all 150 passengers and crew.

If such a situation was to occur over Ireland, what would actually happen, provided there was enough time, is Royal Air Force Typhoon fighter jets would deploy from their UK base and into Irish sovereign airspace to intercept the aircraft and take whatever action is judged necessary. The basis for this is a pre-existing agreement between the UK and Irish governments which allows the RAF to conduct operations in Irish airspace in case of emergencies. The existence and extent of this agreement have been much discussed in Irish media in recent years, but its exact parameters remain mysterious.

According to reports in the *Irish Independent*, the agreement was drawn up after the attacks of September 11 and was kept from even the general in charge of the Air Corps until he demanded to see it. He was then taken into a room where he was allowed to read the document before leaving without a copy.[2] But according to one senior official, a memorandum of understanding on the use of Irish airspace by the RAF has existed since 1952: 'There is a commitment on their part to come to our assistance. It's an agreement. It happens when we request it,' the official said. This memo is approved by the Irish cabinet on a yearly basis, usually without controversy. The official has heard of only one minister raising concerns about the document and its impact on Irish sovereignty, much to the annoyance of the rest of the cabinet.[3]

Support for this can be found in the research of national security expert Professor Michael Mulqueen, who has quoted one Department of Defence official as saying the government would 'call in an air force' in an emergency.[4] When asked in the Dáil in November 2005 if the RAF would intercept a hijacked aircraft over Irish skies, Taoiseach Bertie Ahern confirmed there is 'co-operation and a pre-agreed understanding on those matters'.[5] During the Troubles, British forces also had permission to pursue paramilitaries who had been involved in an attack for up to 5km into Irish airspace, as well as to inspect suspect explosive devices or conduct photographic surveillance of the border region.

Under these agreements, the RAF also has permission to track

Russian military aircraft which enter Irish sovereign airspace. The worry here is less that Russia may be planning an air attack on Irish territory and more that their aircraft may pose a serious risk to civilian air traffic. On several occasions in recent years, Russian Tupolev bombers have been detected skirting Irish airspace while flying with their transponders turned off, rendering them invisible to civilian air traffic. It is believed that some of these aircraft were trailing long cables to allow them to communicate with submarines travelling down below, multiplying the danger to civilian traffic. As has become standard procedure, RAF aircraft have intercepted the bombers and flown alongside them with their transponders on, thereby reducing the chances of a mid-air collision. The prevailing belief within military circles is the bombers are testing the response times of NATO aircraft.[6]

Ireland may benefit extensively from these arrangements, but they are not acts of charity on Britain's part. Irish airspace is a huge hole in the northwest of NATO's air defence network and Britain knows a hijacked airliner or Russian bomber in Irish airspace poses just as much a threat to its interests as Ireland's. It's a mutually advantageous arrangement, but it also poses significant legal and constitutional questions. First, there's the fact that none of these agreements has been approved or even disclosed to the Oireachtas. Several opposition politicians, while seeking information about the agreement, have raised questions on its constitutionality under Article 15.6 ('The right to raise and maintain military or armed forces is vested exclusively in the Oireachtas') and one, Senator Gerard Craughwell, has taken a High Court case over the issue. There are also the legal implications of an RAF jet taking offensive action in Irish airspace. According to Mulqueen, the Air Corps has informed the general staff of the Defence Forces that, under international law, only an Irish Defence Forces officer would have the legal right to attack a civil aircraft over Ireland. Its view was that a diplomatic agreement between the British and Irish governments may not provide sufficient legal protection to any RAF officer responsible for civilian deaths.[7]

Regardless of the legalities, it's clear these secret air defence agreements between Ireland and the UK will continue into the foreseeable future. This is due to the bald fact that Ireland is almost completely defenceless from a military point of view. When asked if there has ever been a point since independence when Ireland was able to defend itself, former Chief of Staff, Vice Admiral Mark Mellett, needed a moment to think before answering, 'Certainly, in the jurisdiction I know best, the maritime, no. Not now, not ever. In terms of the air? Never. In terms of land? Never.'[8] In 2020, Ireland spent 0.3 per cent of its GDP on defence, by far the lowest in the EU. Austria spends roughly twice as much and Switzerland three times as much. The discrepancy is so large that, even if the 50 per cent increase in defence spending announced in September 2022 occurs by the promised date of 2028, Ireland will still be comfortably at the bottom of the table.

This long-standing policy of refusing to invest in national security has run parallel to government claims of military neutrality, meaning the two concepts have become intertwined in the public mind. The biggest advocates of Irish neutrality are almost invariably the loudest opposition voices when the prospect of increased defence spending is raised. The usual and not entirely unreasonable argument is that the money could be better spent somewhere else. 'Twelve airplanes is not going to scare off the Russians or the British or the Americans or the Chinese or whoever, but twelve new housing estates would make a real impact for thousands of people,' People Before Profit–Solidarity TD Paul Murphy told the Dáil in March 2022 in response to the commission's report.[9] He was referring to the commission's most ambitious proposal, the purchase of a squadron of fighter jets, though the government has already signalled this purchase is unlikely to happen, at least in the short to medium term. Several months later Murphy led a Dáil debate calling for neutrality to be enshrined in the Constitution.

PANA Chair Roger Cole said that he believes Ireland should have a well-paid army capable of peacekeeping duties, but that there is no point in equipping it to take on threats from large powers:

> There's not a shred of evidence that the Chinese or the Americans or anybody else for that matter have the slightest interest in

invading us. The only people who have done it are the English and I don't think there's very much evidence that they're going to do it again.[10]

But from some perspectives, neutral countries have a specific legal obligation to defend their neutrality militarily. The 1907 Hague Convention, detailing the rights and obligations of neutral powers, mandates that neutrals cannot allow belligerents to use their territory to move troops or supplies. According to most interpretations, this means a neutral military must be able to stop a warring party from using its ports, coastline, land and airspace. In other words, a neutral country must have an army and navy big enough to deter others from using its territory as a base of operations and an air force capable of intercepting and forcing belligerent aircraft in its airspace to land. Failing to do this in wartime may give a belligerent country the right to invade a neutral country in order to deny it to its enemy.[11]

This is what worried Irish defence planners during World War II when the British repeatedly claimed German U-boats were using the natural harbours on the Irish west coast as a safe haven. On the other hand, it's not at all clear what legal relevance the Hague Convention obligations have in the modern world. In the past, the Irish government has argued it never ratified the 1907 Hague Convention and that the convention's definition of neutrality has been overtaken by the United Nations charter with its focus on collective security. However, the convention is still regarded as customary international law, and the fact that a country has not ratified does not necessarily offer a defence to any breaches.

Everyone seems to have their own theory to explain Ireland's traditional neglect of its national defence. Mellett dates it back to the IRA's ill-fated attack on the Custom House in May 1921, towards the end of the War of Independence. The building was used by Crown civil servants who were dismayed to see it burnt in the fighting. Then one day, these officials suddenly found themselves civil servants in the Department of Finance of the Irish Free State, serving under a Tricolour and taking orders from the same people who had attacked their offices. This animosity, and an assumption that Britain would continue to handle the Free State's defence needs, led to an institutional objection to funding the Irish military. Under Mellett's theory, this animosity became ingrained in the psychological DNA of the Department of Finance over the following decades. It also became codified in law at an early stage: the Ministers and Secretaries Acts 1924 mandated every military purchase, from tanks and aircraft down to telephone cables and water canteens, had to be approved by Finance. Ever since many military officers have been deeply resentful of Finance and its death grip on the Defence Forces' purse strings.

Others have offered different interpretations over the years. The Army Mutiny of 1924 challenged the authority of the government and certainly played a role in creating an atmosphere of distrust. Eunan O'Halpin contends that Finance sought to control the Army by starvation, a policy which remained constant no matter which party was in power.[12] The structures of the new State also served to neuter the military. The Department of Defence was put in charge of all military policy and acted as a buffer between the general staff and the minister of the day, meaning officers rarely had an opportunity to explain their needs or air their grievances first-hand. Everything was filtered through a layer of civil servants. Under this system, senior officers, including the chief of staff, have to get department sign-off for even the most mundane activities. 'We're talking about a situation where if I wanted to send a military vehicle to a local fair, I would have to get sign-off from someone in the department,' said one former senior officer.[13]

In the end, most of these explanations go back to money and the outsized power of the Department of Finance, and more recently, the Department of Public Expenditure and Reform. 'I've seen again and again where the taoiseach wants to do something for defence but if Finance doesn't like it, it doesn't happen,' said one former officer.[14] The great reforming civil servant T.K. Whitaker probably explained Ireland's reluctance for funding defence most concisely when he addressed a group of newly commissioned officers in 1973. He said defence was underfunded simply because the government believed the modernisation of agriculture, industry and education were bigger priorities. With admirable honesty, Whitaker compared Ireland to

> an uninsured, untaxed motorist, skimping on car maintenance. So long as we don't have an accident or are not stopped by the Guards, we will get away with it. As the years go by, all that money that would have been spent on defence would be available to invest in infrastructure, social services and creating employment. It is a gamble, if you like, on peace.[15]

At no stage since independence could the government claim to have been ignorant of Ireland's defence failings. Despite the barrier of civil servants between military officers and ministers, many warnings of the almost perennial dire state of the Defence Forces have been issued over the decades. As early as 1925, just after the government had completed a mass demobilisation of the Army following the Civil War, the Council of Defence warned that the military was not capable of defending the country against any modern force. Like Belgium in World War I, Ireland could not protect its neutrality and would likely become a 'cockpit for belligerents' in any future major conflict. These comments were echoed a decade later by Dan Bryan in his memo 'Fundamental Factors Affecting Saorstát Defence Problem'. 'In the usual European sense the [Irish State] can hardly be said to have a Defence Force at all,' Bryan wrote. He noted neutral states have 'very onerous' obligations to defend their neutrality and, in Ireland's case, failing to do so may give Britain an excuse to invade in the looming war.[16] Little had improved six decades later in 1994, when an audit found the Defence Forces were poorly structured, poorly equipped and, in manpower terms, too old.

Most of these assessments have been carried out in secret, and only declassified years later. But occasionally a senior military figure has felt compelled to speak publicly. A 1982 *Irish Times* interview with retired Lieutenant General Carl O'Sullivan, who had just stepped down as chief of staff, drew criticism from several political parties due to his stark assessment of Irish defence. O'Sullivan believed that Ireland has no neutrality because it has no ability to defend itself from even a minor external attack. If the country wanted a credible defence, it must look at making a military pact with its European neighbours, he argued.[17] The most recent and most public appraisal came from the Army in its submission to the Commission on the Defence Forces in 2021. The Army, it said, 'is not equipped, postured or realistically prepared to conduct a meaningful defence of the State against a full spectrum force for any sustained period'.[18] It's a comment which could have reasonably been made in every decade since independence.

These assessments make for grim reading, but it would be a mistake to say there have been no high points. Most of these are related to the Defence Forces' well-earned reputation in peacekeeping and humanitarian assistance in dangerous places around the world. Irish soldiers have saved lives in many dangerous environments, including the Congo, East Timor, Liberia, and of course, Lebanon. A case in point is the activity of the Irish Naval Service in the Mediterranean between 2015 and 2019 when its sailors saved the lives of almost 20,000 migrants attempting the dangerous sea crossing.

But in recent years, the low points have been more frequent. This is partly because of an emerging trend of ex-military officers energetically pointing out the inadequacies of the Defence Forces in public forums and campaigning for reform. Most prominent has been ex-Army Ranger Wing Commandant Cathal Berry, who resigned his commission to campaign for improved conditions for his former comrades. As an independent TD, he has been a loud voice for improving the military and has been credited with extracting several significant concessions from the government. The other reason the poor state of the Defence Forces has come to the fore in recent years is the organisation is genuinely in crisis. Soldiers, sailors and aircrew are departing the organisation in droves, attracted by better pay and conditions in the private sector, leaving it, by February 2023, with less than 8,000 members.[19] At one stage in 2022, an entire class of Naval Service apprentices departed en masse after being offered more attractive private sector positions.[20]

Without exception, every unit of the Defence Forces is under-strength, but it is the Naval Service that has suffered the most. In 2023, it fell to less than 800 members out of its minimum establishment of 1,095. Over three years, it went from a nine-ship navy to a four-ship navy, partly because of the age of the vessels and partly because it simply did not have enough sailors to crew them. The Naval Service is responsible for patrolling a maritime zone ten times the size of Ireland's landmass. But it frequently has to cancel patrols due to staffing issues. In 2021, 196 patrol days were cancelled due to 'personnel issues', up from 28 the previous year.[21] The Naval Service ordered two inshore patrol vessels from New Zealand in 2022, which will be significantly smaller than the ships they are replacing. But with the current rate of personnel turnover, it is not at all clear whether it will even be able to sufficiently operate these. A programme to acquire a much larger multi-role vessel is still years away from completion.

For retired naval captain Brian FitzGerald, who served as one of the Service's most senior navy officers until his retirement in 2021, the current state of the Naval Service recalls the dark days of the late 1960s when, for a period, it had no ships at all. FitzGerald said that, since its foundation in 1946, the Naval Service has always been resented, not just by the Department of Defence but by the Army, which feared it would draw away scarce resources. FitzGerald described the State's treatment of the Naval Service as 'tokenistic'. At one stage funding was available from the EEC and EU for the purchase of ships for fishery protection but, as Ireland's economic situation improved, the money dried up and the government declined to make the investments itself.

Even after almost 40 years of service, FitzGerald finds it incredible that an island nation, responsible for a massive area of ocean, still cannot find the will to invest in its maritime defence. 'If Russians come along and run an exercise over the subsea cables in our EEZ [Exclusive Economic Zone], Europe expects us to protect them. Neutrality doesn't abdicate you from that responsibility,' he said. It has become an even greater issue since Brexit, he believes, as Ireland's maritime domain is now isolated from those of its EU partners.

The many holes in Irish defence came as little surprise to the military figures assigned to the 2021–2 Commission on the Defence Forces, but some of the members with no military background were shocked by what they learned. 'I was really taken aback by what we found when we started. I was also taken aback by the rigidity of the structures,' said one member. The level of control the Army had over the naval and air forces was also a source of surprise for members. 'For a modern military, that's just a crazy system for strategic planning,' the commission member said.[22] So stark were the problems, that some observers, including army officers, wondered if the Commission was a prelude to abolishing the Defence Forces altogether and replacing it perhaps with a gendarmerie for internal security, backed up by an armed coast guard. There was international precedent for this. In 1948, Costa Rica abolished its military and replaced it with an internal security force. However, unlike Ireland, Costa Rica is an acknowledged member of a collective defence arrangement, namely the Rio Pact, which states any attack on a country in the Americas is considered an attack on all.

The question of why Ireland needs an army at all is one that comes up regularly when defence is discussed, so much so that Dan Harvey, a retired lieutenant colonel and military historian, has taught himself not to get aggravated when it's put to him at social events. 'You may not be interested in war, but war is interested in you,' said Harvey, quoting Leon Trotsky, 'if you don't go abroad, and cut out the causes, it's coming your way.'[23] As well as on-island defence, Ireland requires an 'expeditionary capacity' to travel abroad and help solve problems, which otherwise might arrive on its doorstep later. Harvey is not talking about mounting invasions and toppling dictatorships. Rather, Ireland needs to be able to cooperate with EU partners at very short notice to stabilise dangerous situations before they get worse.

This is what the EU Battlegroups system (a Battlegroup being a military unit adhering to the EU's Common Security and Defence Policy) was designed to do and what its updated version, the EU Rapid Deployment Capacity, will be tasked with. Under the initiative, Ireland will contribute troops to a standing force of 2,000 troops, which will be able to deploy at extremely short notice to trouble spots to stabilise a situation while a longer-term peacekeeping force is generated. Under this concept, EU nations have a humanitarian obligation to help people facing terrorism or civil war. Interventions will also lessen the risks to EU states, by reducing the possibility of international terrorism or mass irregular migration, both problems that have resulted due to widespread unrest in the Sahel region of Africa in recent years.

Harvey gave the example of EUFOR Chad, which was under the leadership of Irish Lieutenant General Patrick Nash. For just over 12 months in 2008 and 2009, a contingent of 4,300 troops from 20 countries, including 450 Irish troops, helped to protect civilians from militants and ensure the safety of food deliveries and UN personnel. 'It was a big experiment and it proved to be a successful experiment. Because the UN subcontracted it to the EU, it was done an awful lot faster,' said Harvey, who helped coordinate the mission from Paris. Despite problems with logistics and tensions with the Chadian government over the involvement of French troops, the mission helped create a stable enough environment that the UN could take over in March 2008. The common consensus in the Defence Forces is that if the mission was to happen today, Ireland would be unable to contribute more than a handful of troops.

The other reason Harvey gives his dinner party guests when asked about the need for an army is 'deterrence'. Realistically, Ireland will never have a large enough military to defeat an invasion by a major power. What it can do is create a force that, in Harvey's words, 'makes the invasion such a massive hassle, that the invader wouldn't try it in the first place'. He pointed to the war in Ukraine as an example of how much damage a small army can inflict on one many times its size. 'Paddy is a nice guy but put him into a corner and he's not such a nice guy. You can train to make it very, very hard for an invasion force to take you. That's something we're very good at. But if we try to play the conventional game, we're lost,' Harvey said. As an example, he referred to Britain's Field Marshall Montgomery, who, early in World War II, was tasked with devising a plan to invade Ireland. But Montgomery had had first-hand experience of the guerrilla warfare employed by the IRA and the terror tactics used by British forces during the War of Independence and said, 'Oh no, we're not going back into Ireland.'[24]

Today's Defence Forces would pose little threat to an invading force, through either conventional or non-conventional warfare. There are also clear signs it is losing its expeditionary capacity. In 2022, it pulled troops out of four EU or UN missions in Africa and there are no signs of it getting involved in any new ones, aside from a small contribution to an EU training mission for Ukraine's military. Serious consideration is also being given to withdrawing the 130 Irish troops assigned to the United Nations Disengagement Observer Force (UNDOF) in Syria to free up resources for the new EU Battlegroup.

The lack of expeditionary capacity was perhaps most clearly shown in August 2021 when Irish Army Ranger Wing operators and diplomats had to catch a ride with the French air force to rescue Irish citizens trapped in Kabul after the fall of Afghanistan to the Taliban. It was highlighted again in July 2022, when there were difficulties evacuating two Irish officers from the Democratic Republic of Congo in the face of mounting violence. One official suggested they escape by renting a car and driving across the border (they were eventually withdrawn by an Air Corp aircraft).[25]

There is some hope for the future though. In its final report, the Commission on the Defence Forces put forward three courses of action or 'levels of ambition' (LOA): LOA 1 involves keeping the status quo, which would leave the Defence Forces 'unable to conduct a meaningful defence of the State against a sustained act of aggression from a conventional military force.'[26] It would also likely mean fewer overseas operations. LOA 2 is a 50 per cent increase in spending, which would fill the 'specific priority gaps in the Defence Forces' ability to deal with an assault on Irish sovereignty' and allow for participation in higher-intensity overseas operations.[27] LOA 3 is the holy grail. Defence spending would increase threefold, bringing it roughly in line with other small EU countries and allowing for the purchase of new ships, fighter jets, air transport capability and improved special forces capability.[28]

As was widely expected, the government opted for LOA 2. This will mean a 50 per cent increase in defence spending by 2028. The government has also committed to recruiting some 6,000 extra permanent and reserve troops, and to restructuring the entire command and control structure. How the former will be achieved when the Defence Forces continue to haemorrhage personnel is as yet unclear, but the intention is there. Unlike previous damning indictments of the country's defence, the government has at last acknowledged there is a problem and has committed to doing something about it. 'I'm disappointed some of the recommendations weren't accepted fully. I just hope it's a trajectory and not an endpoint,' said one member of the commission.[29] Micheál Martin has also suggested a citizens' assembly should be held to discuss the topic of neutrality, something that would assumedly also cover the question of defence. According to a 2022 poll, 70 per cent of people support such an assembly.[30] For Mellett, such an assembly should focus on security rather than neutrality:

> The question we should be asking is, are we willing to resource our security? And if citizens decide, no, we're quite happy to have suboptimal investment in security, then so be it. We're all part of that decision. And we will go where we go. But we have to be willing to accept the consequences.[31]

In short, Ireland needs to ask itself if it wants to be a Costa Rica or a Switzerland. For now, we remain under the unofficial protection of NATO's umbrella. 'That's a reality,' said Mellett, 'but those protections are not guaranteed.'[32]

It's a point echoed by another diplomat, who recalled how, in May 2017, a shudder went down the spines of Irish officials when US President Donald Trump declined to explicitly endorse America's commitments to collective defence under NATO. 'And who's to say he, or someone like him, or worse, won't be back in the White House soon?'[33]

And in the meantime, as we will see next, Ireland is facing increasing security challenges that NATO can't help with.

CHAPTER FIFTEEN

DIRTY TRICKS

*Russia doesn't need to get stronger. All it needs to do is
make the member states of the European Union
look weaker …*
Mark Mellett (2022)[1]

During the worst years of the Troubles, Britain's foreign intelligence service MI6 took to planting stories in newspapers, some with more than a grain of truth, that Charles Haughey was funding terrorist groups and was up to his neck in crooked property deals. This dirty tricks campaign was devised by Maurice Oldfield, the conspiratorial director of the British foreign intelligence service in the 1970s, who was obsessed with Haughey and who believed he posed a serious danger to British national security. The aim was to damage Haughey's reputation and prevent the Fianna Fáil politician from taking power in Ireland. Among the actions taken against Haughey was the leaking of stories to British journalists about his romantic indiscretions, and doctoring pamphlets to make it appear Fianna Fáil had links to the Provisional IRA. Operations like these were the stock in trade of British espionage agents operating in Ireland during the period.[2]

The rumours spread about Haughey were on the less fantastical end of the scale compared to others spread by MI6. At the time, British spies in Northern Ireland were also spreading rumours that the IRA was engaged in witchcraft and black magic and that bomb-making causes cancer. In one operation, they issued a forged order from IRA leadership instructing members to electronically test bazooka rounds before firing them. The hope was that they would blow themselves up in the process. Such was the scale of British rumourmongering that the Army headquarters in Lisburn, County Antrim, became known locally as 'the Lisburn Lie Machine'.[3]

The use of disinformation was by then a well-established tactic among UK intelligence services, having been deployed for decades in its colonies around the world. The general aim was to cause as much confusion, disorder and mistrust among the enemy as possible. Today these tactics would be called 'hybrid warfare', a term which has become common in defence circles to describe any threatening action taken against hostile forces that falls short of outright military aggression and that doesn't involve the actual deployment of military forces. This can include espionage, economic warfare, cyberattacks, state funding of terrorist or separatist groups, disrupting food or energy supplies, spreading disinformation, interfering in elections – the list is endless.

Hybrid warfare may be a new term, but the ingredients have been around as long as warfare itself. As fifth-century BC Chinese tactician Sun Tzu advised in the *Art of War,* 'Indirect tactics, effectively applied, are inexhaustible as heaven and earth.' Five hundred years ago, European powers hired privateers to target their enemies on the high seas, while in the 1700s, the French used local fishermen and priests to inform them of British operations in Spanish Louisiana. The practice become even more common in the twentieth century when deception and disinformation became embedded in modern military doctrines. During World War II, the Allies tricked Germany regarding the location of their invasion of Sicily by planting fake war plans on a dead body which was allowed to wash up on the coast of Spain. During the Vietnam War, US forces attempted to lower enemy morale by playing ghostly sounds in the jungles meant to sound like slain Viet Cong soldiers.

Hybrid warfare goes by many names. The Russians call it the

Gerasimov Doctrine, after former Chief of Staff Valery Gerasimov, who said traditional military operations must go hand in hand with diplomatic, economic and political warfare. Other theorists call it grey zone warfare, new generation warfare, or compound warfare. Much like 'neutrality', the term hybrid warfare is arguably so fuzzy as to be almost useless. But it does serve one purpose: it drives home the point that dangers to a nation's security go far beyond traditional military threats. The risks faced by governments and their citizens are always evolving, and if a government wants to keep its citizens safe, it has to constantly change how it meets those risks.

While it is debatable whether neutrality offers protection against traditional military threats, recent history has shown it is certainly no defence against hybrid threats, whether they be espionage, disinformation or cyber-based. In the modern globalised world, neutrality is not an effective security policy, something noted by Defence Forces Commandant Derek McGourty, who wrote in the 2020 *Defence Forces Review*, 'The policy of preserving Ireland's autonomy and sovereignty through neutrality may not stand up well against state and non-state actors wishing to gain an advantage in an era of hybrid conflict.'[4]

Being a serving officer, McGourty has the discretion not to identify who these state actors may be but France's ambassador to Ireland, Vincent Guérend, had no qualms about naming the country that poses the largest threat to Ireland and the EU today. Russia's actions in recent years pose an 'existential threat' to Europe, he said, and Irish neutrality should evolve to meet this. He believes that Russia has no respect for Irish neutrality, as shown by the country's many recent breaches of international law. France respects Irish neutrality, he said, but added that it 'doesn't mean that this policy cannot evolve … or should not be adapted to a new environment'.[5]

In August 2021, the *Yantar*, a Russian-registered oceanic survey ship, dropped anchor off Ireland's Atlantic coast. Ordinarily, such an event would cause little concern. Oceanic survey ships frequently carry out research in that area of Ireland's EEZ. But the *Yantar* is no ordinary survey ship, rather, it's a 'special purpose ship' from the Russian

Directorate of Underwater Research, and is equipped with sophisticated surveillance equipment, including one manned and several unmanned submersibles capable of interfering with subsea communication cables. In other words, it's a spy ship. What was more worrying for Irish authorities was that the ship had set up shop between two major undersea cables connecting Ireland and Europe to North America. While some expressed fears it may have been seeking to cut or damage the cables, this was probably not on the agenda. Subsea cables have many redundancies built in, meaning cutting one or two would be unlikely to seriously disrupt transatlantic communication.

A more likely scenario, although still unproven, is that the ship was trying to tap into the cables, place interception devices on them, or at least carry out reconnaissance for such operations in the future. If this was the case, there is ample precedent. In 2013, documents released by US whistle-blower Edward Snowden showed the British spy agency GCHQ was engaging in the wholesale tapping of subsea cables serving Ireland under a programme called Tempora. This data was then shared with America's National Security Agency. No solid information has emerged on how Russia or the UK taps into these cables – unsurprisingly they prefer to keep their tradecraft under wraps – but experts have put forward several possibilities. Submersibles that can cut through the cables' outer layer and place a fibre optic listening device inside are one possibility. Intelligence agencies may also target the cables as they make landfall. Russia has reportedly sent intelligence operatives to Ireland on several occasions in recent years to map the landing points of cables.[6]

Worldwide, much of this type of hybrid warfare is made possible through the use of what has become known as 'little blue sailors'. The term is a play on the 'little green men' who took part in the initial invasion of eastern Ukraine in 2014. These were Russian soldiers armed with Russian weapons but who did not wear any markings indicating their military allegiance. This allowed Russia to maintain (barely) credible deniability that it was directly involved in the conflict. Like their land counterparts, little blue sailors work for the Russian military authorities but operate under the guise of engaging in benign maritime activity, such as fishing or scientific research. Again, this is nothing new. Russia and other major powers have been disguising their spy ships as fishing trawlers for decades. But, according to a 2019 report from the Estonian Foreign Intelligence Service (EFIS), Russia is now also increasingly using its civilian fleet for its strategic goals. EFIS warned that more attention should be paid to civilian vessels sailing under the Russian flag. The problem is, with its tiny, under-equipped navy, and scant naval intelligence resources, Ireland is entirely unable to monitor or counter these hybrid maritime threats, something alluded to by Naval Service Lieutenant Ben Crumplin in the 2020 Defence Forces Review:

> Paramilitary forces operating onboard merchant vessels are nigh on impossible to positively identify. Little blue sailors could be operating in Ireland's area of responsibility without the knowledge of Irish authorities and pose a direct threat to Irish sovereignty and interests.[7]

Irish ships have radars extending out just 20km and have no submersibles capable of monitoring subsea cables, meaning the little blue sailors can essentially do what they please in the vast Irish EEZ. Unsurprisingly, just as it does in the air, Britain has decided to take matters into its own hands to protect its interests. The Royal Navy is currently building its own multi-role ocean surveillance ship, which will monitor and protect cables in the Irish EEZ. The Irish Department of Defence has said it has no plans to cooperate with Britain in these operations.[8]

The Irish west coast received a less subtle visit from Russian ships in early 2022, just before Russia launched its full-scale invasion of Ukraine. In late January, the Irish Aviation Authority issued a warning to aircraft that Russian naval vessels were scheduled to engage in live-fire exercises some 240km off the coast of Cork. The exercises would involve the *Marshal Ustinov* – an advanced missile cruiser and one of the largest vessels in Russia's Northern Fleet – along with three other warships. Per Russian naval doctrine, a submarine was also expected to accompany the ships.

There was nothing illegal about Russia's action; the exercises were taking place within the Irish EEZ but outside Ireland's territorial waters. However, their location – the operations were to take place directly above the subsea cables – combined with the tense geopolitical climate regarding Ukraine, meant they were regarded by the Irish authorities as most unwelcome. 'This isn't a time to increase military activity and tension in the context of what's happening with Ukraine at the moment,' Minister for Defence and Foreign Affairs Simon Coveney commented.[9] The Irish government protested to the Russian embassy in Dublin. In response, Russian Ambassador Yury Filatov, who started his career while the Soviet Union still existed, called the concerns a 'hoopla' and said, 'There is nothing really to be disturbed, concerned or anguished about.' Asked if he would call off the exercises in response to Irish government concerns, his reply was succinct: 'Why would we?'[10]

Protests followed from Oireachtas members, both in government and opposition, including a group of TDs and senators who promised to charter a boat to personally observe the exercises. Environmental groups also raised concerns about the impact on marine life in the area. But the loudest objections came from the Irish South and West Fish Producers Organisation, which worried the exercises would disrupt their catch. The group promised to use their fishing boats to peacefully disrupt the exercises. Tensions were increasing by the day. Then something unexpected happened; Filatov invited the fishermen to meet him in the embassy. Afterwards, Brendan Byrne, chief executive of the Irish Fish Processors and Exporters Association, told the media they had reached 'an accommodation where there is a pathway for coexistence for the naval exercises and for our fishing fleet'.[11]

Russian Minister for Defence Sergei Shoigu informed Coveney the exercises would be moved further west into the Atlantic and outside the Irish EEZ. Filatov called it 'a gesture of goodwill' aimed at helping the fishermen.[12] The episode made headlines around the world, with the media focusing on the plucky Irish fishermen's victory over the mighty Russian navy. 'I'm shocked, really,' fisherman Patrick Murphy told CNN. 'I didn't think that little old us … would have an impact on international diplomacy.'[13] A good news story all around which, on the face of it, left everyone happy. The exercises took place outside the EEZ and without too much controversy before the Russian ships sailed for the Mediterranean where they would play a support role in the invasion of Ukraine when it started a few weeks later.

But many in Irish defence circles looked on in concern. They recognised in the embassy's actions a classic example of Russian hybrid techniques; in this case, using the media to make the Irish government look weak. For Mellett, the original plan to stage the exercises within the Irish EEZ was meant to be provocative and increase pressure on the West in the run-up to the war: 'That was an annexation of 5,000sq km, an area the size of Wexford, Wicklow and Dublin, for five days in our jurisdiction. It was unprecedented. It was provocative.' Others saw it as a message that Russia could easily damage the communication cables if Western countries interfered in the plans to invade Ukraine. Mellett said 'the real hybrid part' was moving the exercises after meeting the fishermen:

> It was the most classic hybrid ever. What they did was give the impression that it was fishermen who sorted it, not the government. And that portrays the government as being weak. And that's what hybrid is all about. Russia doesn't need to get stronger. All it needs to do is make the member states of the European Union look weaker.[14]

Filatov has since emphatically rejected this interpretation: 'I do not support conspiracy theories [...] When we saw the reaction from the fishermen we saw it was a problem for them. We thought, "Why make trouble for these people?"' He pointed out that NATO navies and air forces carry out exercises in Ireland's EEZ, yet these rarely cause public controversy. Filatov also said that, contrary to Guérend's view on the matter, Russia does respect Irish neutrality: 'Russia and the Soviet Union has always respected the Irish position of military neutrality [...] Neutrality is a concept which is a positive when there is enough tension in the world.'[15] It's a statement that would be easier to believe if the Russian embassy on Orwell Road at which Filatov is based was not the major Russian espionage centre many believe it to be.

The areas of Irish life at risk from hybrid threats are everywhere. The growing number of technology companies, social media firms and data centres in Ireland present (to borrow a cybersecurity term) a massive 'attack surface' for digital offensives. That attack surface gets larger still when you consider the migration of many areas of public administration online. All of these are at risk from what could be termed 'little digital men' – hackers in hostile states who operate with the permission or active support of their governments and who could potentially cripple Irish society if given the opportunity. The suspects behind the devastating cyberattack on the HSE in May 2021 are believed to operate from within Russia with the tacit support of the Kremlin (although the attack itself is not suspected of being mandated by the government). Many similar groups have been used to launch cyberattacks on Ukraine and the countries supporting it since the war began there. Such groups are also used for the type of election interference seen in the 2016 US presidential election and the Brexit vote in the UK. To date, no evidence has emerged of Russian meddling in Irish elections but it's not hard to envisage interference in some divisive future vote; for example, a potential referendum on a united Ireland. As in previous operations, the goal wouldn't necessarily be to ensure one particular side wins, it would be to cause as much disruption as possible and erode trust in both the final result and the democratic system in general.

Arguably, in 2023, Ireland is already experiencing the impacts of Russian hybrid warfare. Like the rest of Europe, it is accommodating tens of thousands of Ukrainian refugees who have fled the war; desperate people who are arriving at the same time as near-record numbers of asylum seekers from other countries, including many from Syria and the Sahel region, where Russian state-affiliated mercenaries are also behind much of the violence. Not only is this influx a massive drain on state resources, but it is also creating tensions within communities and empowering anti-immigration groups. As a bonus, many of these groups are broadly sympathetic towards the Russian regime. For Russia, it's a beneficial and intentional side effect of the invasion, intended to make Western leaders think twice about their continued support for Ukraine.

The withholding of fuel supplies and the disruption of food shipments from Ukraine, which is considered the breadbasket of Europe, is another instrument in Vladimir Putin's hybrid toolbox. In Ireland, the rise in fuel prices has caused extensive personal hardship and has the potential to stir up significant political discord. That's without considering the economic costs. Again, all of this is intended to weaken western governments' support for Ukraine. Africa has experienced the worst of the food shortages relating to the war, as countries such as Libya, Somalia, and Tunisia import about half their wheat supplies from Ukraine. Russia hasn't been slow in exploiting this. It has waged a disinformation campaign in various African nations, blaming EU countries for causing the food shortages and hoarding grain supplies.[16] This creates tensions between the global north and south and erodes international consensus on how to respond to illegal Russian aggression. As a bonus for Putin, it also further increases irregular migration flows from Africa to the EU.

None of this is new to Russia's immediate European neighbours who have been dealing with hybrid threats for many years. 'To most of our European colleagues, I would say, "Welcome to the club",' Latvian foreign minister Edgars Rinkēvičs told the *Irish Times* in July 2017 as Western EU countries started to wake up to the threat posed by Russian hybrid activities. It's no coincidence NATO's centre of excellence for cyber defence is located in the Estonian capital of Tallinn. In 2007, Estonia suffered a devastating series of cyberattacks that targeted its parliament, banks, civil service and media. This occurred in the midst of a row with Russia over the relocation of a Soviet World War II memorial in Tallinn. The Kremlin has never been conclusively proven as the culprit, but many experts believe, given the sophistication of the attacks, they could only have been carried out with the help of a nation-state. The region has also faced hybrid threats from Belarus, Russia's steadfast ally. Most prominently, the Minsk government has funnelled tens of thousands of asylum seekers from the Middle East through its territory and across the borders of Lithuania, Latvia, and Poland, with the aim of putting the infrastructure in those countries under pressure and creating divisions within the EU.

For Finland, which shares a 1,300km border and a troubled history with Russia, the turning point came in 2013. 'We were told by a friend that somebody is in our cables who was not our friend,' said Liisa Talonpoika, Finland's ambassador on hybrid affairs.[17] Finnish authorities had been informed by a foreign intelligence service that hackers had gained access to the computer systems of the Ministry of Foreign Affairs and had been harvesting sensitive information over the previous four years. Suspicion immediately fell on Russian intelligence agents who the Finns believed were attempting to gather intel on EU deliberations. 'That was a wake-up call for our politicians to say that we have to change the whole legislation,' said Talonpoika. Other types of attacks soon followed, including Russian border guards funnelling refugees over the border and the spread of disinformation targeted at Finnish citizens regarding NATO. Talonpoika said that these activities extended into the most unexpected areas, including interference in international child custody cases involving Finnish citizens. It became apparent that Finland's non-alignment was not protecting it from hybrid threats. More powerful laws to allow for the investigation of cyberattacks were soon passed, and in 2015 the European Centre of Excellence for Countering Hybrid Threats was established in Helsinki.

That is just one small part of the Finnish response to hybrid threats. The country operates a 'whole of society approach' to national security, said Talonpoika: 'It's not only military or civil servants or parliaments which protects us. It's NGOs. It's local authorities. It's the press, and it's the schools.'[18] For example, community leaders regularly undergo training in military colleges on how to deal with hybrid threats on a local level, while national stockpiles of medicine, food and fuel are maintained. For Finnish Ambassador on Cyber Affairs Jarmo Sareva, the most important measure is education. From a young age, children in Finland are taught how to spot propaganda, how to protect themselves from cyber threats and how to use social media safely. This is vital in a world where

Facebook 'is turning our elderly, mild-mannered relatives into blood and soil fascists,' said Sareva.[19] All of this is supported by a vibrant media where national security is regularly discussed and analysed. Unlike in Ireland, Finnish military officers and defence officials frequently speak openly in public forums about the threats facing the country and how to counter them. For example, in early 2022, the Finnish government announced that an unnamed party had hacked their diplomats' phones using the Israeli-developed Pegasus software. Other countries might have been embarrassed to admit such a breach, but Sareva felt that 'this was an opportunity to tell everybody to faithfully follow basics of cyber hygiene.'[20]

Sareva believes that neutrality offers little defence against external threats, particularly modern threats, and while geography perhaps offers Ireland a level of protection that Finland does not enjoy, 'the long arm of the Tsar can reach to your waters'.[21] Furthermore, Ireland is no longer a sole trader in terms of security. Any harm caused to communication cables, energy infrastructure or technology companies here will undoubtedly have a knock-on impact on other EU states. 'It's in everyone's interest that everyone takes care of their own security,' said Talonpoika.[22] Here, she echoes a point made by Mellett, who believes Ireland has taken advantage of the economic benefits of globalisation while failing to live up to the attendant security obligations. 'In this globalised, networked world, the ability to attack infrastructure in Estonia could actually be triggered from a backroom in Capel Street,' Mellett said.[23]

On an EU level, officials have been taking the hybrid threat far more seriously since the 2014 annexation of Ukrainian territory by Russia's little green men. This includes the establishment of the East StratCom Task Force (ESCTF), an agency dedicated to countering Russian disinformation in Eastern Europe. These countermeasures have been beefed up since the launch of the full-scale invasion in February 2022. Russian propaganda channels have been banned, cybersecurity measures have been increased and, most crucially, efforts have begun to wean the EU off Russian gas and oil. Ireland however remains quite a distance behind. It was only after the HSE attack that the government woke up to the need to adequately fund cyber defence, and authorities are still playing catch-up in the area.

Education programmes targeting propaganda and disinformation remain in their infancy while the overall national defence remains a niche subject of discussion in the Oireachtas and the media. There is no single government minister responsible for hybrid or cyber threats, something which is hardly a surprise given at cabinet level the defence portfolio is shared with the foreign affairs brief. Another weakness is energy security. Ireland has no natural gas reserve and is expected to be completely reliant on imported gas by the end of the decade. Perhaps most damning is the fact that, as of February 2023, a national security strategy document promised in 2019 is yet to materialise.

There is cause for optimism though. Once Ireland joins Hybrid CoE in Helsinki, it will take part in wargames and planning exercises aimed at mitigating a broad-front hybrid attack. And the discussion of national security threats has been slowly increasing, both in the media and among the general public, while politicians are also gradually starting to address the topic. Following Russia's deliberate bombing of Ukrainian cities to cause a migration crisis, then Taoiseach Micheál Martin observed in September 2022 that this was 'a new form of hybrid warfare. Now we need to be resilient against that type of warfare.'[24] The term 'hybrid threats' and similar phrases had been used only a handful of times in the Oireachtas between 1998 and 2018, according to research from Cornelia-Adriana Baciu.[25] But a search of the Oireachtas website in 2022 shows the topic has been discussed much more since then (although it remains a niche issue). The 2015 White Paper on Defence mentioned hybrid just three times, but the 2019 update mentions it on 12 occasions. And in September 2022, in a rare public address, Dermot Woods – the State's most senior civil servant responsible for national security – identified hybrid threats as among the most pressing international risks facing Ireland.[26]

There is a growing realisation that neutrality is a poor shield against modern threats, even if concrete actions remain lacking. There is a Finnish proverb that concisely sums up the situation – it roughly translates as 'to be in the Lord's purse' (its Irish equivalent might be 'to be on the pig's back'). 'In the olden days, when life was simpler and less complex,' said Sareva, 'you were safe and sound in this purse. But of course, things have changed. And they will change further still.'[27]

Talonpoika put it more concisely still: 'The purse is now open.'[28]

CHAPTER SIXTEEN

MOUNTAINS, CHOCOLATE AND NUCLEAR WEAPONS

*Landlocked Switzerland: they're nice and neutral only
because they're tiny ...*
Marisha Pessl (2006)[1]

N ear the end of *The Third Man,* a tense noir thriller set in post-World War II Vienna, the dastardly Harry Lime makes an observation:

> In Italy, for thirty years under the Borgias, they had warfare, terror, murder, and bloodshed, but they produced Michelangelo, Leonardo da Vinci, and the Renaissance. In Switzerland, they had brotherly love, they had five hundred years of democracy and peace, and what did that produce? The cuckoo clock.[2]

It's undoubtedly the line of the film, perhaps of any film (it was written by Orson Welles, who played Lime). It's also almost completely wrong. For one thing, cuckoo clocks originated in southwest Germany, not Switzerland. And far from being a haven of brotherly love, Switzerland produced some of the fiercest mercenary soldiers in Europe – there's a reason the brightly coloured, armour-clad men patrolling the Vatican are called the Swiss Guard. Lastly, the country is a far greater producer of weapons of war than it is of timepieces: all of the Irish Defence Forces' Armoured Personnel Carriers come from Switzerland, as does much of its artillery and small arms; the standard-issue Garda handgun is also Swiss-made. Arms manufacturing has always been a mainstay of the Swiss industry. For a brief period, this even extended to nuclear weapons.

By the time the fictional Harry Lime uttered his immortal words in post-war Vienna, planning for the Swiss nuclear programme was well underway. The government wanted a nuclear deterrent against a possible Soviet invasion, something seen as a distinct possibility given that Soviet troops were across the border in Austria and Germany at the time. By 1964, a large amount of nuclear material had been obtained and a decision was made to produce 250 weapons, including ones that could be mounted to a jet and dropped on Moscow. Financial problems led to the programme being shelved shortly afterwards but the programme was not formally wound up until 1988 when the Cold War started to thaw. Even today, Switzerland refuses to sign the 2017 Treaty on the Prohibition of Nuclear Weapons for fear it might limit its future defence options.[3]

Switzerland's large arms industry and historical pursuit of weapons of mass destruction sit uneasily alongside its image as the world's quintessential neutral country. The concept of neutrality is as closely associated with the mountainous federal republic as chocolate and penknives. After all, the country didn't join the United Nations until 2002 over fears it would compromise neutrality. It stayed out of the Council of Europe until 1963 and even shied away from making trade deals with the EEC until 1972 over concerns that preferential dealings with one set of countries might upset the Soviet Union. In the end, Switzerland signed up for the trade deal on the condition it could withdraw during times of war. Unlike in Ireland, the concept of neutrality is well-established and well-understood by the Swiss. But like the Irish, the Swiss have also been willing to stretch its meaning, sometimes beyond breaking point, when it's in the national interest. This raises the question: if Switzerland isn't neutral, who is? Does the word have any meaning at all?

By some measures, the foundations of Swiss neutrality were laid in 1291 when three cantons united to establish a collective defence against interference by its powerful neighbours, particularly the Hapsburgs. However, for much of its early history, the Old Swiss Confederacy engaged in foreign wars just as much as other small European states. Neutrality took on a more definite character after the battle of Marignano in 1515, when the Swiss were beaten so badly by the French that they signed the Treaty of Fribourg (also known as the Treaty of Perpetual Peace), vowing never to attack France again or to support its enemies. In the aftermath of the battle, Switzerland gave up its Italian territory and put a permanent end to its expansionist ambitions. A century later it remained neutral in the Thirty Years' War, a complex and massively destructive conflict between Catholic and Protestant European powers. The decision to remain neutral was taken not due to an ideological commitment but because, given the mixture of faiths in the cantons of Switzerland, involvement would have undoubtedly torn the country apart. The war in ended in 1648 with the Peace of Westphalia, which formally cemented Switzerland's neutrality and its independence from the Holy Roman Empire.

And so, over the next two centuries, Swiss neutrality held out, with the country remaining a comparative island of peace in a violent continent. It remained a source of talented mercenaries for foreign armies but played no role as a state in the many European conflicts during this period.

Then came the French Revolution. Starting in 1790, the Revolutionary government in Paris started to dismantle the Old Swiss Confederacy, first by encouraging internal revolts and then by outright invasion. By 1789, the old aristocratic, federalist government was gone, replaced with the Helvetic Republic and a French puppet regime. Various battles of the French Revolutionary wars would take place on Swiss soil over the following years, but this was only a temporary, if bloody interruption, to Switzerland's experiment with neutrality. In 1815, the Congress of Vienna, which was tasked with reorganising Europe following Napoleon's defeat, guaranteed Switzerland's permanent neutrality. Again, ideology or morals had little to do with it; the victorious powers saw a neutral Switzerland as essential to future European stability as it would act as a buffer between France and Austria.

During World War I, Switzerland was spared invasion by both sides. Germany had initially considered attacking France through Swiss territory under the Schlieffen Plan but in the end fellow neutral Belgium offered an easier path. Maintaining neutrality during the four-year conflict was no easy task for Switzerland and involved the careful positioning of its 450,000-strong army. Even then there were hundreds of incursions into Swiss territory by both sides during the conflict. The greatest threat to neutrality was the Grimm–Hoffmann affair in 1917, when renegade Swiss socialist politician Robert Grimm, with the support of Swiss Federal Councillor Arthur Hoffmann, travelled to Russia to attempt to negotiate a separate peace between Germany and Russia, a move that enraged the Allied powers and forced the Swiss government to engage in some hasty damage control.

Similar challenges presented themselves during World War II. Again Switzerland stood up its army, this time mobilising over 800,000 troops, and again it was subject to many incursions, and occasional bombing, by the belligerents. On multiple occasions, the military shot down Axis and Allied aircraft that strayed into Swiss airspace. This policy of deterrence through force of arms, combined with clever diplomatic and economic manoeuvres and Switzerland's mountainous terrain, meant it saw out the war with its sovereignty intact. Against the odds, neutrality won the day once again.

This whistle-stop tour of Swiss history suggests a country that practices neutrality both in letter and in spirit. Unlike Ireland, Swiss neutrality is deeply embedded in its history and is clearly defined and understood by the population. But dig a little deeper and many exceptions can be found. Swiss neutrality, it turns out, can be just as flexible as the Irish version. Take the League of Nations, for example. Worried about the spread of the Bolshevik revolution, Switzerland signed up as a full member in 1920 and agreed to host the League's headquarters in Geneva. Under the terms of its membership, the League recognised

Switzerland's permanent neutrality and exempted it from any military obligations. However, Switzerland was willing to commit to adhering to economic sanctions mandated by the League, a major departure from pure neutrality. This remained its position until 1938 when, in light of the increasing irrelevancy of the League, it withdrew its commitment to sanctions.

During World War II, it is undoubtable that Swiss economic policies favoured Nazi Germany far more than the Allies. Some of this can be explained, if not excused, by geography – by 1940, Switzerland was entirely surrounded by the Axis powers – but some of it was motivated entirely by greed. Many Swiss companies finished the war with far more wealth than at the start. Swiss banks purchased vast amounts of gold from the Nazis, much of which had been looted from Holocaust victims or the treasuries of occupied countries: 77 per cent of German gold exports were arranged through Switzerland. In return for the gold, Germany received Swiss francs, which it was able to use on the international market to purchase raw materials for the war effort.

A 2002 report commissioned by the Swiss government on its relationship with Nazi Germany said, 'Among the few neutral countries, Switzerland made the greatest contribution towards the German war effort since it was Switzerland which had the greatest presence in both Germany itself and the countries it occupied.'[4] Swiss banks also loaned substantial amounts to German armament companies, while Swiss companies based in Germany availed of Nazi slave labour. In comparison with the financial assistance offered, the sale of Swiss armaments to Germany was small. However, precision Swiss goods, such as bomb sight components and machine tools, were vital to the war effort.

Most shameful was Switzerland's acquiescence in Germany's treatment of its Jewish community. The Swiss government asked Germany to stamp a 'J' on the passports of its Jewish citizens so they could be treated differently from other refugees, and when Hitler stripped citizenship from German Jews, Switzerland declared German Jews living there to be stateless. Some Swiss companies in Germany fired their Jewish employees, even before they were legally required to do so by the authorities. Some even fired Jewish employees who worked back in Switzerland. In 1942, Switzerland stopped admitting refugees, a measure that disproportionately affected Jews and led to thousands being murdered in the death camps. Although not directly relevant to neutrality, these measures showed the lengths the Bern government was willing to go to avoid angering Hitler. For many years after the war ended, Swiss banks continued to make it extremely difficult for Holocaust survivors to claim their savings.

According to a 1986 study of Switzerland's wartime economy by historian Jakob Tanner, 60 per cent of Swiss armaments and 80 per cent of its electrical equipment went to Germany.[5] After the war, Swiss officials defended this record by saying that, while it may have assisted the Nazis, it also assisted the Allies. Like Ireland with Britain, it may have shown a 'certain consideration' for Germany, but this was only in pursuit of the greater goal of avoiding invasion. But that was not how many Allied leaders saw it. Swiss assistance to Germany had 'materially decreased the military effectiveness of (Allied) air attacks on the Axis,' US Admiral William Leahy, chairman of the Joint Chiefs of Staff wrote in 1943, as he urged sanctions be imposed on the country.[6] Curiously, this view was not shared by Winston Churchill, who had been so angered by Irish neutrality. In 1944 he said:

> Of all the neutrals, Switzerland has the greatest right to distinction [...] What does it matter whether she has been able to give us the commercial advantages we desire or has given too many to the Germans, to keep herself alive? She has been a democratic State, standing for freedom in self-defence among her mountains, and in thought, despite of race, largely on our side.[7]

Despite Churchill's glowing endorsement, the status of Swiss neutrality took a beating after the war in light of its preferential treatment of Germany. However, it stood by the policy of neutrality, even as it was abandoned by other small nations that were not lucky enough to avoid invasion. When the United Nations was established in 1945,

Switzerland said it could not become a member unless it received a derogation from the collective security obligations. So it was no surprise when it also declined NATO membership. America was initially keen to have Switzerland as a member but quickly realised this was unlikely and did not issue a formal invitation. Like Ireland, Switzerland would be nice to have, but not essential. It was already surrounded by NATO troops and capable of defending itself against Soviet attack, at least for a time, meaning that from a strategic point of view, America could live with Switzerland's neutrality. At this point, neutrality had become a core tenet of Swiss foreign and security policy, one that was defined by non-membership of international alliances and the maintenance of enough military power to discourage would-be attackers.

But here, too, Swiss neutrality was not as pure as it appeared. It was one of the first countries to sign up to the Marshall Plan – the massive injection of US aid designed to rebuild Europe and prevent the rise of socialist or communist governments. This is despite Switzerland suffering almost no damage in the war. In 1951, Switzerland secretly signed the Hotz-Linder-Agreement, committing it to US-led economic sanctions on the Soviet Union. The agreement, which only became public in 1987, 'clearly contradicted Switzerland's official policy of neutrality', observed Swiss security expert Christian Nünlist.[8] At around the same time, extensive, if unofficial, collaboration was taking place between Switzerland and the Western allies to help the country resist a Soviet attack. For Switzerland, ensuring it was perceived as neutral was sometimes more important than actually being neutral. This meant its coordination with NATO took place in the deepest secrecy.

So secret was this programme that much of the coordination took place during meetings with Britain's Bernard Montgomery, by then a field marshal, while he was ostensibly on skiing holidays in the country. Montgomery's goal was to convince Switzerland to cooperate with the Western European Union (WEU) military alliance in the event of war breaking out. The Swiss government responded that it could only contemplate collaboration if a Soviet invasion of Swiss territory seemed imminent. Nevertheless, it started to expand its airfields so it could accommodate NATO aircraft and began purchasing military equipment in bulk from Britain. Montgomery eventually convinced the Swiss to alter their defence plans so that, rather than simply trying to defend Swiss territory, its army would act in concert with NATO forces in the face of a Soviet invasion.

The country did not enter into an air defence agreement with NATO but that didn't deter the latter from including Switzerland in its defence plans for Western Europe. This suited the Swiss as it allowed them to retain the pretence of neutrality. According to Nünlist, the Swiss Chief of Staff Louis de Montmollin told Montgomery that Switzerland would prefer Western fighters to shoot down Soviet aircraft in its airspace before waiting for an official appeal for help. 'The Swiss would turn a blind eye,' Montgomery was assured.[9] Of course, there is no legal barrier to a neutral country appealing for outside help if it is invaded. But it is difficult to claim neutrality if detailed defence plans are already in place prior to a conflict. Hence the secrecy.

One particularly fascinating deviation from neutrality went by the name Projekt-26, or P-26 for short. This was a top-secret programme launched in 1979, aimed at establishing a 'stay-behind army', which would fight a guerrilla war if the Soviet Union were to overrun the country and defeat Swiss conventional forces. The existence of P-26 emerged in the 1990s at the same time as revelations of shady stay-behind armies in multiple other European countries. The most controversial of these was in Italy, where the secret army took on a specifically anti-communist character and was accused of multiple instances of terrorism and criminal activity. By comparison, the P-26 organisation, which was hidden inside the Swiss intelligence services, was quite benign. Nevertheless, it was found by a 1991 Swiss parliamentary inquiry to be without 'political or legal legitimacy'.

Unlike other stay-behind organisations, P-26 does not appear to have been controlled by NATO and it probably never numbered more than 400 people. However, the inquiry found it engaged in 'intense' collaboration with British forces, including probably the SAS, and that, such was its secrecy, British officials often knew more about it than the Swiss government.[10] As recently as 1987, Swiss troops were travelling to the UK for training in combat, communications, and sabotage. According to Swiss historian Daniele Ganser, this training may have even extended to live operations; one Swiss military instructor claimed to have taken part in a real-world attack on an IRA arms depot during which one paramilitary was killed.[11]

With the end of the Cold War, Switzerland moved towards a policy it called 'security through cooperation'. NATO and EU membership were not considered but, like Ireland, the country opted to increase its cooperation with these organisations. Unlike its Cold War cooperation, this would be done in public. After much public debate, Switzerland signed up to NATO's PfP programme in 1996, two years after fellow neutrals Finland and Sweden and three years before Ireland. On joining, Switzerland said it would not take part in any PfP training relating to collective defence and since then, its participation has focused on the softer types of military operations, such as demining, medical education and, of course, mountaineering. Nevertheless, participation has been highly beneficial to the Swiss military, Nünlist said, particularly the PARP, which has increased interoperability with NATO members.

Entry into PfP coincided with Switzerland's first foray into international peacekeeping when it sent a small contingent of troops under the banner of the OSCE to Sarajevo in Bosnia. It was a tentative step; in a referendum two years before, Swiss voters had rejected the deployment of armed peacekeepers overseas, meaning the troops in Bosnia were entirely unarmed. As a result, they had to be protected at all times by Austrian soldiers. Swiss peacekeeping began in earnest in 1999 when it contributed a company of troops, known as Swisscoy, to the NATO-led peacekeeping mission in Kosovo. Swisscoy remains there today. Swiss law was changed in 2001 to allow these soldiers to carry weapons but they engage only in peace support operations and not peace enforcement.

Like Ireland, Switzerland also contributed a small number of officers to the NATO-led ISAF in Afghanistan in 2001 but withdrew them in 2008 when the operation started to place a greater focus on battling the Taliban rather than reconstruction. Despite the withdrawal, Switzerland remains committed to the NATO-led mission in Kosovo and, aside from some concerns about NATO's confrontational stance towards Russia following the 2014 invasion of Ukraine, it has no intention of withdrawing from PfP. It is notable that Switzerland's major peacekeeping missions have taken place almost entirely under NATO rather than a UN banner. A sign of its continued commitment to NATO as a PfP member was the hosting of the NATO Partnerships 360 Symposium in Geneva in 2022. It was the first time this major NATO summit was held in a non-NATO country.

The other major event in Switzerland's relationship with neutrality occurred in September 2002 when the Swiss cantons voted on finally joining the UN. It was a divisive campaign, with Swiss nationalists arguing it would mean the end of neutrality and even independence. After all, the UN Charter committed members to implement the decisions of the Security Council, including sanctions and military action. These arguments were also made in 1986 when the Swiss voted by a ratio of three to one not to apply for membership. But, as we have seen, much of the UN Charter amounts to little more than words on a page, and in practice, membership imposes no military obligations on countries.

Before the 2002 referendum, the Swiss government campaigned hard for a yes vote. The world had changed since the September 11 attacks, and collective security, even the watered-down version offered by the UN, had become a much less controversial idea. Switzerland was also eager to repair its international reputation following the damaging revelations in the 1990s regarding its wartime Nazi collaboration and allegations of hoarding Jewish gold. The proposal passed by the narrowest of margins, with 12 cantons voting yes and 11 voting no, and Switzerland became the organisation's 190th member. In reality, aside from finally giving it a vote in the General Assembly, UN membership had relatively little practical effect on Swiss foreign policy. It was already a supplier of peacekeepers and election observers and for years it had voluntarily complied with UN sanctions. It was also one of the biggest donors to UN programmes in the world before membership, contributing almost $300 million per year.

Modern Swiss history is replete with examples where neutrality was not strictly adhered to, but it's important not to overstate the point. For every example of Switzerland straying from neutrality, there is another of it sticking rigidly to the concept, sometimes to the point of zealotry. Take its stance on the export of arms to Ukraine for example: under Swiss law, purchasers of Swiss armaments must seek permission from Bern if they wish to transfer the supplies to a third country. After Russia's invasion, Germany and Denmark requested permission to ship Swiss-made infantry, fighting vehicles, and anti-aircraft ammunition to Ukraine's military. Citing neutrality, the Swiss denied the request, saying its arms cannot be supplied to countries engaged in active conflict. Switzerland also refused to grant EU countries permission to fly over its territory when transporting arms to Ukraine. This is despite Swiss arms being used in conflicts around the world, including by Saudi Arabia in Yemen.

And while it did cooperate extensively with NATO, this cooperation pales in comparison to that of some other neutral countries. Sweden, for example, had various top-secret but officially approved cooperation plans with NATO during the Cold War, including prepared plans to rapidly evacuate the royal family to an Alliance country if the Soviets invaded. So intense was the cooperation that Sweden, while outwardly portraying an image of strict neutrality, became known within NATO as its unofficial 'seventeenth member'.[12] The two other major EU neutrals, Austria and Finland, also bent neutrality further than the Swiss. Austria accepted huge amounts of military aid from the US during the Cold War and shared plans for troop manoeuvres with NATO in the event of invasion. Conversely, Finland made every effort to ensure its foreign policies did nothing to aggravate the Soviet bear on its doorstep. Historically, in comparison with the other major European neutrals, Swiss cooperation with NATO was minor. It was perhaps most similar to Ireland's: unofficial, ill-defined, and secretive.

It must also be stressed that, like in Ireland, neutrality remains remarkably popular in Switzerland, with the invasion of Ukraine denting that popularity only slightly. A January 2022 poll found an incredible 97 per cent of people were in favour of the principle of neutrality and only 26 per cent were in favour of joining NATO.[13] Another taken in June 2022, four months after Russia's full-scale invasion, showed 89 per cent in favour of neutrality in principle and 27 per cent in favour of NATO membership. Support for EU membership was even lower, with those in favour of membership never climbing above 20 per cent.[14]

There is a debate going on in Switzerland about what it means to be neutral. Generally speaking, those on the right want to pursue a traditional, pure neutrality, no matter how impractical that may be, while the left favours a more active neutrality involving external cooperation with NATO and the EU on security matters. Unlike in Ireland, this debate is founded on a well-understood definition of what neutrality means in practice. The knowledge base is high thanks in part to the close relationship between the Swiss public and its military. Switzerland is one of the last countries in Western Europe with mandatory military service. At the age of 18, every Swiss male is assessed for suitability for military service and about two-thirds end up enlisting, with the rest having to pay higher rates of tax until they are 37.

Conscripts are expected to serve a certain number of days every year until they are 34 and to take their weapons home with them afterwards. The total size and budget of the military have decreased significantly in recent years, but Switzerland still maintains a force of about 140,000 personnel, with another 1.5 million citizens available for service should the need arise. This translates to about 1.6 military personnel for every 100 people, compared to about 0.2 for Ireland when reservists are included. For the Swiss, the military is part of the fabric of everyday life.

Knowledge of such security issues is also aided by the country's system of direct democracy, where decisions that in any other country would be a matter for government, are put to the people in regular votes. Matters such as conscription, the size of the army and even the acquisition of new equipment are sometimes the subject of referendums. For example, in 2022, there was to have been a public vote on plans to purchase 36 F-35 fighter jets for the Swiss Air Force at a cost of €6.25 billion. It was only called off when the government controversially pushed the deal through so as not to miss the delivery window.

'The majority of the people think of neutrality as part of Swiss identity,' said Ambassador Pälvi Pulli, head of security policy at the Swiss Federal Department of Defence. Pulli has a clear-eyed view of her country's neutrality: Switzerland didn't become neutral for moral reasons; it was made neutral by the Congress of Vienna because it suited the European powers to have a buffer state between France and Austria. Since then neutrality has developed into an effective security policy which allowed the country to avoid the destruction of two world wars.

That's not to say there is not a moral aspect of Swiss neutrality, Pulli added. Its independence from power blocs means Switzerland has been able to maintain a tradition of 'good offices'; in other words, it functions as a peace broker between countries who cannot contemplate talking to each other directly. For example, Switzerland facilitates communications between Georgia and Russia and between Iran and various Western nations. In 2022, it offered to help mediate between Ukraine and Russia, an offer Moscow rejected as it said it no longer viewed Switzerland as neutral due to it signing up to EU sanctions. But being a peacemaker is a helpful side effect of neutrality, not its goal. Besides, as Pulli points out, other decidedly non-neutral countries have also established solid reputations as peacemakers on the world stage, most notably Norway.

De Valera defended neutrality during World War II by arguing that joining the Allied side would tear the country apart, thanks to partition and lingering anger from the War of Independence. For Pulli, neutrality played a similarly historical role in keeping Switzerland together:

> We have major language groups like German speakers and French speakers and even Italian speakers. And if there was a major war going on between France and Germany in the 19th century, there was a risk that the country would be torn apart. So you could say that this was also another function of neutrality.

This is not much of a concern today but as the polls show, Swiss neutrality is not going anywhere. Nevertheless, like in Ireland, the definition is shifting: 'It's been a very lively topic in the recent weeks and months in relation to the war [in Ukraine], much more than there was before,' said Pulli. Switzerland is interested in greater cooperation with EU defence initiatives, particularly PESCO projects, which are open to third countries and it is currently considering signing up to the PESCO cyber defence training project, which could help in better protecting the country's networks. The idea of closer cooperation with NATO is also gaining support and will be the subject of a forthcoming government report. According to Pulli:

> This will look at how far we can push cooperation with these organisations while remaining neutral in the sense of the law of neutrality, which is quite narrowly defined. The law simply means that a neutral country is not supporting militarily a party in armed conflict.

Applying for full NATO membership is, however, not on the cards: 'It seems like a remote possibility due to historical reasons and how neutrality is rooted in Swiss people's DNA,' said Pulli. The country is also facing fewer urgent security fears than other prospective Alliance members. Nestled in the middle of stable, democratic EU states, Switzerland is not in the same geopolitical boat as Sweden and Finland. But, interestingly, Pulli also declined to completely rule out membership: 'The last few months maybe provide us some food for thought that one should never say never.'[15]

If neutrality is a spectrum, Switzerland is much closer to the ideal than Ireland. It at least deals with the topic head-on and is willing to fund the defence of its neutrality. But, as we have seen, it is still far from a pure neutral. It faces many of the same challenges in this area as Ireland, including how to deal with hybrid threats or ensure interoperability with other peacekeeping forces. Both countries have an imperfect relationship with neutrality. Ever-evolving European defence cooperation, a worsening global security environment and the subcontracting of peacekeeping to bodies like the EU and NATO, means this relationship is only set to become more confused.

Because of this, the term 'post-neutral' has become increasingly popular in academic circles as a description for Ireland, Switzerland, Austria, Sweden and Finland. It's certainly an apt description for the latter two countries given their decision to apply for NATO membership in 2022. But some academics go further, arguing that membership or cooperation with the EU, NATO and even the UN is incompatible with neutrality, given the role of all three organisations in collective security. If this is indeed the case, then no one is neutral, and Ireland is much less of an odd one out in Europe than it may at first appear.

CHAPTER SEVENTEEN

SLICING THE SALAMI

*There is no such thing as, if you like, complete military
neutrality ...*
Minister for Defence Michael Smith (January 2003)[1]

Three place names loom large in the minds of EU military officials when they think about security: Rwanda, Srebrenica and Sarajevo. In the 1990s, these places witnessed unimaginable violence directed against civilian populations. The first two were acts of genocide directed against Rwandan Tutsis and Bosnian Muslims respectively and the latter was a three-year siege which killed thousands of civilians. 'There was genocide at our doorstep and we could do nothing about it,' said Brigadier General Ger Buckley, Ireland's representative to the EU Military Committee (EUMC). The ethnic violence in Srebrenica and Sarajevo occurred just a few hours' drive from Vienna but the EU 'absolutely lacked that military or crisis management power to intervene [...] The EU couldn't act and NATO didn't want to act,' he said. Aside from the moral imperative to stop genocide, Buckley believes it is in the EU's interests to maintain stability in its neighbourhood. As demonstrated by the Mediterranean migrant crisis or the seizure of territory by Islamic terror organisations in Africa and the Middle East, violence outside Europe has a way of impacting EU citizens.

For Buckley and his colleagues, Rwanda, Srebrenica and Sarajevo serve as lessons in why the EU requires the ability to intervene in crisis situations in its neighbourhood. More specifically, they believe it's why the Union requires a Rapid Deployment Capacity (RDC) – a military force capable of deploying quickly to trouble spots and stabilising dangerous situations pending the deployment of a more permanent force. According to Buckley, Ireland is to contribute a company of soldiers, numbering up to 120 (rising to some 170 when support staff are included). These will be attached to the German-led group, meaning they will be the first to be activated when the RDC becomes operational. Under current plans, Irish troops will form up in January 2024 for six months of on-island training before going abroad for multinational certification for another six months. They will then remain on standby in Ireland for another year. 'It is quite a contribution for the Defence Forces to make,' said Buckley.[2]

In many ways, the RDC concept mirrors the existing EU Battlegroups system, of which Ireland was also a participant, so much so that many people simply refer to it with the same name. The first EU Battlegroup units were activated in 2005 with a similar purpose in mind – they were designed to deploy at short notice outside EU borders and carry out a wide variety of tasks, including peace enforcement, disarmament, search and rescue and humanitarian tasks – although then they numbered only 1,500 troops and served for six months at a time rather than twelve. Since then, despite numerous crises where they could have been useful, not a single Battlegroup has been deployed on an operation. This has been blamed on a lack of political will as well as bureaucratic barriers. It's also down to the fact that, until 2017, the EU lacked the required military headquarters support. It was decided that a more flexible, powerful capability was needed, supported by a genuine military command structure. As with most things EU-related, negotiations on establishing the replacement for the Battlegroups were slow. But the increasing uncertainty resulting from Brexit, the election of Donald Trump, the rise of the Islamic State, the fall of Afghanistan to the Taliban and increased Russian aggression focused minds and in March 2022, EU leaders reached a final agreement on the RDC concept.

Domestically, Ireland's agreement to participate in the RDC is likely to become the next battleground for neutrality, despite the fact the Defence Forces have been contributing bomb disposal specialists to the Nordic EU Battlegroup since 2006. For Buckley and other senior EU officials, the RDC is required in order to prevent genocide and failed states on the EU's doorstep. For neutrality activists, it's the latest effort by a duplicitous government to erode what remains of Irish neutrality. Inevitably, as occurred when the original Battlegroups were established in 2005, the RDC is being framed by some as the next step towards a European army, an amorphous phrase which means, depending on the needs of the speaker, anything from an EU mutual defence agreement to a massive monolithic military force that will conscript young Irish people and send them to die on foreign battlefields. Raising the RDC concept during a Dáil debate on neutrality in March 2022, Richard Boyd Barrett of People Before Profit–Solidarity called it 'the embryo of a European army'.[3] For the strongest proponents of Irish neutrality, the RDC is the latest example of what is sometimes called 'salami slicing': a gradual reduction of neutrality, slice by slice until there is nothing left.

Looking at the history of the European project to date, it's hard to argue against this. Cooperation between Ireland and NATO, through PfP and otherwise, remains stalled, with Irish governments having neither the will nor the public support for further integration; Irish officials are refusing to move up to even the next phase of PfP, never mind pursuing full NATO membership. EU defence integration is quite a different matter. Since Ireland joined the EEC in 1972, it's been a long road of incremental but ever-increasing defence cooperation, albeit with some major speedbumps along the way, in the form of the Nice and Lisbon treaties. The invasion of Ukraine in February 2022 has accelerated this process further, as demonstrated by Denmark's reversal of its 30-year-opt-out from EU defence matters, and the tonnes of weapons and billions of dollars sent to Ukraine's military through EU institutions. 'It's all changed now since the Russian invasion of Ukraine, which to me is Europe's 9/11,' said Charlie Flanagan, chair of the Oireachtas Committee on Foreign Affairs and a former minister for foreign affairs. He called the invasion 'a wake-up call for Europe … and for Ireland as to where we stand in terms of defence and security and our so-called neutrality.'[4] Flanagan and Boyd Barrett stand at opposite ends of the divide on neutrality, but both seem to be in agreement on the fact that, when it comes to the EU, the concept is at a crossroads.

European leaders have, on occasion, been accused of trying to introduce a defence union by stealth. In fact, for some of the founders of the European project, it's been an overtly stated ambition from the start. One of the forebears of the EEC was the European Defence Community (EDC), a union of France, Italy, West Germany and the Benelux countries. The EDC would have entailed not just a NATO-style mutual defence clause, but a pan-community military comprising 43 divisions; a true European army. These plans died on the vine in 1954 when the treaty establishing the EDC was rejected by the French National Assembly. Just three years later, in 1957, the same countries signed the Treaty of Rome, establishing the EEC and taking the first small step towards a genuine European defence union.

No one can claim Irish leaders were not aware of these intentions from the start. Various Irish leaders made it explicitly clear that they believed EEC membership would eventually entail the abandonment of neutrality at some undefined point in the future. In July 1962, after Ireland made its first unsuccessful bid for membership of the EEC, Taoiseach Seán Lemass, who had always been sceptical of the concept of neutrality, told the *New York Times*:

> We recognise that a military commitment will be a consequence of our joining the Common Market and ultimately we are prepared to yield even the technical label of neutrality. We are prepared to go into this integrated Europe without any reservation as to how far this will take us in the field of foreign policy and defence.[5]

In 1969, Lemass's successor, Jack Lynch, made a similar point, stating that neutrality was not relevant in the decision to join the EEC but that 'being members of that community, we would naturally be interested in the defence of the territories embraced by the communities. There is no question of neutrality there.'[6] The following year, Lynch's Minister for Foreign Affairs Patrick Hillery went further again and said that Ireland 'will be part' of a common defence force if it is a member of a 'fully developed' European Community.[7] This attitude of openness towards a European defence arrangement continued well after Ireland was finally admitted to the EEC in 1972. Being a member of the community does not involve Ireland in any military obligations, but Ireland 'would be prepared to participate in arrangements for its defence, if called upon to do so,' said Minister for Foreign Affairs Brian Lenihan in November 1980.[8] Historian Ronan Fanning noted that during this period, and up to the end of the 1970s, government spokesmen preferred to mention neutrality as little as possible.[9] Much later, former Taoiseach Garret FitzGerald, another neutrality sceptic, said one of the myths of neutrality was that Ireland was somehow in the dark about the eventual defence obligations of the EEC when it first joined.[10] Writing in 1999, he said, 'every Irish taoiseach from 1960 to the 1990s rejected the concept of neutrality and accepted eventual Irish participation in European defence.'[11]

Despite the comments of Lemass and others, when Ireland was finally admitted to the EEC in 1972, the prospect of defence cooperation seemed so remote that most people, government ministers included, believed it did not merit much thought. At the time every other EEC member was also a NATO member, but this also raised little public concern about the implications for Irish neutrality. 'It wasn't a threatening time militarily and it was a period of détente in terms of the Cold War,' said Keatinge. Before the referendum on taking up EEC membership, RTÉ ran a series of televised debates on what it would mean for the country. Keatinge recalls taking part in the debate on neutrality. 'Afterwards, RTÉ lost the can and didn't try to replace it. So they never broadcast on that issue. So I think that was a sign of it not being a huge issue at that time.'[12] The referendum passed with 83 per cent of voters approving membership.

But once in, Irish officials realised there were several immediate factors that could in theory impinge on neutrality. The most significant of these was European Political Co-operation (EPC). This involved reg-ular meetings with member states' foreign ministers, where they would discuss issues of mutual concern and attempt, through consensus, to devise a common EC/EEC position. The most pressing issues it faced were relations with the crumbling Soviet Union and violence in the Middle East. While EPC members did discuss common security con-cerns, this was done in an extremely limited way. For example, military responses to security concerns were strictly off the table. And countries were entirely free to forge their own foreign policy positions, as Ireland frequently did on positions such as disarmament and the issue of sanc-tions against Argentina during the Falklands War. Crucially, the EPC was intergovernmental in nature, meaning that, while ministers tried to work towards joint positions, this took place outside the structures of the EEC/EC. One Irish diplomatic involved in the early days of the EPC recalled that this sometimes resulted in mildly farcical situations, such as in 1973 when foreign ministers met one morning in Brussels as the Council of Ministers, and then all flew to Copenhagen that afternoon for an EPC meeting. Looking back today, the ambitions of the EPC seem almost quaint. It was non-binding, purely intergovernmental and dealt only with the softer end of security issues. But it was also the first step along a path towards making the community a true security actor on the world stage. And Ireland was along for the ride.

The 1980s saw further steps along this path, first in the form of the Single European Act (SEA). Its main objective was to establish the single market but it was also designed to meet an appetite for greater EC foreign policy cohesion through a strengthened EPC structure. Domestically, around the time the SEA was first drafted in 1985, opposition to greater European integration was starting to coalesce around the issue of neu-trality, as well as fears over loss of control over taxation and abortion legislation. Nevertheless, the majority of Irish people still supported closer integration and the economic benefits it promised, and the gov-ernment was confident it would face little opposition to its decision to ratify the treaty in 1986.

These hopes were dashed with the lodging of a Supreme Court

challenge by economist and anti-integration activist Raymond Crotty, who argued that the State could not delegate foreign policy functions to the EPC without it being authorised via referendum.

In a landmark decision in April 1987, the Supreme Court agreed: the SEA, and every subsequent treaty involving a significant change to EC structures, would have to be put to the Irish people. This would put Ireland in the unique position of being able to scupper, or at least stall, any future attempts at integration for the whole European Community. It would also turn every subsequent European treaty into a battleground on the question of Irish neutrality.

The next month, the SEA was put to the Irish people. The result was resounding, with 70 per cent approving. However, for supporters of the European project, the devil was in the detail. The turnout was just 44 per cent, the second lowest in State history until then, and the yes vote was down significantly when compared to the 83 per cent who voted to join the EEC 15 years previously. Furthermore, 40 per cent of the people who voted no said they feared the SEA was a threat to Irish neutrality. Mindful of this demographic, the government set down its first marker in favour of neutrality on the European stage when it ratified the treaty that June. Along with the SEA's ratification instrument, it lodged a 'declaration of neutrality', which referred to 'Ireland's long-established policy of military neutrality' and emphasised that coordination of EC security policy did not include military matters, and did not impede Ireland's right to abstain from anything which might impact neutrality.[13] It was a significant departure from the ambivalent attitudes of Lemass and Lynch.

But the statement did little to assuage the fears of the anti-EC lobby, and the debates that started during the SEA process continued when the Maastricht Treaty was put to a referendum in 1992. As well as transforming the EC into the EU, Maastricht set the stage for what would become known as the Common Foreign and Security Policy (CFSP). This replaced the EPC and placed foreign policy decisions within EU structures. It also required unanimity among member states in decision-making. In the run-up to the vote, opponents such as the Campaign for Nuclear Disarmament argued the CFSP would strip Ireland of any foreign policy independence and would force it to go along with the decisions of its more militaristic neighbours. The prospect of a European army and even the conscription of Irish people were also raised by opposition groups. These concerns were easily dismissed. The treaty contained nothing that could be compared to a standing army, never mind conscription, and on the foreign policy front, member states were still free to pursue their own policy if agreement couldn't be reached within EU structures.

Less easy to discount, however, were the repeated references in the Treaty to 'the eventual framing of a common defence policy, which might in time lead to a common defence'. For the first time, it was spelt out in black and white: the ambition of the EU was to one day transform itself into a NATO-style alliance. But the treaty also contained an important phrase that would become very familiar to Irish people over the coming years: Maastricht stated it 'shall not prejudice the specific character of the security and defence policy of certain Member States'.[14] This maddeningly vague caveat was a way of assuring Ireland, which was still the only neutral member of the union, that nothing would happen regarding common defence without its assent. It was enough for the Irish electorate and the treaty passed with a 69 per cent yes vote, just a hair lower than the SEA vote.

All of this played out again with the Amsterdam Treaty vote in 1998. EU inaction in the face of ongoing violence in Albania, Africa and the former Yugoslavia, had shown up the CFSP as a largely empty suit. More was needed to make the EU genuinely capable of bringing security to its neighbourhood. Amsterdam reiterated its ambition to move towards a common defence union and put in place mechanisms that would allow the EU to deploy armed forces to achieve its security goals. Under the treaty, it would be able to deploy military groupings for tasks ranging from traditional peacekeeping and humanitarian assistance to peacemaking missions, at the point of a gun if necessary. It also laid out plans for cooperation in the field of arms purchases for member states and created the role of a High Representative for the CFSP, a single person who would represent the security interests of the EU.

The treaty also contained the usual caveats that allowed the Irish government to credibly maintain that its military neutrality was unaffected: security matters still required unanimous votes and Ireland could not be forced to take part in a CFSP mission. Importantly for Ireland, Amsterdam also solidified the concept of constructive abstention. This meant Ireland could abstain from a security decision – for example, the deployment of troops to a trouble spot – without blocking it entirely. This allowed it to remain a good EU partner while still having some regard for neutrality.

The referendum campaign played out as before, with neutrality campaigners warning of an increasingly militaristic union intent on embarking on colonial adventures, and the government claiming that neutrality would in no way be impacted. Ministers argued Amsterdam would solidify Ireland's version of 'positive neutrality' by allowing it to contribute peacekeepers on more effective missions through EU structures, while still requiring a UN mandate. As in previous referendums, some of the anti-treaty campaigners put forward far-fetched arguments, including that it would see British troops returning to take over Irish barracks.[15] The impenetrable nature of the treaty made these claims possible; the language was so thick and vague that it was difficult for even politically engaged citizens to understand that these propositions were not based in reality. Nevertheless, in May 1998, on the same day the electorate voted overwhelmingly to accept the terms of the Good Friday Agreement, Irish people approved the Amsterdam Treaty. But, in the sign of things to come, the yes vote had dropped again, with only 62 per cent approving this time.

By the time Amsterdam was approved, a definite pattern was emerging. Every five years or so, a new treaty was presented, which forced the Irish people to consider the nature of neutrality. During this period, the position of successive governments changed from claiming Ireland would support an eventual European defence union to claiming such a thing would never come about. And even if it did, they argued, Ireland had secured such solid guarantees in the treaties that the principle of military neutrality would be in no danger. But, as politicians would find out, there was a growing number of people who were concerned about further EU integration, not just because of neutrality, but also over fears of a loss of Irish sovereignty in general. The government was also failing to appreciate that, for many Irish people, neutrality was about more than non-membership of a military alliance. It was about opposition, not just to war but to the arms trade, great power bullying and militarism in general. Rightly or wrongly, EU policies regarding the acquisition of military equipment and the deployment of troops outside the auspices of the UN were seen by some as just as big a threat to neutrality as joining a formal defence alliance.

Oddly, it took an EU treaty with minimal defence and security implications to drive this message home to the government. Compared to Maastricht and Amsterdam, the Treaty of Nice of 2002 made only incremental changes to EU security policy. All the big-ticket items had already been agreed upon; Nice was about putting down the administrative foundations to make them operational. One of the most controversial issues during the campaign was the proposed European Rapid Reaction Force (ERRF), which would later be known as the EU Battlegroups, the tip of the spear of the CFSP. Ireland would provide 850 troops as part of the Nordic Battlegroup.

But the structures needed for the Battlegroups system had little to do with Nice – these had already been agreed upon prior to the drafting of the treaty. Besides, Irish pro-treaty advocates argued, Irish troops would only be deployed under a UN mandate as per the triple lock system, and the Defence Forces had been carrying out similar tasks for decades. Nevertheless, the Battlegroups, and increased EU militarism in general, became tied up with the debate on Nice. In June 2001, in a shock defeat for the government, the electorate rejected the treaty, with 54 per cent voting no.

In their autopsy, government officials took some comfort from the extremely low turnout of just 35 per cent. The dominant view was that the no vote resulted from a lack of understanding of the treaty and dissatisfaction with other, unrelated government policies. One Department of Foreign Affairs official has since said that the no vote was partly related to anger over the Fianna Fáil Government breaking its promise two years previously to put PfP to a referendum. 'Wriggling out of the debate on the current meaning of Irish neutrality at that time might have seemed like a cute stroke,' Fintan O'Toole wrote in the *Irish Times* after the vote. 'All it did however was to shift that debate into the much less appropriate context of the Nice treaty.'[16] The post-election polling showed neutrality was indeed a factor in the no vote but that it was far from the main one. Just 12 per cent of those who voted no said neutrality was the reason compared with 39 per cent who cited a lack of information and under-standing of what the treaty entailed.[17] However, even if it hadn't been the main issue, neutrality was, without a doubt, on the minds of many of those who went to the polls. Afterwards, 40 per cent of poll respondents said they favoured a 'strengthening of Irish neutrality'.[18]

The government, concerned the vote could make Ireland a pariah in the EU, responded by announcing the Seville Declarations. At a meet-ing of the 14 EU governments in Seville in the aftermath of the no vote, Ireland made a formal declaration that its overseas deployments would be governed by the triple lock; that EU security and defence policy would not 'prejudice its traditional policy of military neutrality'; that there was no move towards an EU army; and that Europe would not activate a mutual defence arrangement without a referendum by the Irish people. For its part, the European Council made similar declarations and repeated the now well-worn phrase that Nice would not impinge the 'specific character of the security and defence policy of certain Member States'.[19] Much to the chagrin of anti-Nice campaigners, another referendum was held on 19 October. This time, voters were asked to approve the referendum and the insertion of an additional provision into the Constitution that the State would not take part in an EU common defence arrangement. While the Seville Declarations were symbolic, this addition to the Constitution put Irish neutrality on a legal footing for the first time in the 80-year history of the State, at least regarding the EU. This, combined with a much more effective yes campaign, was enough to swing the vote. The Treaty of Nice was finally accepted by Irish voters in October 2002, with 63 per cent voting yes.

The following year, the EU's ambitions of becoming a security actor became reality with the deployment of the first mission under the European Security and Defence Policy (later called the Common Security and Defence Policy – CSDP), which was the operational end of EU foreign policy. In March 2003, troops were deployed under an EU flag to the former Yugoslav Republic of Macedonia to monitor the implementation of a peace accord. The mission ended successfully seven months later, with EU High Representative for the CFSP Javier Solana noting that, at the time of Maastricht, few believed 'that only a decade later we would send out men in arms under the EU's flag'.[20]

A much more ambitious mission was launched in June of that year when 1,400 EU troops were deployed to the Democratic Republic of Congo to put a stop to increasing ethnic violence in the Ituri province, a task beyond the capabilities of the beleaguered UN force in the country. By September 2003, the EU force, which included two Irish headquarters officers, had largely secured the area, allowing the UN force to take over. For EU security policy it was a major milestone. For the first time, large numbers of EU troops had been deployed outside the continent, where they prevented what could have become a Rwanda-style massacre. It was the perfect CSDP mission; short and impactful. Over the following years, Irish involvement in these missions became regular. This culminated in the deployment of 400 Defence Forces personnel to keep the peace in Chad and the Central African Republic in 2007 as part of a 3,700-strong mission under the overall command of Irish Lieutenant General Pat Nash. The era of the EU peacekeeper had arrived.

All of these missions took place under a UN mandate, but from the point of view of neutrality campaigners, this was salami slicing in action. The EU was becoming, in part, a military institution, supported by a bewildering array of agencies, offices, taskforces, committees and bureaus. But the biggest slice was still to come, and it would take the form of a treaty agreed upon in Lisbon in December 2007. Most of the previous changes to EU defence and security had focused on what it could achieve outside its borders in terms of peacekeeping and crisis management. The Treaty of Lisbon focused on defending the EU from threats much closer to home. Rather than just stating an ambition, it contained concrete movement towards a genuine common defence arrangement in the form of Article 42.7, also known as the mutual defence clause. It states that, if a member state is a victim of armed aggression on its territory, 'the other Member States shall have towards it an obligation of aid and assistance by all the means in their power, in accordance with Article 51 of the United Nations Charter', which provides for a country's right to self-defence.[21]

The clause was adapted from the WEU, an unambiguous European mutual defence union, which by then was largely defunct. The Treaty of Lisbon included another, somewhat less controversial, provision known as the Solidarity Clause, which bound EU members to assist each other, including militarily if required, if one was the victim of a terrorist attack or natural or man-made disaster. The treaty also introduced the concept of 'enhanced cooperation' to defence matters, allowing groups of member states to move towards military integration without having to get the agreement of the entire bloc. It introduced the system of Permanent Structured Cooperation (PESCO), which would dramatically increase military cooperation on defence projects and procurement and would require members to increase their defence spending at a national level. Finally, it reiterated the ambition towards a full mutual defence union, a prospect that was becoming ever more realistic.

From a neutrality point of view, the actual text of the treaty was dramatic enough. But some anti-treaty campaigners went even further with fresh claims that the Treaty of Lisbon would mean conscription into an EU army. 'People told me their sons and daughters over 16 would be taken and put into this European army,' one pro-treaty campaigner said.[22] All the pro-treaty campaigners could do was point to the caveats built into the text that recognise the 'specific character' of Irish policy in defence matters.

When the referendum took place in June 2008, 53 per cent voted no and the government was back in crisis mode. In response to the rejection, some officials wondered if Ireland should seek a complete opt-out from EU military matters, like Denmark had done years previously. Eventually, the decision was taken to rerun the referendum after obtaining a series of guarantees from the other EU member states that 'Ireland's traditional policy of military neutrality' will be unaffected, as well as guarantees regarding abortion and taxation. Crucially, these guarantees allowed Ireland to determine what kind of assistance it would provide another EU state that came under attack. In theory, that assistance could amount to no more than political statements of support for the impacted country. It was a neat solution, one which did not require the treaty be reopened for negotiation and yet appeared to appease at least some of the no voters. In a second referendum in October 2009, the Treaty of Lisbon was approved with 67 per cent voting yes.

Despite all the opt-outs and caveats, Ireland was now subject to what appeared, on paper at least, to be very similar to a mutual defence clause. Under Article 42.7, if another EU nation was to come under attack, Ireland would be obliged to provide assistance, albeit not necessarily military assistance. While this was technically compatible with the government's increasingly narrow interpretation of military neutrality, it was wholly at odds with every other conceivable definition of the concept. The inclusion of the article in the Treaty of Lisbon was not something the Irish delegation was in favour of, according to one official involved in the negotiations. Its main backer was Greece, which wanted additional protections against possible attack by Turkey, something NATO could not provide as, awkwardly, both countries were members of the Alliance. Ireland went along with the inclusions, partly to be seen as a constructive EU partner, and partly because it was assured by the limited scope of the provision. All assistance would be intergovernmental, meaning EU institutions would not be involved, and Ireland's meagre Defence Forces meant it would be unlikely to be asked to provide military assistance in any event.

Nevertheless, placing Ireland under the obligations of Article 42.7 was arguably the most consequential decision for neutrality since the State refused to join NATO in the early 1950s. It is possible to get an idea of how 42.7 works by looking at the only time it has been invoked. On 13 November 2015, Paris was hit by a series of devastating terrorist attacks by the Islamic State, which left 137 dead. Three days later France invoked

42.7 in its fight against the terrorist group, a request that was granted in a unanimous decision by all 28 EU member states. Why France chose to opt for Article 42.7 instead of Article 222, which specifically deals with terrorist attacks, has been a topic of debate since. Part of the reason, it seems, is that France wanted to send a political signal by forcing member states to take a stand when it came to mutual defence.

France's main request was for help to defeat the Islamic State in the territory the group had claimed in Syria and Iraq. Ireland had neither the will nor the ability to do much in this area, but what it could do was relieve France of some of its UN-mandated tasks in Africa, thereby allowing French troops to be redeployed against Islamic State. In a largely symbolic move, Ireland agreed to increase its existing deployment to the EU Training Mission in Mali from 10 to 18 personnel. The outcome was that Ireland ended up providing military aid to France, albeit indirectly, despite obtaining a specific exemption from doing just that under the Lisbon Treaty. The backfilling of French troops in Africa allowed Dublin to demonstrate its commitment to EU solidarity while avoiding the possibility of sending troops to France, or, even more controversially, to the Middle East to fight the Islamic State.

The Paris attacks showed both the strength and weakness of 42.7. The agreement of all 28 member states to activate the clause sent a powerful message of solidarity. But not everyone took action; the purposely vague wording of the article permitted some EU member states to limit their assistance to flowery words of condolence. Among those who made no concrete offers of assistance were the neutral states of Austria and Malta, and NATO members Bulgaria and Croatia.[23] The episode demonstrated the broad range of interpretations among member states of the meaning of mutual defence. Some NATO members, particularly in Eastern Europe, were worried that further cooperation may undermine the positions of the Alliance as the primary defender of Europe. The Lisbon Treaty attempted to assuage these fears by making it clear NATO still holds supremacy in this area and that if a country activates Article 5 of the North Atlantic Treaty – which states that an attack on one member is an attack on all – it will take precedence over 42.7.

On the other end of the spectrum, Finland and Sweden have always regarded EU membership as entailing a common defence clause, even well before Lisbon. Finland believes its neutrality ended the day it joined the EU in 1995. The country's ambassador to Ireland, Raili Lahnalampi, said that joining the EU 'was predominantly a security-based decision, although that was not said so'. In the years since, her country's officials have been trying to gain clarity on whether other governments believe 42.7 to be a true mutual defence clause. 'Because as it's written, it's the same, if not stronger than Article 5 of NATO,' said Lahnalampi. 'We want to make it stronger, to make the EU members be bound by it.'[24] This is likely to be the case even after Finland formally completes its accession process to NATO. Given its 1,300km land border with Russia, it's not surprising Finland is seeking as much protection as possible. This raises the question of the future of 42.7 and EU common defence in general in the face of the EU's increasingly aggressive neighbours. What would Ireland do if an EU country suffered an armed attack, not by terrorists but by another nation?

Despite the interpretations of the Finnish government, 42.7 is well removed from NATO's Article 5. If someone were to attack an EU member, it would not be regarded as an attack on Ireland. Ireland would be required to send assistance, but the nature of that assistance would be up to the government. Citing legal scholars, Irish neutrality expert Karen Devine argued in 2009 that the caveats inserted in Lisbon to appease Ireland do not exempt it from an obligation to provide military assistance.[25] Events since then, limited though they are, suggest this is probably not the case, at least not from a legal standpoint. Ireland provided indirect military aid to France in 2015 but could have just as easily sat on its hands like Austria and Malta. It's reasonable to conclude that if, for example, Russia attacked Poland, Ireland would not be under any treaty obligations to get involved militarily.

But would the notion of EU solidarity make Ireland want to get involved anyway? Until it happens, it's an unanswerable question, but polling data from recent decades might provide some clues. It's tempting to view the no votes to Lisbon and Nice as ringing endorsements of neutrality when it comes to EU defence. Indeed, they are often framed by pro-neutrality campaigners as such, but the polls bear that out only to a very limited degree. Neutrality was cited as a factor by no voters after both referendums, but only a small minority. After Lisbon, just 10 per cent of no voters cited neutrality as the reason, behind not understanding the treaty (40 per cent), protecting Irish identity (20 per cent), and lack of trust in government (17 per cent). Furthermore, over the last three decades, polling has found that while support for neutrality has remained consistently high, there is also widespread support for increased EU military integration.[26] For some Irish people, EU common defence and neutrality are not mutually exclusive. This suggests either a deeply nuanced view of neutrality or a complete lack of understanding of what it means. Either way, a large proportion of the electorate, sometimes more than half, is comfortable with increasing EU defence cooperation. This proportion would surely only climb significantly if a fellow EU member came under attack.

Statements from EU leaders about the need for a common EU defence policy have become louder and more frequent in recent years. In a 2017 address, then President of the European Commission Jean-Claude Juncker called for a 'fully-fledged European Defence Union' by 2025.[27] Such sentiments, combined with the war in Ukraine, mean countries like Ireland can expect to come under renewed pressure to consider their positions in the years ahead.

CHAPTER EIGHTEEN

THE SLEEPING BEAUTY

It is time to wake the sleeping beauty up!
President of the EU Commission Jean-Claude Juncker (2017)[1]

On 15 October 2022, around 100 people gathered in the charmingly shabby surrounds of the Teachers Club on Parnell Square, just ten doors up from where the first Irish Neutrality League was founded 108 years previously. This group also called themselves the Irish Neutrality League and, like their twentieth-century counterparts, they were gathering that day because of a war in Europe. At the meeting, TD Richard Boyd Barrett reiterated his view that the government was 'just looking for the moment when they can formally and fully abandon neutrality, and they see the Ukrainian crisis as the opportunity to do that'. Minister of State for European Affairs Thomas Byrne, who the previous day had said the invasion had caused Ireland to rethink defence and neutrality, came in for particular criticism. His comments were, as Sinn Féin TD Chris Andrews said at the meeting, part of the 'chipping, chipping, chipping away of Irish neutrality'. Byrne, along with the rest of the 'establishment' and 'most if not all of the mass media' were involved in the 'relentless conditioning of public opinion' to abandon neutrality, Boyd Barrett added.

The audience at the Teachers Club came from a wide variety of backgrounds, albeit all located solidly to the left of the political spectrum.

Among those present were representatives from the Irish Anti-War Movement, PANA and the Irish Communist Party. Most attendees seemed to be from the older generation of peace activists, those who were already seasoned campaigners when they had protested outside Shannon Airport in the early 2000s. There was an urgent need to recruit young people to the cause, Boyd Barrett said. The eventual goal was to secure a referendum aimed at inserting neutrality into the Constitution and taking it once and for all out of the sphere of government policy. Such a referendum might be possible after the next election, Andrews said, but they needed to bring people with them, 'people who we would never otherwise agree with'.

Most of the remainder of the meeting focused on how this could be achieved. Maybe a podcast, one person suggested. Animated videos might also work, said another. In the middle of this, however, an audience member had an awkward question: if Fine Gael was intent on joining military alliances, why has it gutted the Defence Forces? There was a brief silence before Boyd Barrett said he'd have a go at answering the question. He suggested the neglect of the Defence Forces was partly down to austerity, and, less convincingly, partly a way of 'rooting out' older soldiers who were in favour of neutrality. The government also wanted to 'streamline' the military to make it more interoperable with NATO, he suggested.[2]

Boyd Barrett's analysis of the reasons behind the weakness of the Defence Forces' decline may have left something to be desired, but he was correct that following the invasion of Ukraine, the government had been thinking about neutrality more than ever. Then Taoiseach Micheál Martin had spoken of the 'need to reflect on military non-alignment in Ireland and our military neutrality' and suggested that a citizens' assembly should be held on the matter.[3] Around the same time, then Tánaiste Leo Varadkar said there was a need 'to think about deeper involvement in European defence'.[4] The invasion of Ukraine had crystallised many of the abstract discussions on defence and security that had taken place during the various EU treaty debates of the last three decades. A direct EU neighbour had been attacked by a world power in an unprovoked, illegal invasion, and as a result Dublin was now faced with decisions that could dramatically and permanently alter the character of Irish neutrality. As one Department of Foreign Affairs official recalled:

> We were suddenly faced with scenarios we had never had to think about before [...] There was a balancing act. On the one hand we had our treaty commitments, our commitment to EU solidarity and the international rule of law, which is something Ireland places an awful lot of value on. Against that, we had commitments outlined in the programme for government about military neutrality. We also had to consider the view of the public on neutrality, which doesn't necessarily tally with Ireland's actual position.[5]

For the first time since the Treaty of Lisbon, neutrality was front and centre in political decision-making, and this time the results would have immediate effects. That Ireland would assist Ukraine in some way was never really in doubt. It was always going to take a strong diplomatic stance condemning the invasion through the EU and through the UN General Assembly and by using its temporary seat on the Security Council, acquired in January 2021. The real question was if it would offer more concrete assistance. The answer came on 27 February 2022, just three days after the invasion, with the announcement that Ireland would contribute €9 million in military assistance to Ukraine, through the European Peace Facility (EPF), the country's pro-rata share of €500 million EPF funding initially allocated by the EU.

When negotiations regarding the EPF began in 2017, it was seen as a way of providing support to militaries in developing countries, mainly in Africa, where the EU was attempting to play a role in bringing stability. It was designed as a replacement for previous military funding schemes that were legally prohibited from providing lethal equipment to third countries. 'It was really set up with a Mali-type situation in mind, not Ukraine,' said one Irish official familiar with the negotiations, referring to the EU's military training mission in the troubled West African nation.[6] Due to rules preventing the general EU budget from being used for arms purchases, the EPF was to be an off-budget mechanism. During the negotiations, Irish representatives pushed for safeguards that they could point to as protecting military neutrality. These included the inclusion of a reference to the UN Charter and a requirement for a unanimous decision of member states before EPF aid would be activated. Also included at Ireland's behest was a provision allowing countries to 'constructively abstain' from contributing aid.

The EPF was formally launched in March 2021, and over the next year it was used to fund the armed forces of Georgia, Mozambique, Mali, Moldova and Ukraine. However, during this period, despite being mandated to supply weapons, the fund was used exclusively for non-lethal equipment, such as medical and engineering supplies.[7]

That changed after Russian troops launched their invasion in 2022. Announcing that the Peace Facility would now be used to supply weapons of war to Ukraine, the EU's security policy chief Josep Borrell called it a defining moment for Europe: 'A page of history has been turned.'[8] The decision made the EU an active player in a war on its borders, and Ireland was along for the ride. Crucially, however, Ireland had worked out a deal that, while its funding would go towards Ukraine's military, it would not be used to buy weapons. Instead, Irish money would go into a cordoned-off EPF funding stream that would be used to buy fuel, body armour and medical supplies. This was significantly less than what was promised by Finland and Sweden, who agreed to supply large amounts of lethal aid to Ukraine, despite being still regarded internationally as neutrals. However, it was a good deal more than what was promised by Hungary, whose government was sometimes regarded as overly sympathetic to Russia, and by neutral Malta and Cyprus, all of which limited themselves to purely humanitarian aid.

Ireland's decision to provide non-lethal military aid raised some eyebrows domestically, but ministers maintained it was perfectly in line with military neutrality. 'We are not politically neutral and have never been politically neutral in the sense that we uphold democratic values and democratic principles,' Martin said.[9] But surely, some asked, when it comes to neutrality, there is little practical difference between supplying fuel for a tank and supplying explosive shells for its gun? Either way, Ireland was supplying mechanisms designed to take lives. Others questioned why Ireland didn't go the whole hog and just supply lethal weapons. The Defence Forces may be under-equipped, but it had some supplies of anti-tank missiles of the type that were already proving themselves to be highly effective against Russian armour. The government's answer was to point towards the 2020 Programme for Government, which stated, 'Ireland will not be part of decision-making or funding for lethal force weapons for non-peacekeeping purposes.'[10]

Even given this somewhat artificial caveat, this was a sea change for Irish foreign policy. Over the decades, there have been instances where Ireland had donated military supplies to other countries. Once, instead of paying to ship some armoured personnel carriers back from the Congo, the government simply gave them to the Congolese Army. On other occasions, Ireland has provided non-lethal aid through the UN to the militaries of developing countries to assist them with peacekeeping duties. But never before had it provided military supplies explicitly intended for use in a war with another state. As one Department of Foreign Affairs official put it, 'I don't think it was really appreciated at the time, and maybe it still isn't, that this was a pretty major departure.'[11] Irish Defence Forces officers seconded to EU military agencies were also involved in administering the distribution of military equipment, lethal and non-lethal, to Ukraine. This was done through a 'clearing house', which matches requests from Ukraine's military to offers from EU member states.

By January 2023, Ireland had contributed over €77 million worth of military aid to Ukraine, part of a total EPF commitment of €5.6 billion, with more expected in the future. This is not counting other financial and humanitarian commitments, which have received less publicity. These include flying injured Ukrainian soldiers and civilians to Ireland for treatment, and the donation of 19 ambulances, 18 pallets of medicines and thousands of blood bags. On the financial side, Ireland is contributing its pro-rata share to EU budgetary aid for Ukraine, which is likely to be €1.5 billion per month throughout 2023. Then there is Ireland's participation in sweeping, and ever-increasing, sanctions on Russia, including the ban of Russian flights from Irish airspace. Diplomatically, Ireland has expelled four Russian diplomats it had accused of spying. And, of course, there's Ireland's blanket commitment as part of an EU-wide programme to accept refugees fleeing Ukraine without condition. By September 2022, Ireland was in the top eight countries for acceptance of Ukrainian refugees per capita. Germany was the only western European country to take in more per head of population.

Most of this has been facilitated through the EU, which has shown itself more than willing to use its military might to help Ukraine. 'The EU has really stood up to the crisis,' said Brigadier General Buckley. 'To use words which people rarely use about the EU and Common Security and Defence Policy, it is now more coherent, more focused and more united.' Geopolitical factors have meant that NATO had to step back, but the EU successfully filled that gap and has been, in Buckley's words, 'incredibly proactive' in coordinating support for Ukraine. But Ireland was prepared to go further still. In October 2022, in possibly the most controversial step regarding neutrality since the invasion, Simon Coveney, the minister for foreign affairs at the time, announced Ireland would take part in a military training mission for Ukraine under the EU banner.

At the time the mission was being stood up, Buckley explained that the goal was to bring all the existing bilateral training arrangements between EU member states and Ukraine under one command structure in Poland and to 'bring something extra to the table'. But what could Ireland, and indeed the rest of the EU's militaries, have to teach Ukrainian forces, who by that point had already achieved many stunning victories over a much greater force? Ukraine had suffered heavy losses in the war to date, but as Buckley explained, the country has a 'large untapped population [...] So they have a requirement for constant replenishment of personnel'. Ireland can bring something to the table there: Coveney had said at the time that any possible Defence Forces contribution would have to be something Ireland is 'comfortable' with, and for Buckley that meant that 'our contribution needs to be focusing on protecting lives, and helping Ukrainians to protect themselves'.[12]

A week later, details of the EU Military Assistance Mission (EUMAM) in Ukraine were announced. Coveney said Ireland may take part by providing training to Ukrainian forces in bomb disposal and demining, an area in which the Defence Forces are well regarded and where Ukraine had specifically requested Irish assistance. The fact it was a training mission and that only a small Irish contingent would be sent, meant the deployment was not subject to the constraints of the triple lock (which only applies to 12 troops or more). This was vital as Russia would obviously veto any attempt to get a UN Security Council mandate for the mission.

In the debate that followed, the government framed its decision to provide troops largely as a humanitarian one. Irish input could prevent 'horrific injuries' to civilians and soldiers, Coveney said.[13] This stance occasionally became highly defensive. When People Before Profit TD Paul Murphy accused Martin of using the war as a pretext to 'drive a coach and horses through what is left of the idea of neutrality', the taoiseach reacted angrily.[14] Ireland's neutrality 'was of more concern to you than the fact that Iranian drones are raining down on Ukrainian civilians,' Martin responded. 'It makes my blood boil.'[15] It was also frequently pointed out this was not a new departure for the Defence Forces. Irish troops had provided bomb disposal training overseas before, including in recent years to the Malian Army under another EU training mission.

But, rightly or wrongly, Ukraine was a different prospect to Mali. The Mali mission was about building up the country's military to enable it to maintain internal stability, fight Islamic terrorism and take back territory claimed by various armed factions. EUMAM Ukraine on the other hand was about aiding one side in a war between two nations on the EU's border. It was radically different to any previous CSDP mission. This wasn't a peacekeeping or even a peace enforcement mission; there was no peace to enforce.

Unlike other EUMAM contributors, Irish troops would not specifically train Ukrainian troops to take lives. But ordnance disposal and demining, while having humanitarian dimensions, are also crucial combat roles. After all, mines need to be cleared from roads before soldiers can advance towards the enemy. As it did through the EPF, Ireland was committing itself to help Ukraine fight a war against its enemies. As some neutrality activists pointed out, it's not as if Ireland was also training Russian troops in demining. Furthermore, Irish officers would also be involved in the command and control structures, which would coordinate all the training – combat and otherwise.

As well as raising questions about neutrality, the move also raised security concerns. Was Ireland now seen as a viable target by Russia? Could it expect increased hybrid threats such as those seen off the coast of Cork immediately before the invasion? There was now 'no ambiguity about the fact that Ireland is not neutral in the Ukrainian conflict', Russian Ambassador to Ireland Yury Filatov said in a statement shortly after the EUMAM announcement. By engaging with Ukrainian military, 'be it on mines or otherwise, Ireland would clearly be involved in the ongoing conflict in a direct way,' he said.[16] This was probably no more than diplomatic bluster. While there was increased Russian activity in the waters around Ireland in 2022, this was more likely directed at the UK rather than Ireland. Relatively speaking, Ireland is still a minor player when it comes to aiding Ukraine and is viewed by Russia as such. Nevertheless, Filatov's statement in October 2022 was a departure from one he had made in July 2022 when he said, 'Russia, and the Soviet Union before, has always respected the Irish position of military neutrality.'[17]

While all of this was occurring on the international front, the alleged salami slicing of neutrality was still ongoing at home, under PESCO – the permanent structured cooperation. Despite its achingly dull name, PESCO is framed by some as the most significant attempt to militarise the EU in the Union's history. To others, it's merely the latest in a long line of attempts to encourage interoperability between EU militaries and rationalise defence spending. The broad, ambitious and sometimes ambiguous nature of PESCO allowed both camps to frame it to suit their arguments. PESCO is simply 'a way of doing better what we already do,' one senior EU official said.[18] Boyd Barrett claimed it was a way to 'ram through a vote to move towards joining up with an EU army and to quadruple military spending'.[19] In fact, for once, Boyd Barrett was underselling it, at least in one way. PESCO requires defence spending to increase to 2 per cent of GDP, which would actually be a seven-fold increase for Ireland. However, as the government pointed out, this 2 per cent target was for the EU as a whole, meaning Ireland could in theory spend far less while, hopefully, other countries picked up the slack.

PESCO can be best summed up as allowing groups of EU countries to pursue defence projects either as a complete bloc or as smaller groups. Projects may include anything from funding the development of a new type of attack helicopter to setting up joint military training facilities. It would also make hundreds of millions of funding available to such initiatives. First introduced in the Lisbon Treaty, PESCO lay dormant for almost a decade, becoming what EU Commission President Jean-Claude Juncker called the 'sleeping beauty' of European defence.[20] In the mid-2010s, the sleeping beauty was awoken by France and Germany who saw it as a way of increasing EU solidarity and defence in the wake of Brexit. Ireland showed enthusiasm at an early stage and particularly after it obtained the, by now, standard assurances that PESCO could respect the 'specific character' of neutrality.

But initially, Ireland's contribution could scarcely have been more minimal. On PESCO's formal launch in 2017, Ireland signed up to just 2 of the 47 initial projects. It participated in a Greek-led project to upgrade maritime surveillance technology, and a German 'Mission Competence Centre', with the latter being shelved in 2019 after it was determined that it duplicated existing EU structures. 'The view in the Defence Forces was this was a golden opportunity for the development of equipment and competencies that the government just kind of ignored,' said one senior Defence Forces officer. 'In my view they just signed up to show they were part of the club, not to actually do anything with it.'[21] It's a markedly different interpretation than that of many pro-neutrality campaigners who claimed PESCO was the government's way of bouncing Ireland into an EU army.

But, as with so much else, 2022 brought a significant change in government attitudes toward PESCO. In June, Coveney announced Ireland would sign up for another four projects where it had previously held observer status. In the wake of the devastating HSE cyberattack in 2021, Ireland would now take part in an EU 'cyber threats and incident response information-sharing platform' as well as a special forces medical training centre and the development of a deployable disaster relief capability package to support EU's civilian response to natural and man-made disasters. Finally, Ireland would take part in efforts to develop semi-autonomous technology to deal with mines at sea.

The move towards greater PESCO integration was a result of several factors, a Department of Defence official said: 'It had been under consideration for a while but external factors like Ukraine certainly focused minds a bit.'[22] It had also become clear that PESCO was not as controversial as politicians initially feared and that claims of an EU army by stealth were mostly failing to take hold with the public. A 2018 poll found that Irish support for engagement in EU military and defence structures actually increased by 2 per cent after the decision to join PESCO.[23]

This was no doubt helped by the government's limited engagement with the initiative. All of the projects involving Ireland are on the softer end of PESCO's remit. It's reasonable to assume the public would have been much more concerned had Ireland signed up to, for example, the PESCO project to develop a new 'Land Battlefield Missile System' or a 'European Attack Helicopter'.[24] It's noteworthy that Ireland also avoided signing up to any of the various projects focusing on increasing military airlift capabilities, considering the Defence Forces have been found severely lacking in this area.

PESCO is not an EU army, even in embryonic form. It contains no mutual defence obligations, and participation in projects is entirely voluntary. As Ireland has shown, countries can take part in as many or as few of its projects as they see fit. Many of its goals are entirely reasonable. If EU armies are to serve together with increasing regularity on CSDP missions, it makes sense that they can operate together efficiently. It could also save money and create European jobs, rather than outsourcing these to the arms industries in non-EU countries. As Juncker noted when he awakened the sleeping beauty in 2017, EU militaries take an inefficient, expensive 'scattergun' approach to defence spending:

> There are 178 ... different weapon systems in the EU, compared to
> 30 in the U.S. We allow ourselves the luxury of having 17 different
> types of combat tanks while the United States is able to manage
> perfectly well with just one model.[25]

However, PESCO is different from previous attempts at interoperability, in that it places legally binding obligations on those who do decide to join up. These include commitments to regularly increase defence spending, to increase defence research and to submit to annual EU-level reviews. It's also clear that some senior EU leaders view PESCO as a step along the road towards the European defence union envisaged by the Lisbon Treaty. Common defence has been the goal of the European project since its inception and the 'clock is running out on how long we can live in a house half built,' Juncker said in 2017. 'A European Security and Defence Union will help protect our Union, which is exactly what EU citizens expect.'[26] If an EU army does ever come about, historians will point to PESCO as a key enabler.

In the same breath, they will also likely talk about the European Defence Fund (EDF). Not to be confused with the previously mentioned European Peace Facility, the EDF is aimed at bolstering the EU's armaments and defence industry and Ireland has been an eager participant. Launched by Juncker in 2017, the fund's aim is to make EU militaries less reliant on US defence manufacturers. This is part of the 'strategic autonomy' concept, the ability of the EU to act on its own in security matters without the support of the US or NATO.[27] Between 2021 and 2027, the EDF will spend €8 billion on research and development across various military projects, towards which the Irish taxpayer will contribute about €150 million. Some of these projects, such as maritime and cyber defence will be of interest to Ireland. Others, such as advanced jet fighter engines, will likely not. But Ireland does not get a choice in where its contribution goes, meaning it will be indirectly funding things like research into improved warheads and unmanned ground combat vehicles, whether it wants them or not.

The government sees the EDF as a growth opportunity for Irish businesses, specifically the growing 'dual-use' sector, which produces technology capable of being used for both civilian and military applications. Examples include virtual reality software that can train both fighter pilots and firefighters or drones that can be used to carry out reconnaissance of the enemy or monitor oil spills at sea. As the government frequently points out, Ireland does not have a traditional arms industry. There are a few companies that make small parts – such as Timoney Technology in County Meath, which produces components for armoured personnel carriers – but that's as far as it goes. However, Ireland is highly active in the dual-use sector: by one metric, the value of the Irish dual-use export market in 2019 was €2.4 billion, which easily exceeds the value of Ireland's beef export market.

It's a sector that has experienced remarkable growth in recent years. The value of military equipment exported from Ireland increased from €42.3 million in 2019 to €108.5 million in 2020. It's no surprise then that the Department of Defence is trying to bolster the industry further, including by hosting conferences where major international arms manufacturers meet with Irish entrepreneurs. These events have been described as 'arms fairs' by peace activists but the truth is not as interesting. These conferences are little more than networking events interspersed with a few banal speeches. However, they do reflect a desire by the government for Irish businesses to get a bigger slice of the EDF pie and, in the eyes of neutrality activists at least, make Ireland an essential part of the global arms industry.[28]

In 1985, Keatinge said EC membership was the most significant qualification to Irish neutrality, while noting that this qualification was 'vague in the extreme'.[29] In the last few years, the war in Ukraine, the development of PESCO and increasing calls for an EU common defence arrangement, have caused this qualification to grow rapidly and to become at least somewhat less vague. The government currently defines Irish neutrality as simply meaning that the country does not enter military alliances. But arguably, through membership of the EU, Ireland is already in a military alliance. The EU is funding a war in a third country, while rapidly developing its expeditionary capabilities and organising intense cooperation between its member states' militaries in myriad ways. It also has a mutual assistance clause compelling, at least on paper, countries to come to each other's aid if attacked. Ireland participates in all of this to one extent or another. On the other hand, the mutual assistance clause is far weaker than NATO's, and Ireland could limit its assistance to Ukraine to humanitarian aid if it so wished. Participation in things like PESCO is entirely optional, as is taking part in overseas CSDP missions and donating military aid to third countries.

It seems a better definition of Ireland's stance in this area may be that it is a member of a military alliance, but one with so many caveats and opt-outs that it can still pursue a broadly independent foreign policy if it chooses. Of course, that doesn't roll off the tongue as easily as saying 'we're militarily neutral', but it's much more accurate.

CHAPTER NINETEEN

CROSSROADS

I do think neutrality needs to evolve
Leo Varadkar (December 2022)[1]

Mary Lou McDonald, the leader of Sinn Féin, agrees with Fianna Fáil and Fine Gael on neutrality in more ways than you might expect, or than she might admit. Like the leaders of the government parties, she has no desire for Ireland to enter NATO but she believes that it is correct to send non-lethal military aid to Ukraine. 'My personal view is that assisting Ukraine in that way was the right decision and the right call,' she said in an interview, although she believes it's a fine line between funding weapons of war and non-lethal military aid. On the proposals, still in their infancy in late 2022, to send Irish troops to train Ukrainian soldiers in demining and ordnance disposal, the Sinn Féin leader said:

> Others might reflect that that is crossing a line and taking a side, but Russia is the aggressor and one which has broken international law [...] They're bombarding a civilian population. So I think there is the basis for those interventions.

But she feels that the government is pushing the margins and 'sailing close to the wind'.

Like the government, McDonald believes the Defence Forces need significant extra funding to protect national security. Capabilities like radar and cyber defence badly need to be upgraded, she said, as well as conditions for serving members. 'You could not defend some of the circumstances in which they are asked to serve. So of course, there needs to be an adequate spend in all of those capacities,' she said. Sinn Féin endorses the recommendation of the Commission on the Defence Forces to move to LOA 2 and increase defence spending by 50 per cent. If that's the case, however, it will take a long time to get there under Sinn Féin's most recent proposals. In its alternative budget for 2023, the party proposed a 7 per cent increase in capital defence spending, compared to the government's 25 per cent increase, which itself was criticised in some quarters as unambitious.

Furthermore, McDonald makes clear that LOA 2 is an end state for Sinn Féin, not a step towards LOA 3, which would triple spending and bring Ireland roughly in line with other small EU countries. 'Others might have that ambition, but since we're not for joining NATO, that's not an issue for us,' she said, ignoring the fact that the LOA 3 is designed to equip the military to offer a minimum, independent defence to an external attack and has little to do with joining NATO.

While she differs on how fast and to what extent Ireland should increase its national defence, McDonald has broadly the same definition of neutrality as her opposite numbers. When the leaders of the three largest parties, plus Simon Coveney who was minister for defence and foreign affairs during the first year of the Ukraine war, were asked how they defined Irish neutrality, all four described it as a military neutrality that is dependent on Ireland not being a member of a military alliance. To varying extents, all four also said that Ireland's neutrality was a positive or active one, which involves a commitment to multilateralism, the international rule of law and peacekeeping. In other words, Irish neutrality is, and should be, of a non-isolationist nature and one which allows it to take sides in conflicts, but not direct military intervention. Even the leader of Sinn Féin, the most pro-neutrality major party, believes this definition can accommodate sending military aid and trainers to an ally such as Ukraine.

At first glance, these similarities suggest there is not much disagreement between the main opposition party and coalition government on the topic. But when it comes to EU defence, there are fundamental differences between the government and opposition on how much integration is too much. For example, Sinn Féin remains adamantly opposed to Irish participation of any kind in PESCO; neither is McDonald a fan of the EU taking a leading role in peacekeeping projects, even those under a UN mandate. 'They're problematic for us,' she said. 'The best flag to enter anywhere as a peacekeeping entity is under the United Nations flag.' McDonald believes there is an ambition in some quarters to make the EU a global security actor to rival the US, but that this is 'not what the world needs right now.' Crucially, she believes there should be no move towards a proper common defence agreement at EU level; that, given that most EU countries are NATO members, entering such an arrangement with them wouldn't make sense for Ireland.

One of McDonald's goals if Sinn Féin takes power, is to place Irish neutrality in the basic law of the EU in a way that goes far beyond the 'specific character' reference contained in the Lisbon Treaty. Such a move would put Irish neutrality on par with the Swiss version in terms of international legal recognition of its status. It's an ambitious proposal and one that could perhaps damage Ireland's standing in the EU. It would certainly upset French and German officials who have recently attempted to reinvigorate the push towards common EU defence. But in McDonald's view, enshrining the right of members to remain neutral in law would strengthen the EU, not weaken it. She believes Ireland could form part of a network of EU neutrals, which would add 'another string to the EU's diplomatic bow', and that this network could take the lead in EU conflict resolution efforts in situations where the involvement of EU NATO members could prove counter-productive.

Listening to comments by Sinn Féin TDs in recent years, it would be reasonable to assume the party is for immediately pulling Ireland out of initiatives like PESCO, the EU Battlegroups and NATO's PfP. Withdrawing from these programmes would be a complex task. Not only would the programmes themselves be impacted, severely damaging diplomatic and military relations in the process, but the Defence Forces would also suffer. Millions already pumped into interoperability projects would go to waste. The military would become isolated from advances in technology and doctrine and increasingly unable to serve alongside peacekeeping partners overseas. In every overseas posting, Irish troops work with foreign militaries, often relying on them for basic functions such as transport, intelligence and reconnaissance. It's easy to see how the Defence Forces falling behind in areas such as, for example, surveillance drone technology, could damage its ability to carry out its overseas mission and perhaps even place its personnel in unnecessary danger.

However, the Defence Forces may have less to fear from a Sinn Féin government than first appears. McDonald takes a more pragmatic approach to Irish participation in EU and NATO projects than her party has in the past: 'I would not be advocating a sudden pulling out. Nothing dramatic like that,' she said. The party would instead examine each initiative 'very, very carefully to see if it were possible for Irish participation to continue without a leeching into the NATO system'.

So, under a Sinn Féin government, participation in PfP or the Battlegroups or even PESCO might continue based on these assessments? It's a possibility McDonald leaves open: 'It might require a little bit of reengineering,' she said. McDonald believes it is important the Defence Forces remain capable of serving overseas in peacekeeping and humanitarian roles. Participation in military partnerships may be a cost she is willing to pay for this – 'We live in the real world and so it'd be a case of balancing those things,' she said – but one thing is not up for discussion: while Sinn Féin may accept that Ireland would have to remain in the PfP programme, there would be no further integration with NATO structures if the party were in government. In other words, under a Sinn Féin government, there is no chance of Ireland moving to the second level of PfP, as countries like Finland, Sweden and Ukraine have done in recent years.[2]

So is the party line on neutrality softening? Its members, including McDonald, would reject such an assertion, but there is additional evidence of shifting points of view since the invasion of Ukraine in February

2022. In 2018, the government expelled a Russian diplomat in a show of solidarity with the UK following the Salisbury poisonings. In response, McDonald immediately accused the government of disregarding Irish neutrality. She demanded to know the national security reasons behind the expulsion and said that the government was 'asking us to trust Boris Johnson, which, dare I say, might not be the wisest course of action.'[3] Two years later, the day after Russia's full-scale invasion of Ukraine, McDonald changed tack entirely. In response to the invasion, she called for the expulsion not merely of a faceless Russian diplomat or two, but of the Russian ambassador himself, which would effectively end diplomatic relations between the two countries. It's a call she has made several times since. This time, however, the government is the one arguing for restraint, saying it is important to keep diplomatic channels open.

When asked about this in November 2022, McDonald had a simple explanation, which echoes Sinn Féin's long-standing distrust of British intelligence. She said that, after Salisbury, the Irish government made a national security decision based on an assessment by MI5, 'which, let it be remembered, does not have a great track record in this country or indeed others for always being entirely accurate.'[4] On the other hand, the illegality of the invasion of Ukraine was clear for all to see. Ireland didn't need British spooks to tell it what was happening. Therefore, for McDonald, the two situations are not comparable. The contention that internal security decisions should not be made based on assessments by other countries' intelligence agencies is a reasonable one of course. But it also ignores the fact that Ireland lacks an intelligence service capable of carrying out its own assessment of such matters and must therefore place some trust in the intelligence provided by the old enemy.

If Sinn Féin has become softer on neutrality, it isn't the only one. As recently as 2017, the Green Party were some of the most vocal opponents of Ireland signing up to PESCO, with party leader Éamon Ryan arguing that PESCO would imperil our status as a 'neutral, non-aligned country'.[5] In July 2022, as part of the coalition government, Ryan and his colleagues voted to expand Ireland's participation in PESCO from one project to four. Separately, before entering government, Ryan supported a referendum to enshrine neutrality in the Constitution on three separate occasions. When a fresh proposal was put forward by Boyd Barrett in March 2022, all Green Party TDs voted against it.

By comparison, Sinn Féin's apparent move towards the middle ground on neutrality has been far less dramatic. Unlike the Greens, all Sinn Féin TDs voted in favour of Boyd Barrett's March 2022 proposal. His bill proposed adding three clauses to the Constitution. These would bar Ireland from joining any common defence alliance, be it through NATO or EU; end the use of Irish facilities such as Shannon by the US military or any other foreign power; and, most dramatically, prevent the State from participating in 'any war or other armed conflict' or helping a foreign state to prepare for such a conflict (the only exception is if Ireland itself is attacked).[6] It's easy to see how the latter clause could prevent Ireland from sending supplies or trainers to assist Ukraine, or possibly even taking part in sanctions against a rogue state such as Russia.

McDonald said putting neutrality on a constitutional footing is one of Sinn Féin's priorities. She did not say what form this would take, but that the clause would likely set out a commitment to military non-alignment, multilateralism and the international rule of law. Asked if this could limit Ireland's freedom to help countries like Ukraine, McDonald said a 'great deal of thought' would have to be put into the proper formula of words. 'We would have to be very careful.' It seems then that any future Sinn Féin proposal would not be as strongly worded as Boyd Barrett's bill or any of the five previous failed attempts by Sinn Féin to insert neutrality into the Constitution (there have been nine attempts in total, including one by the Greens and one by Labour).

Once neutrality is placed on a constitutional footing, Sinn Féin intends that it will stay that way. But what if it becomes a sticking point in the progression towards Irish unification, a process McDonald believes will begin within the next decade? For example, what if northern unionists don't want to leave the protection of NATO? 'Our position as a neutral is absolutely fundamental to our identity domestically and internationally,' McDonald said. On the other hand, if the issue does arise in this context 'it will have to be discussed'. She's not convinced it will emerge as a sticking point, however. McDonald said neutrality and NATO membership has yet to come up during her many dealings with people north and south on the topic of unification. The health service, pensions, the currency: these are the issues that concern people when it comes to unification, she said, not neutrality.

If neutrality is to find a place in the Constitution, surely McDonald agrees with proposals from Micheál Martin for a citizens' assembly on the topic? 'I was kind of surprised when he said that, because we have a backlog of citizens' assemblies, some of them really, really urgent at this stage,' she said. McDonald suspects the Fianna Fáil leader made the suggestion in the wake of the Russian invasion because he believed Irish public opinion had dramatically shifted away from neutrality. That hasn't happened. McDonald feels that, if there is to be a citizens' assembly, it should be as a step towards enshrining neutrality in the Constitution, rather than moving further away from it.

Unlike others in her party and on the left in general, McDonald doesn't accuse the government leaders of trying to secretly bounce Ireland into NATO. Not in so many words anyway. But she does believe Fianna Fáil and Fine Gael are 'at best lukewarm' on neutrality and that there has been a 'chipping away' of it. 'It's the truth they are fearful to say out loud,' she said. In her view, these parties have only ever stood up for neutrality after being forced to by the public, such as following the rejections of the Nice and Lisbon Treaties. Furthermore, she believes some members of the government parties, she doesn't say who, 'would prefer to be playing with the big boys', referring to NATO.[7]

Is this fair? None of the politicians, diplomats or military leaders cited here has said they believed Ireland's interests are best served by joining NATO. Even the most military-minded Dáil members, including former Army Ranger Wing commander turned independent TD Cathal Berry, are not in favour of joining NATO as it stands. The same goes for Micheál Martin, Simon Coveney and Leo Varadkar. Coveney's term in office as minister for foreign affairs and defence saw a massive upheaval in the global threat picture. While still in that post, Coveney said that joining NATO would not 'add significantly to Ireland's foreign policy in terms of capacity to influence world affairs'. His view was that Ireland is not Finland. It doesn't have a 1,300km land border with a predatory autocratic behemoth of a state. Instead, Ireland is an island in the Atlantic with the US on one side and the UK and EU on the other, neither of which currently poses a security threat. 'We have natural protections and we don't have very many natural enemies. That is no reason to be complacent, but Ireland is unlikely to have a conventional military attack,' Coveney said.

Unlike McDonald, however, Coveney doesn't shut the door on NATO membership completely. Right now there is no strong appetite to join but 'obviously, circumstances could change that', for example, if there is 'some catastrophic turn of events in the context of the war in Ukraine which left Irish people feeling very vulnerable. That of course could change things.'[8] It's a comment that might cause some concern on the Irish left, but it should be remembered that Swiss security official Pälvi Pulli expressed a similar view, and Switzerland remains one of the few European countries further away from NATO membership than Ireland. If Ireland is hoping to move into NATO in the near future, it's a process that would have to start by, at the very least, moving up to the next level of PfP. And there is zero sign of this happening.

Speaking in December 2022, a few days before rotating back into the position of taoiseach, Varadkar concurs with Coveney – his Fine Gael colleague and occasional rival – that NATO membership is 'not on the horizon. [...] When I see opinion polls from time to time suggesting 30 or 35 per cent support for it, I'm actually quite surprised it's even that high.' For Varadkar, not being a NATO member has definite advantages when it comes to peacekeeping and work in the UN, 'but at the same time, I do think neutrality needs to evolve.' Sweden and Finland joining NATO changes the dynamic in Europe. On a purely practical level, it means that when EU NATO leaders meet, Ireland will be outside of the room with just three other small nations. 'It's one thing being outside the room when there's a few of you. It's another when it's just you, Austria, Cyprus and Malta,' he said.

In December 2022, Varadkar hosted Austrian officials in Dublin and asked if they were planning a change in their neutrality policy in light of recent events. He was relieved to hear the conversation in Vienna is similar to that in Ireland and there is no major shift towards NATO membership. 'They were describing it as almost part of the country's political identity. Perhaps in a way that's true here too,' Varadkar said. Indeed, a few weeks before that visit, Austria's defence minister Klaudia Tanner had suggested the remaining EU neutrals form a diplomatic quartet that could help to mediate peace between Russia and Ukraine, a very similar suggestion to that made by McDonald. 'It is very important that we coordinate more closely with the neutral countries or those that do not belong to an alliance like NATO,' Tanner said.[9]

In early January 2023, not long after he had rotated back into the position of tánaiste and minister for foreign affairs and defence, Micheál Martin said Ireland's neutrality has evolved over the years, including allowing participation in EU military projects, but that he does not envisage the country ever joining NATO – 'I very much see our security and defence policy evolving within the context of Europe's security policy and defence policy,' he said – but he is also clearly annoyed by accusations from some on the opposition benches that NATO is a malevolent force or is somehow responsible for the war in Ukraine. Referencing previous Dáil debates, Martin said some on the 'far left' have a habit of issuing 'a pro forma condemnation of Russia and then pivoting very quickly to sort of outrageous statements that NATO is using the war in Ukraine to militarise further'.[10]

For his part, Varadkar feels that, while it would be naive to minimise the importance of the EU neutrality club getting smaller, Ireland's policy towards NATO is unlikely to change.[11] Like Coveney, Varadkar believes our fortunate geography means there is no pressing need to join the Alliance. But both men see a need for a fresh look at Ireland's approach to collective security and both seem to believe this should occur through EU structures. Coveney believes that Ireland's policy on non-alignment is unlikely to change anytime soon, 'but I do think we will see Ireland being perhaps more involved in collective approaches towards security and defence in areas where we choose to do so.' For him, this means EU humanitarian intervention and crisis management of a military nature. Involvement in things like PESCO and the EU Battlegroups are also important in reminding Ireland's EU neighbours of its commitment to the bloc and international peace and security, Coveney argues. Ireland can't expect other EU countries to take on these tasks while it sits on the sidelines.

Regarding PESCO, Varadkar is, unsurprisingly, strongly in favour; he was taoiseach when Ireland first signed up in 2017. For him, it is not a slippery slope nor is it salami slicing, although he understands why people might view it as such. 'It's an evolution of our foreign and defence policy and neutrality,' he said. He does not see why neutrality should not adapt to the changing world around it. The type of neutrality Ireland pursued in the depths of the Cold War may not be the type that best suits it today. But, he stressed, this does not mean an EU army: 'When you talk about that in Brussels, they always kind of shrug their shoulders and laugh and ask, "What's a European army? There's no NATO army."'

Obviously, a united army of European nations is not on the table, either in Ireland or anywhere else. But what about a true EU common defence pact similar to NATO's Article 5? Here Varadkar leaves the door slightly ajar. 'I think that's possible, but I don't see it in the short to medium term [...] I don't think it's impossible, given how far the European Union has come in 50 years,' Varadkar said. He mentioned the solidarity clauses already in the Lisbon Treaty, though noted they stop well short of common defence in the military sense.

Against this however is the fact that Sweden and Finland joining NATO has cemented its status as the primary security provider in Europe, Varadkar noted. Despite the invasion of Ukraine, an EU common defence pact is perhaps further away than ever. Russia's actions may have increased EU solidarity, but they have also strengthened NATO. Varadkar believes that it would likely take something 'very strange', such as the US pulling out of NATO, for an EU common defence clause to become reality anytime soon. However, he concedes that, even if common defence remains in the realms of the hypothetical, Ireland would be obliged to provide ample assistance to any EU country that comes under attack. For example, in the unlikely event an Eastern EU country was attacked by Russia, 'we would certainly have to do at least what we've done [for Ukraine],' Varadkar said. 'But I wouldn't envisage us sending combat troops, nor would I think they would expect it.'[12]

Martin is even more doubtful that Ireland will join a common EU defence pact or that there will ever be such a pact to join. 'I see an evolution of [the EU CSDP]. But I'm not clear that it'll ever move to a formal defence pact given the scale and size of Europe.' But like his government colleagues, he doesn't rule anything out. 'I can't predict the future, but I don't see it happening,' he said. 'I'm a pragmatist in some respects. I think we have to work within the frameworks we have.' In any event, there needs to be a 'proper, informed discussion' on the issue, Martin said.[13]

Unsurprisingly, given their voting record on the issue, Martin, Coveney and Varadkar are against enshrining neutrality in the constitution. Coveney believes that it's vital that decisions regarding foreign affairs and defence remain in the realm of government policy. It's Coveney's position that Ireland needs to be able to take sides in a conflict if it wishes, just as it has always done. In any event, he believes neutrality is already adequately protected by the Constitution. There are clauses committing Ireland 'to the ideals of peaceful and friendly cooperation', he said, as well as requiring a referendum before any commitment to an EU common defence. But it must remain up to the government to decide which side, if any, to take in a conflict. 'And I think Irish people are very comfortable with the Irish government taking sides when there's a clear aggressor that's breaking international law.' After all, he said, 'there have been many other conflicts elsewhere that Ireland has taken sides on.' But he concedes Ukraine is different: 'It is very unusual for us to take sides to the extent that we are actively funding a military on one side.' The fact we are doing so in Ukraine is because there is 'such a strong view in government of the rights and wrongs of this conflict,' he said.[14]

Varadkar believes that putting something like neutrality in the Constitution means it will be the judges of the Supreme Court who will decide its meaning, not the Oireachtas. 'This is just my own political philosophy but I'm always cautious about what you put in the Constitution,'

Varadkar said, pointing to instances in the past where Irish society has been held back by overly prescriptive constitutional clauses, including in the areas of gay marriage and abortion. 'All those things required a referendum because the Constitution prevented the Oireachtas from doing what the people wanted it to do.' Furthermore, before you put neutrality in the constitution you have to define it, he added, 'and that would interesting'.[15]

Proponents of a neutrality clause would say it's relatively easy to frame one in a coherent way; there are plenty of previous versions to work from. But it's also easy to see how a provision barring Ireland from aiding one side in an armed conflict, such as that contained in the March 2022 bill, could be used to handcuff the government to an extent that even Sinn Féin would be uncomfortable with.

For Martin, having a 'dynamic constitution', capable of being changed relatively easily through a referendum, is one of Ireland's great strengths, but at the same time, he believes that TDs elected to the Dáil every five or so years should enjoy a level of freedom to make policy regarding neutrality without being 'straight-jacketed' by a constitutional amendment. 'I think the parliament deserves flexibility in relation to issues like Battlegroups, training and peacekeeping missions. I'm not saying a constitutional amendment could jeopardise that, but one doesn't know.'[16]

Martin first proposed a citizens' assembly on neutrality in March 2022, just a fortnight after Russia invaded Ukraine, saying that Ireland needed to take account of a fundamentally changed security situation in Europe. He has since been accused, including by Mary Lou McDonald, of using a proposed assembly as a Trojan horse to get rid of neutrality. This is probably unfair. While Martin sees neutrality as something that should 'evolve', he also believes any citizens' assembly on the issue should consider the positive aspects as well as the drawbacks. Neutrality has allowed Ireland to act as an 'honest broker' in international affairs, Martin believes, and was a crucial factor in the pursuit of the nuclear non-proliferation treaty in the UN. 'So we just need to weigh that up and assess it.' The assembly should also do more than examine the concept of neutrality, he added, it should look at security and defence issues. In particular, Ireland has 'coasted along' on defence and has underspent on its military.[17]

Varadkar and Coveney also see neutrality as something that must evolve with global conditions. Both also believe there must be more debate on the issue. So they must welcome Martin's suggestion of a citizens' assembly? Varadkar seemed lukewarm on the idea: 'I don't think it's a bad idea but if we were to do it, I would do it on the wider issue of defence and security.' He pointed out, as McDonald did, that there are several other citizens' assemblies to get through first. 'I don't see one being set up this side of 2024, if at all.'[18]

Coveney warned against 'boxing off' the debate into a citizens' assembly. Instead, he feels that there needs to be a wider public debate involving citizens, politicians and non-governmental groups about Ireland's place in the world; that such a debate should focus on: 'What neutrality means today; what it should mean in the future; how Ireland should take sides when there are conflicts in different parts of the world; and what is our moral compass?' He said he is 'not saying no' to a citizens' assembly, and that it could be a useful tool. But it should take place within a wider context.[19]

Neutrality is at a crossroads. It appears both the government and the main opposition leader agree that Irish neutrality is a relatively narrow concept centred on non-involvement in military alliances. And neither side believes NATO membership is in Ireland's interest. But the similarities largely end there. Varadkar is, in theory, open to the idea of EU common defence one day, while the Sinn Féin leader rules it out entirely. McDonald is deeply sceptical of EU military structures (although she will look at them on a case-by-case basis if Sinn Féin takes power) and wants to enshrine neutrality both in the Constitution and the EU's basic law. The government wants Ireland to become more enmeshed in the EU military system, including through PESCO and the Rapid Deployment Capacity, and believes neutrality is best left as a matter of policy, which can be altered as needed. The results of the 2025 general election, as well as events on the EU's eastern border, will determine which road Ireland will travel down.

CONCLUSION

Despite the shibboleth of neutrality, and the claims of the
Irish themselves, Ireland has never been truly neutral.
Trevor Salmon (1989)[1]

Over the course of fighting nine general elections, Fine Gael TD Charlie Flanagan has knocked on a lot of doors. But from his first campaign in 1987, right up to the most recent in 2020, not once has anyone raised the issues of security or defence with him. This is remarkable given that during his time as a TD he has witnessed, to name just a few events, the end of the Cold War, referenda on multiple EU treaties directly impacting neutrality, the September 11 attacks, the decimation of the Defence Forces and the use of Shannon by the US military to prosecute what many believed to be an illegal war. It's even more remarkable considering that, in the last decade, Flanagan has held the posts of minister for foreign affairs and minister for justice and that his constituency office is just a few hundred metres from Portlaoise Prison, the State's only maximum-security facility, which is guarded around the clock by the Army.

'Nobody I've encountered on the doorsteps has ever raised with me either foreign affairs policy or our defence policy. Nobody. It's bread and butter issues that come up,' said Flanagan, who currently chairs the joint Oireachtas Committee on Foreign Affairs and Defence. Incidentally,

Flanagan's view is that Ireland needs to increase defence cooperation with the EU: 'What is worth joining is worth defending,' he said. On the other hand, while he is 'unashamedly pro-American', Flanagan believes there is no appetite here for NATO membership.[2]

Flanagan's experience on the doorsteps is not unusual. Several of the politicians interviewed for this book specifically remarked upon how little their constituents seem to think about defence, security or neutrality, even in the weeks and months after controversial issues such as the Treaty of Nice vote, or Ireland joining Partnership for Peace or PESCO. It's reasonable to assume then that the matter is largely settled and neutrality is not something up for debate. This is backed up by the countless opinion polls over the years showing overwhelming support for neutrality. But, given the tumultuous events of the last few years, there are signs neutrality may not be as established as it once appeared.

Following the September 11 attacks, conservative US columnist George Will famously wrote in the *Washington Post* that the 'holiday from history', which began with the end of the Cold War a decade previously, was at an end.[3] The previous certainty that the world was moving towards a more peaceful, more stable and wealthier state was shattered the instant the first plane hit the towers in New York. It was a neat way of interpreting such a horrific event but it was not wholly accurate, at least when it came to Europe. Despite the wars in the Middle East and terrorist attacks of its own, the EU and Ireland remained in holiday mode for at least another decade. Peace in Northern Ireland and the former Yugoslavia, combined with a weakened Russia, meant debates about neutrality were largely confined to the abstract constructs of EU treaties. Any debates about an EU common defence union could be put safely on the long finger.

Saying exactly when Europe's holiday from history came to an end is tricky. Perhaps it was Russia's initial invasion of eastern Ukraine in 2014, the 2015 Paris attacks by Islamic State or the combined shock of Brexit and Trump's election a year later. The holiday was certainly over by 24 February 2022, the day Russian troops launched a full-scale invasion of the rest of Ukraine and tried to take Kyiv. With a large-scale war once again on the continent, questions about what Irish neutrality means and what obligations Ireland owes its European neighbours are tangible again, while a more in-depth look at polling numbers suggests public opinion isn't as confirmed as it first appears.

Support for the vague concept of neutrality remains as high as 80 per cent, even after the February 2022 invasion. But when people are asked about more specific measures that would impact neutrality, that support gets much softer. According to one survey, in January 2022, just 34 per cent of Irish people supported joining NATO; by March, that had risen to 48 per cent. Confusingly, the same poll also showed 57 per cent of people were in favour of neutrality.[4] The same poll shows 46 per cent of people support sending Irish troops to serve in an EU army.[5] Another Europe-wide poll, carried out in January 2022, showed that Irish support for an EU army, at 47 per cent, was greater than in all other neutral countries except Cyprus.[6]

The war in Ukraine has no doubt focused minds, but other factors have also played a role in reopening the debate, including recent Russian activity in Irish-controlled waters, newly renewed EU military structures and an increasingly complex peacekeeping and humanitarian situation in Africa, one which is only likely to get worse as a result of climate change. At the same time, the report from the Commission on the Defence Forces showed clearly just how defenceless Ireland was against both conventional and hybrid attacks. It also served to increase public knowledge and discussion about security issues, albeit from a very low base. (At a wedding in 2022, I had the unusual experience of engaging in a detailed discussion with other guests about the benefits of a primary radar system – it was more fun than it sounds.) With all that in mind, it seems that now is a good time for a real debate on the question, 'Is Ireland neutral?'

It's a surprisingly tricky question given the many different flavours of neutrality out there. First, the easy one: neutrality as it's defined in international law. The neutrality described in the 1907 Hague Convention applies only to a time of war – a country's actions regarding peacetime alliances are not relevant. International law does recognise Switzerland's claim to permanent neutrality, but this is not something Ireland has ever sought to claim. By this definition, by not being a party to the many wars fought over the centuries, the vast majority of countries have been neutral, including Ireland. Therefore, the only war of relevance to Ireland, as it was occurring partly in Irish waters and skies, is World War II. The many secret concessions offered to the Allies and, in particular, the Irish approach to the internment of belligerents meant that Ireland cannot credibly claim to have been legally neutral in that conflict, despite official attempts to fudge the issue. Also in allowing US troops to transit through the country to fight its various wars, Ireland did not abide by the obligations of the Hague Convention. So, in summary, Ireland has been legally neutral for most of its independent history, simply because the matter didn't arise. The couple of times it did arise, it failed the test.

But the Hague Convention is over a century old and was never signed by Ireland. Developments in technology, along with the concept of collective security practised through the United Nations have made it a legal relic and not a particularly useful way of defining neutrality in the modern world. So, what about the more general and amorphous definition of neutrality, the one that means not taking a side in foreign conflicts, either militarily, economically or politically? Ireland does not meet this definition today and has rarely done so in the past. It was not neutral in the various international crises of the League of Nations era and was even less neutral in World War II, the Cold War and all of the United States' wars in the Middle East. And Ireland is certainly not neutral in the current war in Ukraine. Neutrality in this broad sense is not a policy Ireland adheres to, and as it is a member of the EU and UN, it is also not one that is possible, or desirable, to adhere to.

What about the 'military neutrality' espoused by recent governments, which, according to the 2015 White Paper on Defence is 'characterised by non-membership of military alliances and non-participation in common or mutual defence arrangements.'[7] This narrow definition is the one we are closest to meeting. We are not a member of NATO, nor is there any political will to make us one. At the EU level, there has been a push in recent years to realise the long-standing ambitions of establishing a true common defence union. But Irish officials have long fought to retain a veto in this regard and real progress is unlikely without a referendum. It's early days but Sweden and Finland's decision to join NATO is also likely to weaken the push towards an EU common defence structure.

On the other hand, while Ireland is not a member of a military alliance in the strictest sense, it is an active and enthusiastic member of various EU military structures, including the European Defence Agency and the planned updated battlegroup system. And while it is not obliged to send military support to an EU country under attack, most readings of the Lisbon Treaty suggest it is obligated to provide some sort of assistance. Ireland has already done so by sending troops to Chad to relieve French soldiers in the aftermath of the 2015 Paris attacks. Is Ireland *militarily* neutral? Yes, but with caveats.

At times Ireland has been closer to the general definition of neutrality than it is now, but even on those occasions, neutrality was rarely the government's original aim. When Irish leaders have tried to pursue a policy of neutrality, it has often been the fallback position after the original goal proved elusive. De Valera adopted a strictly neutral position regarding the Spanish Civil War after he lost faith in the League of Nations, and he declared neutrality in World War II after failing to convince the British to end partition. The same barrier prevented Ireland from joining NATO in the late 1940s and early 1950s, while Margaret Thatcher's rejection of Haughey's overtures about a defence alliance likely precipitated Ireland's neutral position in the Falklands War. Throughout the twentieth century, neutrality is what happened when other plans did not pan out.

On balance, therefore, when taking the country and its history as a whole, it's reasonable to conclude that Ireland is not neutral. But then again, is anyone? If we apply the same requirements to other 'neutral' countries as we have to Ireland, it seems no one passes the test, not even Switzerland. This is the position taken by academic Karen Devine, who has studied Irish neutrality in detail. Devine is a supporter of Irish neutrality (she was one of the speakers at the Irish Neutrality League rally in October 2022) and she takes issue with the argument that Ireland has never been neutral just because it doesn't meet a set of overly prescriptive criteria. She is particularly critical of another neutrality academic, Trevor Salmon, who argued that Ireland's actions, particularly during World War II, means it does not comply with any type of neutrality, even those prefixed with words like limited, messy or qualified. Devine contends Salmon's approach is overly legalistic and prescriptive and 'has effectively defined neutrality out of existence'. Ireland may have sometimes strayed from the strict definition of neutrality during World War II, argues Devine, but its approach to the matter was 'arguably as clear-cut, legally circumspect and sufficiently deterring, credible, recognised and respected as that of the other neutral European states ... if not more.'[8] Historian Patrick Keatinge, heavily referenced throughout this book, falls somewhere in the middle, arguing that Irish neutrality does exist in some form, but that it comes with many caveats.

Perhaps then, rather than taking a prescriptive approach and running the risk of 'defining neutrality out of existence', it is more useful to view neutrality as a spectrum. At one extreme are neutral nations who are not members of any alliance, military or otherwise, and who take every conceivable effort to play no role whatsoever in foreign conflicts of any kind. On the other end are the nations locked into explicit military alliances and who regularly pursue aggressive war as a legitimate foreign policy tool. The first group is entirely fictional, the second arguably less so. But it's a useful thought experiment nonetheless. It would be tough to get two people to agree on where exactly Ireland is on that spectrum, but most would probably put us closer to the pure neutral end than the warmongering end. However, events like the war in Ukraine and further EU integration mean Ireland's place on the spectrum is in flux and perhaps slowly moving towards the middle.

That brings us to another question: *should* Ireland be neutral? Or to put it another way, where on the neutrality spectrum should Ireland be? This is something the citizens' assembly proposed by the government may consider in the coming years. In deciding the question, it's important to realise, for the most part, that neutrality is not a moral question. In neutral countries, the policy has been a tool for pursuing foreign policy goals, ensuring national security and avoiding social unrest at home. In

Ireland's case, all three apply. In theory, neutrality can be brave or it can be cowardly but these are concepts which have little meaning in international relations. The moral arguments in favour of joining the Allied side in World War II are a match for the arguments in favour of staying neutral. Was it right for Ireland to stand by while the Nazis persecuted millions of Europeans based on their religion or ethnicity? On the other hand, would it have been moral for de Valera to expose his own citizens to German bombing and invasion to join a war which, at the time, did not threaten Ireland?

Indeed, neutrality has often allowed countries to contribute positively towards world affairs. Sweden's reputation as a 'moral superpower' is at least somewhat connected to its previous neutral status, while Switzerland has been able to act as an honest broker in many global disputes for the same reason.[9] In Ireland's case, the benefits of 'positive neutrality' have often been overstated, but not being a member of NATO unquestionably allowed it to take the lead in pursuing global nuclear non-proliferation. However, these benefits are a side effect of the neutrality of European countries rather than the reason the policy was adopted in the first place. Depending on the circumstances of a situation, neutrality could be described as cowardice or an act of humanity. But it's always primarily an act of self-interest.

If we accept neutrality is about self-interest, then the best way to approach it is from a pragmatic fashion, stripped of ideology. Ireland's unique position and history mean the best approach is not chasing the unattainable goal of pure neutrality or joining military alliances. Instead, Ireland should pursue policies which allow its people the freedom to act in specific situations as best suits their interests. The benefits of this approach were best summarised by Charlie Haughey when he addressed the Dáil as taoiseach in March 1981:

> In thinking about our defence policies, we should not resort either to emotionalism or ideology, but rather should we calmly and realistically consider every aspect from the point of view of our own fundamental interests.

The duty of the government was not to serve neutrality but, Haughey said, to 'establish firmly and to maintain Irish sovereignty and independence and to preserve the safety of our people.' That policy must be clearly stated and based on the changing international environment, he added.[10] It was perhaps the most clear-eyed statement on Irish neutrality ever made in the Dáil. What's remarkable is it came from a man who at other times was more than happy to wield neutrality as a blunt political weapon.

In many ways, a commitment to maintaining freedom of action is not a million miles away from Ireland's current foreign policy. As it stands, Ireland does not face the prospect of getting dragged into any wars due to membership in NATO and its EU commitments are non-military in nature and something most people seem happy to live with. The Irish government chose to send military supplies to Ukraine and to take part in a mission to train its army but it was under no obligation to do so. Ireland could also have refused to join sanctions against Russia or expel its diplomats. EU treaty obligations certainly create their own pressures to act in a certain way, but member states retain vetoes on foreign policy matters and, despite some protests from Germany, there is little sign of this changing soon.

The biggest obstacle to Ireland's freedom to act is probably the triple lock, which effectively grants countries like Russia and China control over where Ireland sends its peacekeepers. Even that only arises in very limited circumstances, however, and, if the will is there, it would be easy to change. But if it truly wants the freedom to act, Ireland needs to be capable of defending itself without relying on unspoken agreements with NATO or EU nations. That doesn't mean funding the Defence Forces to be able to fight off an invasion by a major power – that would be unworkable and probably unwise – but it does mean funding it to deter such an invasion and, perhaps more pressingly, to respond to the many lower-level threats that exist in this increasingly unstable world.

Is Ireland neutral? The somewhat awkward answer is no, but then again, no one is. In Ireland's case at least, it is closer to being neutral than non-neutral. The Irish people just need to decide if that's somewhere they're happy to be.

ACKNOWLEDGEMENTS

Writing a book on a topic as complex and controversial as Irish neutrality would not have been possible without the patient advice and counsel of many people. I would like to acknowledge the various academics and experts who answered my questions, entertained my theories and directed me towards obscure sources. I especially want to thank Prof. Patrick Keatinge, a dedicated and brilliant academic who has been ploughing a lonely furrow in this area for decades. Also invaluable were the staff in the National Library and National Archive. Their assistance always came with a smile and a word of encouragement. Thanks also goes to Seán Hayes and his team at Gill Books for their guidance and for taking a gamble that some people might want to read a book on Irish neutrality.

Some 50 people were interviewed for this book from the worlds of diplomacy, government, military, peace activism and others. Some were happy to be quoted, some have remained anonymous, and some provided background information and context. Most had little to gain from talking to me and I want to thank all of them of their time and assistance. Special acknowledgement goes to those members of the Defence Forces, both serving and retired, who took time from their busy schedules to speak with a nosy journalist. In particular, Commandant Gemma Fagan and her team in the Press Office could not have been more helpful.

I'm grateful to my *Irish Times* colleagues for their support and guidance throughout the process, particularly Jack Horgan Jones and Simon Carswell whose advice on writing a book was invaluable. I also want to acknowledge my news desk, led by Mark Hennessy, for not questioning too much why all my articles seemed to suddenly be about neutrality.

None of this would have been possible without the support of my family and friends, who picked up the slack while I was buried under a pile of dusty books in a library or cycling to an interview. Most importantly I want to thank the love of my life Alanna for putting up with me while also moving house, having a baby and somehow still working a full-time job. I will always be in awe.

Lastly, I want to mention my son Teddy, who arrived into our world at the start of the year, not because he has been particularly helpful in writing this book – quite the opposite in fact – but because he has been a shining light in our lives. For his sake, I hope Ireland, neutral or not, continues to know peace and to stand for justice.

ENDNOTES

CHAPTER 1

1   Temple Lang, John. 'The Proposed Treaty Setting up the
    European Union: Constitutional Implications for Ireland and
    Comments on Neutrality.' *Irish Studies in International Affairs*,
    vol. 2, no. 1, 1985, p. 159.

2   Aan de Wiel, Jérôme. 'French Military Intelligence and Ireland,
    1900–1923.' *Intelligence and National Security*, vol. 26, no. 1, 2011,
    pp. 46–71.

3   'Address by H.E. Ursula von der Leyen, President of the European
    Commission.' Dáil Debates, 1 December 2022. *KildareStreet*,
    https://www.kildarestreet.com/debates/?id=2022-12-01a.317.

4   Temple Lang.

5   Wall, Martin and Gallagher, Conor. 'Ireland's Defence Spending
    Set to Rise by at Least 50%, Says Coveney.' *Irish Times*, 28 April
    2022.

CHAPTER 2

1   Tone, Theobald Wolfe. *Spanish War!: An Enquiry How Far Ireland
    Is Bound, of Right, to Embark in the Impending Contest on the
    Side of Great-Britain? Addressed to the Members of Both Houses of
    Parliament.* Printed by P. Byrne, 1790.

2   Tone. p.5.

3   Greenhalgh Albion, Robert and Barnes Pope, Jennie. *Sea Lanes in
    Wartime – The American Experience, 1775–1942.* W.W. Norton &
    Co., 1942. p.134.

4   Müller, Leos. *Neutrality in World History*. Routledge, 2019, p.43.

5   Chernow, Ron. *Alexander Hamilton*. New York: Penguin Press, 2004. p.435.

6   Müller, Leos. *The Golden Age of Neutrality*. Routledge, 2014.

7   'The Avalon Project: Peace Conference at the Hague 1899 – Rescript of the Russian Emperor August 24 (12, Old Style), 1898.' *University of Minnesota Human Rights Library*, Peace Resource Center. Yale Law School, Lillian Goldman Law Library, https://avalon.law.yale.edu/19th_century/hag99-01.asp.

8   Abbenhuis, Maartje. *The Hague Conferences and International Politics, 1898–1915*. Bloomsbury Academic, 2020. Location 725/10054 (Kindle).

9   'Hague Convention (V) Respecting the Rights and Duties of Neutral Powers and Persons in Case of War on Land.' *University of Minnesota Human Rights Library*, Peace Resource Center, http://hrlibrary.umn.edu/peace/docs/con5.html.

10   Ibid. Article 1.

11   The Avalon Project: 'Judgment: The Law Relating to War Crimes and Crimes Against Humanity.' *Yale Law School, Lillian Goldman Law Library*, http://avalon.law.yale.edu/imt/judlawre.asp.

12   Keatinge, Patrick. *A Place Among the Nations*. Institute of Public Administration, 1978. p.85.

13   Mansergh, Nicholas. *The Irish Question: 1840–1921*. Routledge, 2022. p.293.

14   Hobson, Bulmer. *A Short History of the Irish Volunteers, Vol. 1*. Candle Press, 1918. p.23.

15   Mitchell, Angus. *Casement*. Haus Publishing, 2003. p.85.

16   Doerries, Reinhard R. *Prelude to the Easter Rising: Sir Roger Casement in Imperial Germany*. Routledge, 2000. (Quoted in Mitchell. p.56.)

17   Casement, Roger. 'Letter to Irish Independent.' *Irish Independent*, 5 October 1914. (Quoted in Mitchell. p.94.)

18   Casement, Roger. 'Ireland, Germany and the Next War.' *Irish Review*, vol III, July 1913.

19   Mitchell. p.102.

20   Townshend, Charles. *Easter 1916: The Irish Rebellion*. Penguin, 2015. p.136.

21   Ibid.

22   Heffer, Simon. *Staring At God: Britain in the Great War*. Random House, 2019. p.263.

23   Fanning, Ronan. 'Irish Neutrality: An Historical Review.' *Irish Studies in International Affairs*, vol. 1, no. 3, 1982, pp. 27–38.

24   Lyons, F.S.L. *Ireland Since the Famine*. Fontana, 1971. p.393.

25   'Redmond Urges Irish Volunteers to Join the British Army.' *Ireland's National Public Service Media | Meáin Náisiúnta Seirbhíse Poiblí Na hÉireann*. https://www.rte.ie/centuryireland/index.php/articles/redmond-urges-irish-volunteers-to-join-the-british-army.

26   Keatinge (1978). p.45.

27   Nevin, Donal. *James Connolly: A Full Life*. Gill and Macmillan, 2006. p.604.

28   Ibid.

29   *The Somme. Volume II. The Second Battle of the Somme (1918)*. Impr. Kapp, 1921. *Bibliothèque Nationale de France*. https://gallica.bnf.fr/ark:/12148/bpt6k6531651x/textebrut.

30   Hennessey, Thomas. *Dividing Ireland: World War One and Partition*. Routledge, 1998. p.221.

31   Tone. p.11.

CHAPTER 3

1   Fanning, Ronan. *Éamon de Valera: A Will to Power*. Harvard University Press, 2016. p.86.

2   'Message to the Free Nations of the World Dáil Éireann Debate – Tuesday, 21 Jan 1919.' *House of the Oireachtas*, https://www.oireachtas.ie/en/debates/debate/dail/1919-01-21/13/.

3   Ibid.

4   'Declaration of independence.' *Documents on Irish Foreign Policy, Royal Irish Academy*, https://www.difp.ie/volume-1/1919/declaration-of-independence/1/#section-documentpage; 'Debates.'

Dáil100 | Houses of the Oireachtas, 21 Jan. 1919, www.dail100.ie/en/debates/1919-01-21/1903.

5   Fanning. *Éamon de Valera*. p.85.

6   Fanning. *Éamon de Valera*. p.86.

7   Fanning. *Éamon de Valera*. p.84.

8   Keatinge, Patrick. *A Place Among the Nations*. Institute of Public Administration, 1978. p.52.

9   Fanning. *Éamon de Valera*. p.85.

10   'Éamon de Valera to Arthur Griffith (for Cabinet) (Dublin) (Copy).' *Documents on Irish Foreign Policy*, Royal Irish Academy, 17 Feb. 1920. http://www.difp.ie/volume-1/1920/eamon-de-valera-to-arthur-griffith-for-cabinet/30.

11   McCartan, Patrick. *With de Valera in America*. New York: Bretano, 1932; Francis M. Carroll, *American Opinion and the Irish Question*. St. Martin's Press, 1978. p.151.

12   Coogan, Tim Pat. *De Valera: Long Fellow, Long Shadow*. Random House, 2015. p.276.

13   Griffith, Arthur. Quoted in Moylett, Patrick. 'Statement by Witness: Document No. W.S. 767.' Bureau of Military History, 1913–21. *Military Archives*. p.63. https://www.militaryarchives.ie/collections/online-collections/bureau-of-military-history-1913-1921/reels/bmh/BMH.WS0767.pdf.

14   Coogan. p.167.

15   Fanning. *Éamon de Valera*. p.86.

16   Ibid.

17   'David Lloyd George to Éamon De Valera (Dublin).' *Documents on Irish Foreign Policy*, Royal Irish Academy, 29 Sept. 1921. https://www.difp.ie/volume-1/1921/anglo-irish-treaty/156.

18   'David Lloyd George to Éamon De Valera (London) (Copy).' *Documents on Irish Foreign Policy*, Royal Irish Academy, 20 July 1921. https://www.difp.ie/volume-1/1921/david-lloyd-george-to-eamon-de-valera/141.

19   Ibid.

20 Hawkings, F.M.A. 'Defence and the Role of Erskine Childers in the Treaty Negotiations of 1921.' *Irish Historical Studies*, vol. 22, no. 86, 1980, pp. 251–70.

21 Hawkings. p.255.

22 'Draft Treaty Proposals Taken by the Irish Delegation to London', No. 159 NAI DE 2/304/1. *Documents on Irish Foreign Policy*, Royal Irish Academy, Dublin, 7 October 1921. https://www.difp.ie/books/?volume=1&docid=159.

23 Hawkings. p.260.

24 Ibid.

25 Sloan, Geoffrey. *The Geopolitics of Anglo-Irish Relations in the Twentieth Century*. Bloomsbury Academic, 1997. p.180.

26 Canning, Paul. 'Yet Another Failure for Appeasement? The Case of the Irish Ports.' *The International History Review*, vol. 4, no. 3, 1982, pp. 371–92.

27 Hawkings. p.260.

28 Ibid.

29 Hawkings. p.11.

30 'Memorandum by the Irish Representatives for the sub-committee on naval and air defence (S.F.C. 11) (Secret)(Copy)', No. 169 NAI DE 2/304/1. London, *Documents on Irish Foreign Policy*, Royal Irish Academy, 18 October 1921. https://www.difp.ie/books/?volume=1&docid=169.

31 Friemann, Gretchen. *The Treaty: The Gripping Story of the Negotiations that Brought about Irish Independence and Led to the Civil War*. Merrion Press, 2021. p.94.

32 Hawkings. p.264.

33 Hawkings. pp.265–6.

34 Hawkings. p.265.

35 'Final text of the Articles of Agreement for a Treaty between Great Britain and Ireland as signed', No. 214 DE 2/304/1. London, *Documents on Irish Foreign Policy*, Royal Irish Academy, 6 December 1921. http://www.difp.ie/volume-1/1921/final-text-of-the-articles-of-agreement-for-a-treaty-between-great-britain-and-ireland-as-signed/214/.

36   Ibid.

37   Ibid.

38   Ibid.

39   'Proposed Alternative Treaty of Association Between Ireland and the British Commonwealth Presented by Mr Éamon de Valera to a Secret Session of Dáil Éireann on 14 December 1921.' *Documents on Irish Foreign Policy*, Royal Irish Academy, 14 December 1921. https://www.difp.ie/volume-1/1921/proposed-alternative-treaty-of-association-between-ireland-and-the-british-commonwealth-presented-by-mr-eamon-de-valera-to-a-secret-session-of-dail-eireann-on-14-december-1921/217.

40   Fanning. 'Irish Neutrality.' p.29.

41   Frank Pakenham Earl of Longford. *Peace by Ordeal: An Account, from First-hand Sources of the Negotiation and Signature of the Anglo-Irish Treaty 1921*. Sidgwick and Jackson, 1972. p.148.

42   'Debate on Treaty.' Vol. T No. 6. Dáil Éireann debate, Monday, 19 Dec 1921. *Houses of the Oireachtas*. https://www.oireachtas.ie/en/debates/debate/dail/1921-12-19/2/.

43   MacCarron, Donal. *Silent Sentinels: The Irish Treaty Forts*. History Press, 2008. p.86.

CHAPTER 4

1   Lord Chancellor Viscount Cave, 'Irish Free State Constitution Bill.' Volume 52: debated on Friday 1 December 1922. *Hansard*. https://hansard.parliament.uk/Lords/1922-12-01/debates/c9be76d1-c7cb-4857-8c6b-9b60ae9510c0/IrishFreeStateConstitutionBill.

2   'British Troops Fired on at Queenstown.' *Irish Times*, 22 March 1924.

3   'British Troops Shot Down at Queenstown.' *Irish Times*, 29 March 1924.

4   'British Troops Fired on at Queenstown.' *Irish Times*, 22 March 1924.

5   MacCarron. p.70.

6   'Blot on Irish Honour.' *Irish Times*, 25 March 1924.

7   MacCarron. p.70.

8   'Blot on Irish Honour.' *Irish Times*, 25 March 1924.

9   MacCarron. p.76.

10   Broderick, Mary. *A History of Cobh (Queenstown)*. 1989. Mary
     Broderick, p.133; MacCarron, pp.55–9; Walding, Richard. 'Royal
     Navy Harbour Defences – Berehaven and Queenstown.' *Indicator
     Loops*, http://indicatorloops.com/ireland.htm.

11   MacCarron. p.71.

12   MacCarron. p.76.

13   O'Halpin, Eunan. *Defending Ireland*. Oxford University Press,
     2001. p.95.

14   Cave. 'Irish Free State Constitution Bill.'

15   'Money Resolution – Defence Forces (Temporary Provisions)
     Bill, 1927.' Dáil Éireann debate – Thursday, 17 Feb 1927. *Houses
     of the Oireachtas*, https:// www.oireachtas.ie/en/debates/debate/
     dail/1927-02-17/15.

16   'Department of the President to each member of the Executive
     Council enclosing schedule on Defence Policy (Secret)', No. 333
     NAI DT S4541. Dublin, 28 October 1925. *Documents on Irish
     Foreign Policy*, https://www.difp.ie/books/?volume=2&docid=669.

17   O'Halpin. *Defending Ireland*. pp.56–7.

18   Keatinge, Patrick. *A Singular Stance: Irish Neutrality in the 1980s*.
     Humanities Press, 1984. p.14.

19   'In Committee on Finance. Vote 64—Army.' Vol. 26 No. 10.
     Dáil Éireann debate – Wednesday, 31 October 1928. *Houses of
     the Oireachtas*, https://www.oireachtas.ie/en/debates/debate/
     dail/1928-10-31/37/..

20   Farrell, Theo. '"The Model Army": Military Imitation and the
     Enfeeblement of the Army in Post-Revolutionary Ireland, 1922–
     42.' *Irish Studies in International Affairs*, vol. 8, 1997, pp. 111–27.

21   Valiulis, Maryann Gialanella. 'The "Army Mutiny" of 1924 and
     the Assertion of Civilian Authority in Independent Ireland.' *Irish
     Historical Studies*, vol. 23, no. 92, November 1983 pp. 354–66.
     p.360.

22   Farrell. p.115.

23   FitzGerald, Garret. 'Articles and Speeches About Michael Collins
     – Reflections on the Foundation of the Irish State: Cumann na
     nGaedheal – Government and Party.' University College Cork,
     April 2003. *General Michael Collins*, https://web.archive.org/
     web/20110319151530/http://www.generalmichaelcollins.com/
     Cumann_na_nGael/Garrett_Fitzgerald.html.

24   Duggan. p.147.

25   Farrell. p.116.

26   'Memorandum by the Council of Defence on Irish Defence Policy
     (Secret)', No. 323 NAI DT S4541. Dublin, 22 July 1925. *Documents
     on Irish Foreign Policy*, https://www.difp.ie/volume-2/1925/
     memorandum-dept-of-defence/659/.

27   Ibid.

28   'Department of the President to each member of the Executive
     Council enclosing schedule on Defence Policy (Secret)', No. 333
     NAI DT S4541. Dublin, 28 October 1925. *Documents on Irish
     Foreign Policy*, https://www.difp.ie/books/?volume=2&docid=669.

29   O'Halpin. *Defending Ireland*. pp.93–5.

30   Irish League of Nations Society. *Why Ireland Should join the
     League of Nations* (pamphlet), 1923.

31   Keatinge, Patrick. 'Ireland and the League of Nations.' *Studies: An
     Irish Quarterly Review*, vol. 59, no. 234, 1970, pp. 133–47. p.135.

32   Keatinge. 'Ireland and the League of Nations.' p.136.

33   McGee, Owen. *A History of Ireland in International Relations.*
     Irish Academic Press, 2020. p.84.

34   Kennedy, Michael. *Ireland and the League of Nations, 1919–1946:
     International Relations, Diplomacy, and Politics.* Amsterdam,
     Netherlands, Amsterdam UP, 1996. p.222.

35   'Letter from Joseph P. Walshe to Diarmuid O'Hegarty (Dublin)',
     No. 66 NAI DT S4714A. Dublin, 8 March 1927. *Documents on
     Irish Foreign Policy*, https://www.difp.ie/volume-3/1927/naval-
     disarmament-conference/782/.

CHAPTER 5

1   Fanning, Ronan. 'De Valera, Éamon ("Dev")' *Dictionary of Irish Biography*, https://www.dib.ie/biography/de-valera-eamon-dev-a2472.

2   Kavanagh, Martha. 'The Irish Free State and Collective Security, 1930–6' *Irish Studies in International Affairs*, vol. 30, 2019, pp. 103–22, p. 110. Project MUSE, https://muse.jhu.edu/article/845126/pdf.

3   Longford, Frank Pakenham, and Thomas P. O'Neill. *Éamon de Valera*. Hutchinson Radius, 1970. p.336.

4   *Irish Examiner*, 17 September 2005.

5   Keatinge, Patrick. 'Odd Man Out? Irish Neutrality and European Security' *International Affairs*, vol. 48, no. 3, 1972, pp. 438–49. The Royal Institute of International Affairs – Oxford University Press. pp. 438–9.

6   'Speech by Éamon de Valera at the League of Nations Assembly (Copy)', No. 347 NAI DFA 26/94. Geneva, 2 July 1936. *Documents on Irish Foreign Policy*, https://www.difp.ie/volume-4/1936/failure-of-the-league-of-nations/1716.

7   Kennedy, Michael. 'Prologue to Peacekeeping: Ireland and the Saar, 1934–5' *Irish Historical Studies*, vol. 30, no. 119, 1997, p. 425.

8   'Committee on Finance – Vote 67—External Affairs' Dáil Éireann debate – Thursday, 18 Jun 1936' *Houses of the Oireachtas*, https://www.oireachtas.ie/en/debates/debate/dail/1936-06-18/15.

9   Salmon, Trevor. *Unneutral Ireland: An Ambivalent and Unique Security Policy*. Clarendon Press, 1989. p.102.

10   Fanning, Ronan. 'De Valera, Éamon ("Dev")' *Dictionary of Irish Biography*, https://www.dib.ie/biography/de-valera-eamon-dev-a2472.

11   'A League of His Own – The Story of Sean Lester' *BBC Radio Ulster*, BBC, 22 December 2013. *BBC*, https://www.bbc.co.uk/programmes/b03d5cnv.

12   Roberts, Geoffrey, and Brian Girvin. *Ireland and the Second World War*: Politics, Society and Remembrance. Four Courts Press, 2000. p.1.

13 'Eire (Confirmation of Agree Ments) Bill.' *UK Parliament Hansard*, 5 May 1938, https://hansard.parliament.uk/Commons/1938-05-05/debates/8fa1314f-7ff2-4f46-bd2f-769c33561e27/Eire(ConfirmationOfAgreeMents)Bill.

14 O'Shea, Joe. 'Spooky photos show long-abandoned school on Spike Island as former pupil tells of island life.' *CorkBeo*, 5 October 2021.

15 Salmon. p.100.

16 Fisk, Robert. *In Time of War: Ireland, Ulster, and the Price of Neutrality*, 1939–45. A. Deutsch, 1983. p.77

17 O'Halpin. *Defending Ireland*. pp.136–7.

18 O'Halpin. *Defending Ireland*. pp.138–9.

19 Salmon. p.115.

20 Salmon. p.117.

21 Dwyer, T. Ryle. *Behind the Green Curtain: Ireland's Phoney Neutrality During World War II*. Gill & Macmillan, 2009. p.9.

CHAPTER 6

1 Fisk. p.156.

2 Fanning, Ronan. *Independent Ireland*. Vol. 9. Educational Company of Ireland, 1983. p.127.

3 Lyons. p.554.

4 Department of External Affairs. 'Code Telegram From the Department of External Affairs to Francis T. Cremins (Geneva) (No. 19) (Copy).' *Documents on Irish Foreign Policy*, 4 October 1939. https://www.difp.ie/volume-6/1939/telegram-external-affairs-to-cremins/3044.

5 'Memorandum from Michael Rynne to Joseph P. Walshe (Dublin) "The Legal Basis of Ireland's Neutrality"', No. 211 NAI DFA Legal Adviser's Papers. Dublin, 14 July 1942. *Documents on Irish Foreign Policy*, https://www.difp.ie/books/?volume=7&docid=3634#s1.

6 Dwyer. *Behind the Green Curtain*. pp.15, 19.

7 Kennedy, Michael J. *Guarding Neutral Ireland: The Coast Watching Service and Military Intelligence, 1939-1945*. Four Courts Press Ltd, 2008. p.238.

8   Kennedy. *Guarding Neutral Ireland.* p.217.

9   Dwyer. *Behind the Green Curtain.* p.247.

10   'Memorandum by Joseph P. Walshe'. No. 349 NAI DFA Secretary's
       Files A26. Dublin, 29 November 1943. *Documents on Irish Foreign
       Policy*, https://www.difp.ie/volume-7/1943/internment-of-
       belligerent-aircraft-and-airmen/3772/.

11   'Cranborne Report'. *Malin Head*, https://www.malinhead.net/
       Cranborne_Report.htm

12   Fisk. p.132.

13   Maxwell, Nick. 'Britain, Ireland and the Second World War.'
       History Ireland, Issue 1, Jan/Feb 2011.

14   'Memorandum by Joseph P. Walshe "Help Given by Irish
       Government to the British in relation to the Actual Waging of the
       War" (Most Secret)', No. 76 NAI DFA Secretary's Files A3. Dublin,
       24 May 1941. *Documents on Irish Foreign Policy*, https://www.
       difp.ie/volume-7/1941/assistance-given-by-ireland-to-britain-in-
       relation-to-the-waging-of-the-second-world-war/3499/.

15   'Éire signs and the "Emergency"'. *Royal Irish Academy*, 8 August
       2018. https://www.ria.ie/news/documents-irish-foreign-policy/
       eire-signs-and-emergency.

16   Kennedy. *Guarding Neutral Ireland.* p.62.

17   McMahon, Paul. *British Spies and Irish Rebels: British Intelligence
       and Ireland, 1916–1945.* Vol. 1. Boydell Press, 2008. p.413.

18   McMenamin, Marc. *Codebreaker: The Untold Story of Richard
       Hayes, the Dublin Librarian Who Helped Turn the Tide of World
       War II.* Gill & Macmillan Ltd, 2018.

19   *Richard Hayes, Nazi Codebreaker.* Produced by Marc McMenamin
       with Donal O'Herlihy. October 2017, *RTÉ Radio 1*, https://www.
       rte.ie/radio/doconone/2017/1003/909437-richard-hayes-nazi-
       codebreaker/.

20   O'Halpin, Eunan, ed. *MI5 and Ireland, 1939–1945:* The Official
       History. Irish Academic Press, 2003. pp.74–5.

21   Maxwell.

22   O'Halpin. *MI5 and Ireland.* p.xiii.

23   Dwyer. *Behind the Green Curtain.* p.247, pp.288–91.

24   Dwyer. *Behind the Green Curtain.* p.92.

25   O'Riordan, Ellen. 'US Honour for 98-year-old Woman Whose Mayo Weather Report Changed D-Day Landing.' *Irish Times,* 20 June 2021.

26   Fisk. p.242.

27   Fisk. pp.364–38

28   McMahon. p.405.

29   Fisk. pp.178–9.

30   McCullagh, David. *De Valera: Rule: 1932–1975.* Gill & Macmillan Ltd, 2018. p.227.

31   Fisk. p.203.

32   Fisk. p.255.

33   Fisk. p.156.

34   McGreevy, Ronan. 'Number of Irish in Both Wars Unknown.' *Irish Times,* 9 June 2014.

35   Fisk. p.ix.

36   Lysaght, Charles. 'Churchill Criticism of Irish Neutrality Touched a Raw Nerve.' *Irish Times,* 13 May 2020.

37   Ibid.

38   Dwyer, Ryle. 'US Minister David Gray couldn't grasp subtlety of Irish neutrality.' *Irish Examiner,* 22 February 2019.

39   Dwyer, Ryle. 'Ireland's Phoney Neutrality During World War II.' *Irish Examiner,* 24 February 2014.

40   O'Halpin. *MI5 and Ireland.* pp.32–3.

40   Fanning. *Independent Ireland.* p.124.

41   Dwyer. *Behind the Green Curtain.* p.338.

CHAPTER 7

1   'Membership of United Nations Organisation—Motion.' Vol. 102 No. 10. Dáil Éireann debate – Wednesday, 24 July 1946. *Houses of the Oireachtas,* https://www.oireachtas.ie/en/debates/debate/dail/1946-07-24/14/.

2   'Letter from Seán MacBride to Ernest Bevin (London) (Copy).'
    No. 291 TNA DO 35/3974. Dublin, 9 March 1949. *Documents on
    Irish Foreign Policy*, https://www.difp.ie/volume-9/1949/letter-
    macbride-to-bevin/4891/.

3   Lyons, F.S.L. *Ireland Since the Famine*. Fontana Press, 1979. p.558.

4   Keane, Elizabeth. '"Coming Out of the Cave": The First Inter-
    party Government, the Council of Europe and NATO.' *Irish
    Studies in International Affairs*, vol. 30, no. 1, 2019. p.172.

5   'Letter from Seán MacBride to Ernest Bevin.' No. 291 TNA DO
    35/3974.

6   'Membership of United Nations Organisation.' Vol. 102 No. 10.

7   'Extracts from a memorandum (possibly by Col. Dan Bryan, G2).
    "The North Atlantic Pact and Ireland"', No. 223 NAI DFA/10/A89.
    Dublin, undated. *Documents on Irish Foreign Policy*, https://www.
    difp.ie/books/?volume=9&docid=4823.

8   Keane. p.179.

9   McCabe, Ian. *A Diplomatic History of Ireland, 1948–49: The
    Republic, the Commonwealth and NATO*. Irish Academic Press,
    1991. p.98.

10 Salmon. p.64.

11 Keane. p.179.

12 Salmon. p.166.

13 McCabe. p.99.

14 Salmon. p.63.

15 'Letter from Seán MacBride to Lester B. Pearson (Ottawa)
    (Personal)', No. 257 NAI DFA Ottawa Embassy D/3. Dublin,
    7 February 1949. *Documents on Irish Foreign Policy*, https://www.
    difp.ie/books/?volume=9&docid=4857.

16 McCabe. p.111.

17 Salmon. p.159.

18 Salmon. p.179.

19 'Extract from the minutes of a meeting of the Cabinet
    "Schedule: Aide-Mémoire" (GC 5/67) (Item 2) (S14291) (Top
    Secret)', No. 261 NAI TSCH/2/2/10. Dublin, 8 February

1949. *Documents on Irish Foreign Policy*, https://www.difp.ie/books/?volume=9&docid=4861.

20 'Schedule: Aide-Mémoire', No. 261 NAI TSCH/2/2/10.

21 Ibid.

22 Keane. p.180.

23 Wylie, Paula L. *Ireland and the Cold War: Diplomacy and Recognition, 1949-63*. Irish Academic Press, 2006. p.43.

24 Wylie. p.44.

25 Keane. p.168.

26 Keane. p.176.

27 'Membership of United Nations Organisation—Motion' Dáil Éireann (12th Dáil), Wednesday, 24 Jul 1946. *Houses of the Oireachtas*, https://www.oireachtas.ie/en/debates/debate/dail/1946-07-24/14/?highlight%5B0%5D=bretton&highlight%5B1%5D=woods&highlight%5B2%5D=amend&highlight%5B3%5D=agreement&highlight%5B4%5D=agreement.

28 Montgomery, Rory. Interview. Conducted by Conor Gallagher, 29 June 2022.

CHAPTER 8

1 McCullagh, David. 'Neutral – but Not Neutral.' *RTÉ*, www.rte.ie, 27 February 2022. https://www.rte.ie/news/2022/0227/1283020-ireland-neutrality-ukraine-david-mccullagh/.

2 McCue, Ken. Interview. Conducted by Conor Gallagher, 9 July 2022.

3 Keatinge, Patrick. 'The Europeanisation of Irish foreign policy,' in Drudy, P. J. and Dennot McAleese (eds). *Ireland and the European Community: Irish Studies 3*. Cambridge University Press, 1984. pp.33–56.

4 McCullagh.

5 O'Riordan, Michael. *Pages from History: On Irish–Soviet Relations*. Pamphlet, 1977.

6 Dwyer, Ryle. 'A Politician Who Always Put the National Interest First.' *Irish Examiner*, 5 October 2017.

7   Kennedy, Michael. 'Envisaging the Unthinkable: Planning for Armageddon in 1950s Ireland.' *History Ireland, Issue* 1, Jan/Feb 2017.

8   'Lemass Authorised Aircraft Searches During Cuban Crisis.' *Irish Times*, 28 December 2007.

9   Kennedy, Michael, et al., editors. *Documents on Irish Foreign Policy*. Royal Irish Academy, 2020. pp. 653–60.

10   Quinn, Michael. *Irish–Soviet diplomatic and friendship relations, 1919–80*. 2014. NUI Maynooth, PhD thesis. pp. 46–55.

11   'Extract from a memorandum from Colonel Dan Bryan to Denis R. McDonald (Holy See) concerning the development of Communism in Ireland (G2/C/203)', No. 54 NAI DFA Holy See Embassy 14/73. Dublin, 6 May 1948. *Documents on Irish Foreign Policy*, https://www.difp.ie/books/?volume=9&docid=4654.

12   O'Halpin. *Defending Ireland*. p.283.

13   O'Halpin. *Defending Ireland*. p.285.

14   Quinn. p.65.

15   Andrew, Christopher, and Vasili Mitrokhin. *The Mitrokhin Archive: The KGB in Europe and the West*. Penguin UK, 2015. p.210.

16   'Misgivings about Soviet diplomatic links.' *History Ireland*, Issue 1, vol. 10, spring 2002.

17   Quinn. p.119.

18   'Expulsion of Russian diplomats marks low point in Irish relations with Moscow.' Interview by Conor Gallagher. *Irish Times*, 29 March 2022.

19   'Ex Trinity Student Was CIA's Irish Link, Records Show.' *Irish Times*, 28 December 2007.

20   Maxwell, Nick. 'The 1972–3 Dublin Bombings.' History Ireland, 26 March 2019; 'Joint Committee on Justice, Equality, Defence and Women's Rights (Sub-Committee on the Barron Report) Debate – Thursday, 27 Jan 2005.' *Houses of the Oireachtas*, 27 Jan. 2005, https://www.oireachtas.ie/en/debates/debate/joint_committee_on_justice_equality_defence_and_womens_rights/2005-01-27/2/.

21   'MI6, the Spy in the Irish Police Force, Jack Lynch and Britain – an Insight into Anglo-Irish Relations a Year After Bloody

Sunday.' *The Broken Elbow*, 27 Jan. 2014, https://thebrokenelbow.com/2014/01/26/mi6-the-spy-in-the-irish-police-force-jack-lynch-and-britain-an-insight-into-ango-irish-relations-a-year-after-bloody-sunday.

22   Maxwell.

23   Mulhern, Robert, and Ronan Kelly. *Ireland and the KGB. RTÉ*, 23 September 2017, https://www.rte.ie/radio/doconone/2017/0911/903835-ireland-and-the-kgb.

24   Ibid.

25   FitzGerald, Garret. *All in a Life: Garret FitzGerald, An Autobiography.* Gill and Macmillan, 1991. p.603.

26   Quinn. p.106.

27   Kennedy. 'Envisaging the Unthinkable.'

CHAPTER 9

1   Dorr, Noel. 'Do we know what we mean by Ireland's "traditional neutrality"?' *Irish Times*, 15 March 2022.

2   Irish Department of Foreign Affairs, National Archives, Dublin 417/33/V, 20 May 1953.

3   'United Nations Charter, Chapter I: Purposes and Principles.' *United Nations*, https://www.un.org/en/about-us/un-charter/chapter-1.

4   Skelly, Joseph Morrison. 'Ireland, the Department of External Affairs, and the United Nations, 1946–55: A New Look.' *Irish Studies in International Affairs*, vol. 7, 1996, pp. 63–80.

5   Skelly. p.76.

6   'Charter of the United Nations. Chapter VII — Action with respect to Threats to the Peace, Breaches of the Peace, and Acts of Aggression: Article 42.' *Repertory of Practice of United Nations Organs*, https://legal.un.org/repertory/art42.shtml.

7   Skelly.

8   DFA 417/33/v.

9   Irish Department of Foreign Affairs, National Archives, Dublin. DFA 417/33/11, 24 September 1946.

10   'Committee on Finance. Vote 58—External Affairs.' Vol. 159 No. 1. Dáil Éireann debate, Tuesday, 3 July 1956. *Houses of the Oireachtas*, https://www.oireachtas.ie/en/debates/debate/dail/1956-07-03/33/.

11   Keatinge. *Singular Stance*. p.22.

12   Dorr. 'Do we know what we mean…?'

13   Duggan. p.250.

14   O'Halpin. *Defending Ireland*. p.271.

15   'The Veto: UN Security Council Working Methods: Security Council Report.' https://www.securitycouncilreport.org/un-security-council-working-methods/the-veto.php.

16   Snow, Donald M. *Peacekeeping, Peacemaking and Peace-enforcement: The US Role in the New International Order*. DIANE Publishing, 1993. p.3.

17   'Private Members' Business. – Despatch of Irish Army UN Contingent to Somalia: Motion.' Dáil Éireann Debate – Tuesday, 6 July 1993'. *Houses of the Oireachtas*, https://www.oireachtas.ie/en/debates/debate/dail/1993-07-06/29.

18   Gallagher, Conor. 'Irish peacekeeping future: More specialised, complex and dangerous.' *Irish Times*, 5 July 2021.

19   Gallagher, Conor. 'Senior Irish general says peacekeeping becoming more dangerous.' *Irish Times*, 6 December 2021.

20   'Leo Varadkar Says Fine Gael Should Oppose "Triple Lock" on Irish Troops Being Sent Abroad.' *Irish Independent*, 30 March 2022.

21   'Mechanism Governing Dispatch of Irish Troops Abroad Has to Be Reviewed, Says Micheál Martin.' *Irish Times*, 9 February 2023.

22   Anonymous. Interview. Conducted by Conor Gallagher, 2022

23   Montgomery, Rory. Interview. Conducted by Conor Gallagher, 29 June 2022.

CHAPTER 10

1   'The Falklands Crisis: Statement by Taoiseach.' Dáil Éireann Debate – Tuesday, 11 May 1982. 11 May 1982, *Houses of the Oireachtas*, https://www.oireachtas.ie/en/debates/debate/dail/1982-05-11/10.

2   Ibid.

3   'Ireland "not neutral" – Haughey.' *Belfast Telegraph*, 30 December 2011.

4   Dorr, 'Do we know what we mean…?'

5   'Ireland "not neutral" – Haughey.'

6   Lillis, Michael. Interview. Conducted by Conor Gallagher, 3 June 2022.

7   'Britain and the US "Rejected" Irish Defence Proposals.' *Irish Times*, 21 November 1997.

8   Lillis.

9   O'Connell, Hugh. 'After Falklands Invasion, Thatcher Sought Haughey's "Urgent Help".' *TheJournal.ie*, 28 December 2012.

10   Dorr, Noel. Interview. Conducted by Conor Gallagher, 6 May 2022.

11   Allison, George. 'Britain Was Right to Sink the Belgrano.' *UK Defence Journal*, 27 May 2021. https://ukdefencejournal.org.uk/britain-was-right-to-sink-the-belgrano.

12   'The Irish government said today it was appalled by…' *United Press International*, 4 May 1982. https://www.upi.com/Archives/1982/05/04/The-Irish-government-said-today-it-was-appalled-by/8962389332800/.

13   Borders, William. 'Falkland Crisis is Staining British–Irish Relations.' *New York Times*, 12 May 1982.

14   Irish Department of Foreign Affairs, National Archives, Dublin 2018/28/503, May 1982–Jun 1982.

15   Riegel, Ralph. 'Government Feared an All-out British Boycott of Irish Goods.' *Irish Independent*, 22 January 2013.

16   Bréadún, Deaglán de. 'Guinness Wary of Falklands Backlash.' *Irish Times*, 28 December 2012.

17   Ibid.

18   Lillis, Michael. 'Mr Haughey's Dud Exocet.' *DRB*, 6 January 2021, https://drb.ie/articles/mr-haugheys-dud-exocet.

19   'Edging Towards Peace.' *DRB*, 6 Jan. 2021, https://drb.ie/articles/edging-towards-peace.

20   Dorr. Interview.

21   Kelly, Stephen. Interview. Conducted by Conor Gallagher, 6 May 2022.

22   Dorr. Interview.

23   Bew, John. 'Haughey Seen as Using Neutrality "as a Cloak to an anti-British Attitude."' *Irish Times*, 28 December 2012.

24   Ibid.

25   Dorr. Interview.

CHAPTER II

1   Ishizuka, Katsumi. *Ireland and International Peacekeeping Operations 1960-2000: A Study of Irish Motivation*. Routledge, 2005. p.160.

2   Lane, Ray. Interview. Conducted by Conor Gallagher, 5 July 2022.

3   Roache, Daire. Interview. Conducted by Conor Gallagher, 24 June 2022.

4   Ibid.

5   Ibid.

6   Gallagher, Conor. 'Ireland Considering Closer Nato Co-operation in Hybrid and Cyber Spheres.' *Irish Times*, 23 June 2022.

7   Anonymous. Interview. Conducted by Conor Gallagher, 8 July 2022.

8   Brennock, Mark. 'Whatever We're Having Ourselves of the PfP.' *Irish Times*, 25 October 1996.

9   'Partnership for Peace | an Phoblacht.' *anphoblacht.com*, 8 April 1999, https://www.anphoblacht.com/contents/4759.

10   Keatinge, Patrick. *A Singular Stance*. p.80.

11   'NATO Expansion: What Yeltsin Heard.' *National Security Archive*, 16 March 2018, https://nsarchive.gwu.edu/briefing-book/russia-programs/2018-03-16/nato-expansion-what-yeltsin-heard.

12   NATO. 'Partnership for Peace: Invitation Document Issued by the Heads of State and Government Participating in the Meeting of the North Atlantic Council' *NATO*, https://www.nato.int/cps/en/natohq/official_texts_24468.htm?mode=pressrelease.

13   'White Paper on Foreign Policy: Statements.' Dáil Éireann debate
     – Thursday, 28 Mar 1996. *Houses of the Oireachtas*, https://www.
     oireachtas.ie/en/debates/debate/dail/1996-03-28/6.

14   Anonymous. Interview. Conducted by Conor Gallagher, 8 July
     2022.

15   'Stabilisation Force (SFOR) in Bosnia and Herzegovina: Motion.'
     Dáil Éireann debate – Wednesday, 14 May 1997. *Houses of
     the Oireachtas*, https://www.oireachtas.ie/en/debates/debate/
     dail/1997-05-14/5.

16   Ishizuka. p.160.

17   Department of Foreign Affairs. 'Ireland and the Partnership for
     Peace An Explanatory Guide.' Pamphlet. May 1999. p.10.

18   Hedgecoe, Guy. 'Referendum Would Have to Be Held Before
     Ireland Joined Nato, Taoiseach Says.' *Irish Times*, 29 June 2022.

19   Anonymous. Interview. Conducted by Conor Gallagher, 8 July 2022.

20   Mellett, Mark. Interview. Conducted by Conor Gallagher,
     30 August 2022.

21   Roache. Interview.

22   Anonymous. Interview. Conducted by Conor Gallagher, 8 July
     2022.

23   Stoltenberg, Jens. Interview. Conducted by Conor Gallagher,
     12 July 2022.

24   Ibid.

25   Roache. Interview.

26   *Report of the Commission on the Defence Forces*. Commission on
     the Defence Forces, 9 February 2022. p.vi. *Gov.ie*, https://www.
     gov.ie/en/publication/eb4co-report-of-the-commission-on-
     defence-forces/.

27   Cunningham, Kevin. 'Poll: Sands Beginning to Shift on Irish
     Neutrality.' *Irish Independent*, 6 March 2022.

28   Mahon, Brian Political Reporter. '70% of Voters Are Against
     Ireland Joining Nato.' *Ireland | The Times*, 25 April 2022.

29   'Ireland's Views on Neutrality and NATO.' https://www.
     behaviourwise.ie/irelands-views-on-neutrality-and-nato.

CHAPTER 12

1   Fisk, Robert. 'Turning Our Backs on the Fire of Life.' *Irish Times*, 19 October 1999.

2   O'Driscoll, Mervyn. '"We are trying to do our share": the Construction of Positive Neutrality and Irish Post-War Relief to Europe.' *Irish Studies in International Affairs*, vol. 30, 2019. p.27. Project MUSE, https://muse.jhu.edu/article/845131/pdf.

3   Molohan, Cathy. 'Humanitarian Aid or Politics?' *History Ireland*, Issue 3, Autumn 1997.

4   Ibid.

5   O'Driscoll. p.33.

6   O'Driscoll. p.25.

7   O'Driscoll. p.37.

8   O'Driscoll. p.24.

9   de Búrca, Senator Déirdre. 'The Place of Neutrality in Irish Politics.' Atack, Iain and Seán McCrum, eds. *Neutrality Irish Experience European Experience*, May 2009. p.8. *Quaker Council for European Affairs*, https://www.qcea.org/wp-content/uploads/2011/07/rprt-neutrality-en-may-2009.pdf.

10   Department of the Taoiseach. *Programme for Government: Our Shared Future*. October 2020, p.115. https://www.gov.ie/en/publication/7e05d-programme-for-government-our-shared-future/.

11   McSweeney, Bill. 'Out of the Ghetto: Irish Foreign Policy Since the Fifties.' *Studies: An Irish Quarterly Review*, vol. 75, no. 300, 1986, pp. 401–12.

12   Dorr, Noel. *Ireland at the United Nations: Memories of the Early Years*. Institute of Public Administration, 2010. pp.130–43.

13   '37. Letter From Chairman Khrushchev to President Kennedy.' Foreign Relations of the United States, 1961–1963, Volume VI, Kennedy–Khrushchev Exchanges. *Office of the Historian*, https://history.state.gov/historicaldocuments/frus1961-63v06/d37.

14   Bureau of Public Affairs. *American Foreign Policy, Current Documents,*. US Printing Office, 1963. p.1400.

15 Dorr, Noel. 'How Ireland Sowed Seeds for Nuclear Disarmament.'
   Irish Times, 14 April 2010.

16 Keatinge. *Singular Stance*. p.50.

17 Anonymous. Interview. Conducted by Conor Gallagher, 26 July
   2022.

18 Anonyomous. Interview. Conducted by Conor Gallagher, 5 July
   2022.

19 Ibid.

20 Anonymous. Interview. Conducted by Conor Gallagher, 26 July
   2022.

21 Gerard Buckley. Interview. Conducted by Conor Gallagher,
   13 October 2022.

22 Dan Mulhall. Interview. Conducted by Conor Gallagher, 14 July
   2022.

23 Anonymous. Interview. Conducted by Conor Gallagher, 26 July
   2022.

24 Hachey, Thomas E. 'The Rhetoric and Reality of Irish Neutrality.'
   New Hibernia Review / Iris Éireannach Nua, vol. 6, no. 4, 2002,
   pp. 26–43.

25 Anonymous. Interview. Conducted by Conor Gallagher, 26 July
   2022.

26 de Bréadún, Deaglán. 'Foreign policy entering new phase.' *Irish
   Times*, 29 December 2006.

27 Anonymous. Interview. Conducted by Conor Gallagher,
   September 2022.

28 Sinnott, Richard. 'Ireland and the Diplomacy of Nuclear Non-
   Proliferation: The Politics of Incrementalism.' *Irish Studies in
   International Affairs*, vol. 6, 1995, pp. 59–78.

29 Ibid.

30 Irish Neutrality League. Launch of Irish Neutrality
   League. 21 September 2022. uploads-ssl.webflow.
   com/61f7ee611d3fce1125869ac7/63176e4e2b828c67ae69e63e_
   Irish%20Neutrality%20League%20Leaflet.pdf.

31   Williams, Dan. 'Israel Switches From U.S. Cluster Bombs,
      Buys Local.' *Reuters*, 30 September 2008. https://www.
      reuters.com/article/us-israel-weapons-clusterbomb-
      idUSTRE48T2N020080930.

32   Montgomery. Interview.

33   Tonra, Ben. 'Security, defence and neutrality: the Irish dilemma.'
      Irish Foreign Policy, 2012, pp.221–41. p.227.

34   Ibid.

35   Montgomery. Interview.

36   Anonymous. Interview. Conducted by Conor Gallagher, 25 July
      2022.

37   Montgomery. Interview.

38   Murphy, Séamus. 'Neutrality: An Immoral Option?' Studies: *An
      Irish Quarterly Review*, vol. 81, no. 322, 1992, pp. 158–62.

39   Coveney, Simon. Interview. Conducted by Conor Gallagher,
      10 October 2022.

40   Fanning, Ronan. *Irish Neutrality*. p.33.

41   *The Good Country Index*, https://index.goodcountry.org/.

CHAPTER 13

1   Montgomery. Interview.

2   Hayes, Isabel. 'US Army Veterans Convicted of Interfering With
      Shannon Airport Operations.' *Irish Times*, 3 May 2022.

3   Dodd, Eimear, and Jessica Magee. 'Peace Activists Spared Jail
      Over Trespassing at Shannon Airport.' *Irish Times*, 25 January
      2023.

4   'Horgan v. An Taoiseach and Others.' 28 April 2003. *International
      Law Reports*, Volume 132. Cambridge Core, Cambridge University
      Press. p.16.

5   Devine, Karen M. 'Public Opinion and Irish Neutrality:
      A Theoretical and Empirical Test of the "Rational Public"
      Hypothesis,' [thesis], Trinity College (Dublin, Ireland).
      Department of Political Science, 2007. p.181. *Trinity's Access to
      Research Archive*, http://www.tara.tcd.ie/handle/2262/78346.

6   Cole, Roger. Interview. Conducted by Conor Gallagher, 3 August 2022.

7   Brennock, Mark. 'Poll Shows Disapproval of Shannon Use by US Forces.' *Irish Times*, 15 February 2003.

8   Ibid.

9   O'Brien, Carl. 'Ahern Signals Use of Shannon for US War.' *Irish Examiner*, 27 May 2020.

10   'Foreign Conflicts: Motion.' Dáil Éireann Debate – Thursday, 20 Mar 2003. *Houses of the Oireachtas*, https://www.oireachtas.ie/en/debates/debate/dail/2003-03-20/4.

11   Ibid.

12   Ibid.

13   Montgomery. Interview.

14   'Foreign Conflicts: Motion.'

15   Montgomery. Interview.

16   Devine. 'Public opinion.'

17   Woulfe, Jimmy. 'Ireland Only Loser if US Military Use of Shannon Ends.' *Irish Examiner*, 30 May 2020.

18   Kearns, Nicolas. 'Horgan v. An Taoiseach and Ors.' [2003] IEHC 64 | High Court of Ireland, Judgment, Law.

19   'State Must Pay Half Costs of Shannon Case.' *Irish Times*, 3 May 2003.

20   Healy, Alison. 'Official Criticises Use of Shannon for Attack Helicopters.' *Irish Times*, 10 April 2006.

21   Dwane, Mike. 'American Assurances Over Shannon Warplane Landing "Worthless".' *Limerick Live*, 3 November 2015. https://www.limerickleader.ie/news/local-news/140451/American-assurances-over-Shannon-warplane-landing.html.

22   'State Airports.' Priority Questions – Wednesday, 14 Dec 2005. *Houses of the Oireachtas*, https://www.oireachtas.ie/en/debates/question/2005-12-14/section/13.

23   Ó Beacháin, Donnacha. 'Ireland's Foreign Relations in 2014.' *Irish Studies in International Affairs*, vol. 26, 2015, pp. 275–320. p.305.

24   'This Week They Said.' *Irish Times*, 2 December 2006.

25   Carswell, Simon. 'Shannon Played Vital Logistical Role in Rendition Circuits, Say Researchers.' *Irish Times*, 10 December 2014.

26   'Rendition Flights "used Shannon".' *Irish Times*, 17 December 2010.

27   Montgomery. Interview.

28   Phelan, Shane. 'WikiLeaks Cable Reveals US Tension Over Shannon.' *Irish Independent*, 30 November 2012.

29   Montgomery. Interview.

30   Devine. 'Public opinion and Irish neutrality.'

31   McEnroe, Juno. 'Poll Finds Most People Oppose Military Use of Shannon.' *Irish Examiner*, 23 May 2020.

32   'Daly and Wallace Join US Stopover Protest.' *Irish Independent*, 10 June 2013.

CHAPTER 14

1   Lee, Dorcha '"A gamble on peace" – Dorcha Lee on TK Whitaker and defence spending.' *Irish Times*, 30 December 2021.

2   Lavery, Don. 'Government's Secret Plan to Ask Britain for Help if Attacked.' *Irish Independent*, 24 November 2012.

3   Anonymous. Interview. Conducted by Conor Gallagher, June 2022.

4   Mulqueen, Michael. *Re-Evaluating Irish National Security Policy: Affordable Threats?* Manchester University Press, 2009. p.76.

5   'National Security' Debate – Wednesday 16 November 2005. Houses of the Oireachtas, https://www.oireachtas.ie/en/debates/question/2005-11-16/1.

6   Wall, Martin and Gallagher, Conor. 'The "Gaping Gap" in Ireland's Airspace Defence.' *Irish Times*, 19 June 2021.

7   Mulqueen. p.76.

8   Mellett. Interview.

9   'Report of the Commission on the Defence Forces: Statement. Dáil Éireann Debate – Wednesday, 16 Feb 2022. *Houses of the Oireachtas*, https://www.oireachtas.ie/en/debates/debate/dail/2022-02-16/16.

10 Cole. Interview.

11 See Falk, Richard A. 'III. McDougal and Feliciano on Law and Minimum World Public Order.' *Legal Order in a Violent World*, Princeton: Princeton University Press, 1968, pp.80–96; Tucker, Robert W. 'The Law of War and Neutrality at Sea: The General Principles of the Laws of War.' *International Law Studies* vol. 50, no. 1, 1955; and Robertson Jr, Horace B. 'The "new" Law of the Sea and the Law of Armed Conflict at Sea.' *International Law Studies*, vol. 68, no. 1, 1996.

12 Mulqueen. p.39.

13 Gallagher, Conor. 'The "Cold War" Between the Irish Military and the Civilians in Charge of Them.' *Irish Times*, 20 February 2021.

14 Anonymous. Interview. Conducted by Conor Gallagher, August 2022.

15 Lee, Dorcha 'A gamble on peace.'

16 O'Halpin. *Defending Ireland*. pp.136–7.

17 'Dedicated Soldier, Officer and Loyal Servant to the State.' *Irish Times*, 20 September 2008.

18 *Commission on the Defence Forces.* p.15.

19 Lally, Conor. 'Defence Forces Crisis Deepens as Strength Drops Below 8,000 Personnel.' *Irish Times*, 2 February 2023.

20 Gallagher, Conor. 'Entire Class of Naval Service Recruits Leaves for Private Sector as Retention Crisis Worsens.' *Irish Times*, 30 September 2022.

21 'Naval Service.' 2 February 2023: Written Answers. *KildareStreet*, https://www.kildarestreet.com/wrans/?id=2023-02-02a.38.

22 Anonymous. Interview. Conducted by Conor Gallagher, 25 July 2022.

23 Harvey, Dan. Interview. Conducted by Conor Gallagher, 14 July 2022.

24 Ibid.

25 Gallagher, Conor. 'Rent-a-car Escape Plan Considered for Evacuating Irish Troops From Restive DRC.' *Irish Times*, 22 October 2022.

26   *Commission on the Defence Forces.* p.28.

27   *Commission on the Defence Forces.* p.28.

28   *Commission on the Defence Forces.* p.29.

29   Anonymous. Interview. Conducted by Conor Gallagher, 25 July 2022.

30   Glennon, Seána. 'Citizens' Assembly Is the Ideal Forum to Resolve the Issue of Irish Neutrality.' *Irish Times*, 28 March 2022.

31   Mellett. Interview.

32   Ibid.

33   Anonymous. Interview. Conducted by Conor Gallagher, July 2022.

CHAPTER 15

1   Mellett. Interview.

2   Burke, David. *An Enemy of the Crown: The British Secret Service Campaign Against Charles Haughey.* Mercier Press, 2022.

3   Cormac, Roy. 'Secrets and lies: Britain's dirty war in Ireland.' *Irish Times*, 17 May 2018.

4   Irish Defence Forces, *Defence Forces Review 2020.* ISSN 1649-7066. p.17. *Military.ie*, https://www.military.ie/en/public-information/publications/defence-forces-review/review-2020.pdf.

5   Gallagher, Conor. 'Russia Does Not Respect Irish Neutrality, Says French Ambassador.' *Irish Times*, 23 May 2022.

6   Mooney, John. 'Russian agents plunge to new ocean depths in Ireland to crack transatlantic cables.' *The Times*, 18 February 2020.

7   *Defence Forces Review 2020.* pp. 172–3.

8   Gallagher, Conor. 'British surveillance ship to monitor subsea cables in Irish Economic Zone.' *Irish Times*, 28 July 2022.

9   Press Association. 'Russian Military Exercises off Coast of Ireland "Not Welcome", Says Coveney.' *BreakingNews.ie*, 24 January 2022. https://www.breakingnews.ie/ireland/russian-military-exercises-off-coast-of-ireland-not-welcome-1247552.html.

10   Gataveckaite, Gabija. 'Russian Ambassador says "nothing to be concerned about" on planned military exercises off Irish coast.' *Irish Independent*, 24 January 2022.

11 McCurry, Cate. 'Fishermen given "guarantee" of no disruption during Russian navy exercises.' *Irish Examiner*, 27 January 2022.

12 Burns, Sarah. Carswell, Simon. 'Russia Moves Naval Exercises Outside Ireland's Exclusive Economic Zone.' *Irish Times*, 29 January 2022.

13 O'Sullivan, Donie. Shelley, Jo. 'How a Group of Irish Fishermen Forced the Russian Navy Into a U-turn.' *CNN*, 31 January 2022. https://edition.cnn.com/2022/01/31/europe/ireland-fishermen-russia-navy-intl/index.html.

14 Mellett. Interview.

15 Filatov, Yury. Interview. Conducted by Conor Gallagher, 28 July 2022.

16 Peters, Jeremy. 'Food Supply Disruption Is Another Front for Russian Falsehoods' *New York Times*, 19 September 2022. https://www.nytimes.com/2022/09/19/business/media/russia-war-food-supply-chain-disinformation.html.

17 Talonpoika, Liisa. Interview. Conducted by Conor Gallagher, 24 February 2022.

18 Ibid.

19 Sareva, Jarmo. Interview. Conducted by Conor Gallagher, 24 February 2022.

20 Ibid.

21 Ibid.

22 Talonpoika. Interview.

23 Mellett. Interview.

24 McGee, Harry and Wall, Martin. 'Taoiseach Condemns Putin's "Threat of Nuclear Deployment" in Ukraine.' *Irish Times*, 21 September 2022.

25 Baciu, Cornelia-Adriana. 'Security Transformation and Multilateralism: The Future of Irish Defence and Foreign Policy.' *Irish Studies in International Affairs*, vol. 29, 2018, pp. 97–117.

26 Gallagher, Conor. 'Spying and Right-wing Extremism Listed Among Main National Security Threats to Ireland.' *Irish Times*, 23 September 2022.

27   Sareva. Interview

28   Talonpoika. Interview.

CHAPTER 16

1   Pessl, Marisha. *Special Topics in Calamity Physics*. Penguin Books, 2007. p.454.

2   *The Third Man*. Directed by Carol Reed, performances by Orson Welles, Joseph Cotton, Alida Valli, Trevor Howard, Ernst Deutsch, Bernard Lee, British Lion Film Corporation, 1949.

3   Fischer, Michael. 'When Switzerland Wanted an Atomic Bomb.' *Swiss National Museum – Swiss History Blog*, 15 July 2022. https://blog.nationalmuseum.ch/en/2019/04/plans-for-a-swiss-atomic-bomb/.

4   Independent Commission of Experts Switzerland. *Switzerland, National Socialism and the Second World War Final Report*. Pendo Verlag GmbH, 1999. https://www.uek.ch/en/schlussbericht/synthesis/ueke.pdf. p.307.

5   Blocker, Joel. 'Europe: Was Switzerland Really Neutral During World War II?' *RadioFreeEurope/RadioLiberty*, 9 April 2008. https://www.rferl.org/a/1083095.html.

6   Ibid.

7   Halbrook, Stephen P. 'The Swiss were prepared to fight facism to the bitter end.' *pbs.org*, 1997. www.pbs.org/wgbh/pages/frontline/shows/nazis/readings/halbrook.html.

8   Nünlist, Christian. 'Switzerland and NATO: From Non-relationship to Cautious Partnership.' Cottey, Andrew, ed. *The European Neutrals and NATO: Non-alignment, Partnership, Membership*. Springer, 2017. p.186.

9   Nünlist. p.185.

10   Norton-Taylor, Richard. 'UK trained secret Swiss force.' *Guardian*, 20 September 1991.

11   Ganser, Daniele. *NATO's Secret Armies: Operation GLADIO and Terrorism in Western Europe*. Routledge, 2005.

12 Schmidt, Gustav. *A History of NATO: The First Fifty Years.*
    Palgrave MacMillan, 2001. p.105.

13 Afp. 'Swiss Warm to NATO, EU Security Links: Survey.' *The
    Defense Post*, 14 July 2022. https://www.thedefensepost.
    com/2022/07/14/swiss-nato-eu-security.

14 Keystone-Sda/Jdp. 'Voter Analysis: Swiss Youth Less Interested
    in EU Membership.' *SWI swissinfo.ch*, 23 September 2022. https://
    www.swissinfo.ch/eng/business/voter-analysis--swiss-youth-less-
    interested-in-eu-membership/47923704.

15 Pulli, Pälvi. Interview. Conducted by Conor Gallager, 18 July 2022.

CHAPTER 17

1   'Smith's Line on Neutrality is Criticised.' *Irish Times*, 17 January
    2003.

2   Gerard Buckley. Interview. Conducted by Conor Gallagher,
    12 October 2022.

3   'Thirty-ninth Amendment of the Constitution (Neutrality) Bill
    2022: Second Stage [Private Members].' Dáil Éireann Debate –
    Wednesday, 30 Mar 2022. *Houses of the Oireachtas*, https://www.
    oireachtas.ie/en/debates/debate/dail/2022-03-30/10/?highlight.

4   Flanagan, Charlie. Interview. Conducted by Conor Gallagher,
    21 June 2022.

5   O'Toole, Fintan. 'No Call for Us to Be Defensive About Our
    Neutrality.' *Irish Times*, 22 March 1996.

6   FitzGerald, Garret. 'Myth of Irish Neutrality Not Borne Out by
    Historical Fact.' *Irish Times*, 24 April 1999.

7   Fanning, Ronan. 'Bertie Leaps in Where De Valera Feared to
    Tread.' *Irish Independent*, 13 May 2007.

8   'European Communities (Amendment) Bill, 1986: Committee
    and Final Stages.' Dáil Éireann Debate – Thursday, 11 Dec. 1986.
    Houses of the Oireachtas, https://www.oireachtas.ie/en/debates/
    debate/dail/1986-12-11/21.

9   Fanning. 'Irish Neutrality.' p.37.

10   FitzGerald. 'Myth of Irish Neutrality'.

11   Ibid.

12   Keatinge, Patrick. Interview. Conducted by Conor Gallagher, 12 July 2022.

13   Keatinge, Patrick. 'Ireland's Foreign Relations in 1987.' *Irish Studies in International Affairs*, vol. 2, no. 4, 1988, pp. 77–104.

14   European Union. Consolidated versions of the Treaty on European Union and the Treaty on the Functioning of the European Union [2016] OJ C202/1 (TFEU).

15   Clarity, James F. 'Ireland Weighs Trading Neutrality for Europe's Military Pact.' *New York Times*, 17 May 1998. https://www.nytimes.com/1998/05/17/world/ireland-weighs-trading-neutrality-for-europe-s-military-pact.html.

16   O'Toole, Fintan. 'Uneasy Electorate Gives the Establishment a Bloody Nose.' *Irish Times*, 9 June 2001.

17   Keatinge, Patrick and Ben Tonra, 'The European Rapid Reaction Force.' *Institute of European Affairs*, 2002. Academia, https://www.academia.edu/341945/The_European_Rapid_Reaction_Force.

18   Murphy, Eithne. 'The Nice Treaty and the Irish Referendum: What Values Are at Stake?' *Studies: An Irish Quarterly Review*, vol. 91, no. 362, 2002, pp. 114–24.

19   European Union. Consolidated versions of the Treaty on European Union and the Treaty on the Functioning of the European Union [2016] OJ C202/1 (TFEU).

20   Solana, Javier. 'A joint effort for peace and stability.' *Eleftherotypia* (GR) and *Der Tagesspiegel* (DE), 16 December 2003. *Council of the European Union*, https://www.consilium.europa.eu/uedocs/cms_data/docs/pressdata/en/articles/78480.pdf.

21   European Union. *Treaty of Lisbon Amending the Treaty on European Union and the Treaty Establishing the European Community*, 13 December 2007, 2007/C 306/01, available at: https://www.refworld.org/docid/476258d32.html.

22   McGee, Harry. 'Second referendum cannot be held, says O'Rourke.' *Irish Times*, 18 June 2008.

23   Sophie Cramer, Clara. 'What EU sanctions policy can learn from
      European mutual defence.' *European Council on Foreign Relations*,
      13 September 2021. https://ecfr.eu/article/what-eu-sanctions-
      policy-can-learn-from-european-mutual-defence/.

24   Lahnalampi, Raili. Interview. Conducted by Conor Gallagher,
      27 July 2022.

25   Devine, Karen. 'Irish Neutrality and the Lisbon Treaty.' Atack,
      Iain and Seán McCrum, eds. *Neutrality Irish Experience European
      Experience*, May 2009. p.31. https://www.qcea.org/wp-content/
      uploads/2011/07/rprt-neutrality-en-may-2009.pdf.

26   Leahy, Pat. McLaughlin, Dan. 'Overwhelming support for
      retention of Ireland's military neutrality.' *Irish Times*, 15 April 2022.

27   Boffey, Daniel. 'Juncker Says EU Will "move on" From Brexit in
      State of Union Speech.' *Guardian*, 3 February 2020.

CHAPTER 18

1   Juncker, Jean-Claude. 'Speech by President Jean-Claude Juncker
      at the Defence and Security Conference Prague: In defence of
      Europe.' *European Commission*, 9 June 2017. https://ec.europa.eu/
      commission/presscorner/detail/en/SPEECH_17_1581.

2   Contemporaneous notes. Taken by Conor Gallagher, 15 October
      2022.

3   Hosford, Paul (Political Correspondent). 'Ireland Needs to "Reflect"
      on Military Neutrality – Taoiseach.' *Irish Examiner*, 8 June 2022.

4   McQuinn, Cormac. 'Taoiseach: "Neutrality Is a Policy Issue That
      Can Change at Any Time."' *Irish Times*, 2 March 2022.

5   Anonymous. Interview. Conducted by Conor Gallagher, October
      2022.

6   Anonymous. Interview. Conducted by Conor Gallagher, 26 July
      2022.

7   Fotidiadis, Apostolis and Nico Schmidt. 'The European Peace
      Facility, an unsecured gun on EU's table.' *Investigate Europe*,
      29 March 2022. https://www.investigate-europe.eu/en/2022/
      european-peace-facility-controversy/.

8   'Informal videoconference of Foreign Affairs Ministers: Remarks by High Representative/Vice-President Josep Borrell at the press conference.' *European Union External Action*, 27 February 2022. https://www.eeas.europa.eu/eeas/informal-videoconference-foreign-affairs-ministers-remarks-high-representativevice-president_en.

9   Killeen, Molly. 'Irish PM: Non-lethal aid to Ukraine not against military neutrality.' *Euractiv*, 1 March 2022. https://www.euractiv.com/section/politics/short_news/irish-pm-non-lethal-aid-to-ukraine-not-against-military-neutrality/.

10   Gallagher, Conor. 'Irish soldiers: Idle anti-tank missiles should be sent to Ukraine.' *Irish Times*, 2 March 2022.

11   Anonymous. Interview. Conducted by Conor Gallagher, October 2022.

12   Buckley. Interview.

13   O'Leary, Naomi, and Gallagher, Conor. 'Ireland Set to Provide Training for Ukraine to Clear Russian Landmines.' *Irish Times*, 17 October 2022.

14   O'Halloran, Marie. '"It makes my blood boil": Taoiseach rejects accusation Putin's war being used to address Irish neutrality.' *Irish Times*, 25 October 2022.

15   Ibid.

16   Gataveckaite, Gabija. 'Russian Ambassador Says State Would Be Getting Involved in War in Ukraine "In a Direct Way" by Assisting Landmines Clearance.' *Irish Independent*, 28 October 2022.

17   Filatov. Interview.

18   Smyth, Patrick. 'Government hopes to engage Ireland in new EU military framework.' *Irish Times*, 9 November 2017.

19   O'Halloran, Marie. 'Dáil hears claims Ireland "selling out" neutrality for EU support on Brexit.' *Irish Times*, 5 December 2017.

20   Juncker. 'In defence of Europe.'

21   Anonymous. Interview. Conducted by Conor Gallagher, October 2022.

22 Anonymous. Interview. Conducted by Conor Gallagher, November 2022.

23 Smyth, Patrick. 'More than 90% of Irish people want to stay in EU, poll reveals.' *Irish Times*, 8 May 2018.

24 'PESCO Projects: Air Power.' *Permanent Structured Cooperation*, https://www.pesco.europa.eu/project/air-power/.

25 Juncker. 'In defence of Europe.'

26 Ibid.

27 European Parliament. 'EU Strategic Autonomy 2013–2023: From Concept to Capacity.' *Think Tank | European Parliament*, https://www.europarl.europa.eu/thinktank/en/document/EPRS_BRI(2022)733589.

28 Gallagher, Conor. 'Is Ireland funding the military adventures of its European Neighbours?' *Irish Times*, 25 April 2022.

29 Keatinge. *Singular Stance.* p.84.

CHAPTER 19

1 Varadkar, Leo. Interview. Conducted by Conor Gallagher, 8 December 2022.

2 McDonald, Mary Lou. Interview. Conducted by Conor Gallagher, 16 November 2022.

3 Ibid.

4 Ibid.

5 'Permanent Structured Cooperation: Motion.' Dáil Debates. *KildareStreet*, 7 December 2017. https://www.kildarestreet.com/debate/?id=2017-12-07a.365.

6 'Thirty-Ninth Amendment of the Constitution (Neutrality) Bill 2022.' *Houses of the Oireachtas*, 23 March 2022. https://www.oireachtas.ie/en/bills/bill/2022/34.

7 McDonald. Interview.

8 Coveney, Simon. Interview. Conducted by Conor Gallagher, 10 October 2022.

9 Pleschberger, Johannes. 'With Finland and Sweden Set to Join NATO, Austria Seeks Neutral Allies.' *Euronews*, 13 October 2022.

https://www.euronews.com/2022/10/13/with-finland-and-sweden-set-to-join-nato-austria-seeks-neutral-allies.

10   Martin, Micheál. Interview. Conducted by Conor Gallagher, 7 January 2023.

11   Varadkar. Interview.

12   Ibid.

13   Martin. Interview.

14   Coveney. Interview.

15   Varadkar. Interview

16   Martin. Interview.

17   Ibid.

18   Varadkar. Interview.

19   Coveney. Interview.

CONCLUSION

1   Salmon. p.309.

2   Flanagan. Interview.

3   Will, George. 'The End of Our Holiday From History.' *Washington Post*, 12 September 2001.

4   Pogatchnik, Shawn. 'Poll: More Irish want to join NATO in wake of Ukraine invasion.' *Politico*, 27 March 2022. https://www.politico.eu/article/poll-more-irish-want-to-join-nato/.

5   Brennan, Michael. 'Poll shows 46% in favour of Irish troops serving in European army.' *Business Post*, 26 March 2022.

6   Reynié, Dominique. 'Freedoms at risk: the challenge of the century.' *Fondation Pour L'Innovation Politique*, January 2022. https://www.fondapol.org/en/study/freedoms-at-risk-the-challenge-of-the-century/.

7   'White Paper on Defence.' 16 October 2015 (updated 10 March 2021). *Gov.ie*. p.24. https://www.gov.ie/en/policy-information/bee90a-white-paper-on-defence/#.

8   Devine, Karen. 'A Comparative Critique of the Practice of Irish Neutrality in the "Unneutral" Discourse.' *Irish Studies in International Affairs*, vol. 19, 2008, pp. 73–97.

9   Dahl, Ann-Sofie. 'Sweden: Once a Moral Superpower, Always a
     Moral Superpower?' *International Journal*, vol. 61, no. 4, 2006,
     pp. 895–908.

10   'Defence Policy: Motion.' Dáil Éireann Debate – Wednesday,
     11 Mar 1981. *Houses of the Oireachtas*, https://www.oireachtas.ie/
     en/debates/debate/dail/1981-03-11/19.

INDEX